THIS BOOK BELONGS TO
The Library of

....

....

I can't tell you how grateful I am that you decided to read my book. My most heartfelt thanks that you took time out of your life to choose my work and I hope you find benefit within these pages. There are so many books available today that offer similar content so that makes it even more humbling that you decided to buying mine.

Tell me what you thought! I am eager to hear your opinion and ideas on what you read as are others who are looking for a good book to buy. Leave a review on Amazon.com so others can benefit from your wisdom!

With much thanks.

Table of Contents

SUMMARY

The Joy of Crocheting for Babies is a comprehensive guidebook that caters to the needs of crochet enthusiasts who are passionate about creating beautiful and practical items for babies. This book is a treasure trove of patterns, techniques, and tips that will inspire and empower crocheters to embark on exciting projects for the little ones in their lives.

The book begins with an introduction to the art of crocheting, providing a brief history and explaining the basic tools and materials required. It then delves into the specific techniques and stitches used in baby crochet, ensuring that even beginners can follow along and create stunning pieces. From simple stitches like single and double crochet to more intricate techniques like shell stitch and popcorn stitch, this book covers it all.

One of the highlights of The Joy of Crocheting for Babies is its extensive collection of patterns. Whether you're looking to make adorable baby blankets, cozy hats, snug booties, or charming toys, this book has a pattern to suit every taste and skill level. Each pattern is accompanied by clear and concise instructions, as well as detailed charts and diagrams, making it easy for crocheters to visualize the steps involved.

In addition to the patterns, the book also offers valuable guidance on choosing the right yarns and colors for baby projects. It provides insights into the importance of using soft and hypoallergenic materials that are gentle on a baby's delicate skin. Furthermore, it offers suggestions for incorporating different colors and textures to create visually appealing and stimulating items for babies.

The Joy of Crocheting for Babies goes beyond just providing patterns and instructions. It also includes helpful tips and tricks to enhance the crocheting experience. From time-saving techniques to troubleshooting common mistakes, this book equips crocheters with the knowledge and skills to overcome any challenges they may encounter during their projects.

Moreover, this book recognizes the sentimental value of handmade items and the joy they bring to both the creator and the recipient. It emphasizes the importance of crocheting with love and care, and encourages readers to infuse their projects with personal touches and customization. Whether it's adding a special stitch pattern or incorporating a unique embellishment, this book inspires crocheters to create one-of-a-kind pieces that will be cherished for years to come.

Texture plays a crucial role in baby crochet, as it not only enhances the overall aesthetic appeal of the finished product but also provides numerous benefits for the baby. When it comes to baby items, comfort and safety are of utmost importance, and texture can greatly contribute to both aspects.

One of the primary advantages of incorporating texture into baby crochet is the added sensory stimulation it provides. Babies are naturally curious and constantly exploring their surroundings through touch. By using textured stitches or incorporating different yarns with varying textures, such as soft and fuzzy or bumpy and ribbed, baby crochet items can offer a rich tactile experience for the little ones. This sensory stimulation can help promote their cognitive development, as they learn to recognize and differentiate between different textures.

Furthermore, texture in baby crochet can also serve a practical purpose by improving the functionality of the items. For instance, using textured stitches in baby blankets or clothing can create a more breathable fabric, allowing air circulation and preventing overheating. This is particularly important for newborns, as they have limited ability to regulate their body temperature. Additionally, textured stitches can provide extra insulation, keeping the baby warm during colder months.

Another significant benefit of texture in baby crochet is its ability to enhance grip and promote fine motor skill development. As babies grow, they start to grasp objects and explore their dexterity. By incorporating textured stitches or adding embellishments like buttons or loops, baby crochet items can provide a tactile surface that aids in developing their hand-eye coordination and fine motor skills. This can be particularly beneficial when it comes to items like baby toys or teething rings, where the texture can provide a soothing sensation for the baby's gums.

In terms of safety, texture in baby crochet can also play a crucial role. Smooth and slippery surfaces can pose a risk of items slipping out of a baby's grasp, especially during teething or when they are learning to hold objects. By incorporating textured stitches or using yarns with grip, baby crochet items can provide a secure and safe grip for the baby, reducing the chances of accidents or choking hazards.

Overall, the importance of texture in baby crochet cannot be overstated. From providing sensory stimulation and promoting cognitive development to enhancing functionality and safety, texture adds a whole new dimension to baby crochet items. Whether it's a cozy blanket, a cute hat, or a soft toy, the incorporation of texture not only makes the item visually appealing but also ensures that it serves its purpose effectively and contributes to the overall well-being of the baby.

The output for the input A. Pattern 1: Classic Granny Square Blanket is a detailed description of the classic granny square blanket pattern.

The classic granny square blanket is a popular crochet pattern that has been around for decades. It is a versatile and timeless design that can be customized to suit any color scheme or size preference.

To create this blanket, you will need a crochet hook and yarn in your desired colors. The pattern starts with a center square, which is typically made up of multiple rounds of double crochet stitches. This square serves as the foundation for the rest of the blanket.

Once the center square is complete, you will begin working on the granny square motif. This motif consists of clusters of double crochet stitches separated by chain stitches. The number of clusters and chain stitches can vary depending on the desired size of the blanket.

To expand the blanket, you will continue working additional rounds of the granny square motif, increasing the number of clusters and chain stitches with each round. This creates a beautiful and intricate pattern that is characteristic of the classic granny square design.

The blanket can be made as large or as small as you like, depending on your preference. You can also experiment with different color combinations to create a unique and personalized look.

Once you have completed the desired number of rounds, you will finish off the blanket by adding a border. The border can be as simple or as elaborate as you like, and can be made using any stitch pattern of your choice.

The classic granny square blanket is not only a beautiful and functional piece, but it is also a great project for beginners to learn and practice their crochet skills. The repetitive nature of the pattern makes it easy to memorize and follow along, and the end result is always stunning.

Whether you choose to make a small lap blanket or a large bedspread, the classic granny square blanket is sure to be a cherished heirloom that will be passed down for generations to come.

The Cozy Baby Cardigan is a delightful knitting pattern that is perfect for keeping your little one warm and stylish. This pattern features a classic cardigan design with a twist, as it is specifically designed for babies, making it the ideal garment for your little bundle of joy.

The pattern begins with the instructions for the back panel of the cardigan. It provides detailed guidance on how to cast on the required number of stitches and then proceed with the knitting process. The pattern includes clear instructions on how to create the ribbing at the bottom of the back panel, which adds a touch of texture and elegance to the overall design.

Moving on to the front panels, the pattern provides step-by-step instructions on how to create the buttonholes and shape the neckline. This ensures that the cardigan is not only functional but also easy to put on and take off. The pattern also includes instructions on how to create the ribbing on the front panels, which matches the ribbing on the back panel, creating a cohesive and polished look.

The sleeves of the Cozy Baby Cardigan are also carefully detailed in the pattern. It provides instructions on how to create the ribbing at the cuffs, which adds a touch of sophistication to the overall design. The pattern also includes guidance on how to shape the sleeves to ensure a comfortable fit for your little one.

Additionally, the pattern includes instructions on how to sew the various pieces of the cardigan together, ensuring a seamless and professional finish. It also provides guidance on how to attach the buttons securely, ensuring that they do not come loose during wear.

The Cozy Baby Cardigan pattern is suitable for knitters of all skill levels. It provides clear and concise instructions, making it easy for beginners to follow along. For more experienced knitters, the pattern offers opportunities for customization and personalization, allowing you to add your own unique touch to the design.

Overall, the Cozy Baby Cardigan pattern is a must-have for anyone looking to create a beautiful and cozy garment for their little one. With its detailed instructions and versatile design, this pattern is sure to become a favorite in your knitting repertoire.

The output for Pattern 7, the Adorable Baby Hat, is a detailed set of instructions on how to create a cute and cozy hat for a baby. This pattern is perfect for those who enjoy knitting or crocheting and want to make something special for a little one.

The instructions begin by listing the materials needed for the project, including the type and amount of yarn, the recommended needle or hook size, and any additional supplies such as buttons or ribbons. This ensures that the crafter has everything they need before starting.

Next, the pattern provides step-by-step instructions on how to create the hat. It starts with the foundation, which could be a magic ring or a chain stitch, depending on the chosen technique. The pattern then guides the crafter through the process of increasing or decreasing stitches to shape the hat, ensuring a perfect fit for the baby's head.

The instructions also include details on how to create any special features of the hat, such as ear flaps, pom-poms, or decorative stitches. These additional elements add a touch of uniqueness and charm to the finished product.

Throughout the pattern, there are helpful tips and tricks to assist the crafter in achieving the best results. These may include suggestions on how to maintain consistent tension, how to weave in loose ends neatly, or how to customize the hat to fit different sizes or styles.

The pattern concludes with instructions on how to finish the hat, such as binding off the stitches and securing any embellishments. It may also provide guidance on how to care for the finished hat, such as washing instructions or recommendations for storing it.

Overall, the output for Pattern 7, the Adorable Baby Hat, is a comprehensive and detailed set of instructions that enable crafters to create a beautiful and functional hat for a baby. With clear guidance and helpful tips, this pattern ensures a successful and enjoyable knitting or crocheting experience.

The Soft and Squishy Baby Rattle is a delightful and engaging toy designed specifically for infants. This rattle features a unique pattern, known as Pattern 10, which adds an extra element of visual stimulation for your little one.

One of the standout features of this baby rattle is its soft and squishy texture. Made from high-quality, baby-safe materials, the rattle is designed to be gentle on your baby's delicate skin. The softness of the rattle also makes it easy for your baby to grip and hold onto, promoting their fine motor skills development.

The Pattern 10 design on the rattle is visually captivating for babies. The combination of vibrant colors and interesting shapes stimulates their visual senses, encouraging them to explore and engage with the toy. This pattern is carefully crafted to provide just the right amount of visual stimulation without overwhelming your baby.

In addition to its visual appeal, the Soft and Squishy Baby Rattle also produces a gentle rattling sound when shaken. This auditory stimulation helps to capture your baby's attention and encourages them to interact with the toy. The soft rattling sound is not too loud or jarring, ensuring a pleasant and soothing experience for your little one.

The Soft and Squishy Baby Rattle is also designed with safety in mind. It is free from any small parts that could pose a choking hazard, making it suitable for even the youngest of infants. The materials used in its construction are non-toxic and meet the highest safety standards, giving you peace of mind as your baby explores and plays with the rattle.

Overall, the Soft and Squishy Baby Rattle with Pattern 10 is a fantastic choice for parents looking for a safe, engaging, and visually stimulating toy for their little one. Its soft and squishy texture, captivating pattern, gentle rattling sound, and emphasis on safety make it a must-have for any baby's toy collection.

The output for Pattern 13: Baby Layette Set includes a sweater, booties, and a hat. This adorable set is specifically designed for babies, providing them with warmth, comfort, and style.

The sweater is the main component of the layette set, and it is carefully crafted to fit a baby's delicate body. It features a soft and cozy fabric that will keep the baby warm during colder seasons. The sweater is designed with a button-up front, making it easy to put on and take off. It also has long sleeves to provide full coverage and protection for the baby's arms.

The booties included in the set are designed to keep the baby's feet warm and snug. They are made with the same soft fabric as the sweater, ensuring maximum comfort for the baby. The booties have an elasticized opening, allowing for easy slip-on and a secure fit. They also feature a non-slip sole, providing traction and stability as the baby starts to explore their surroundings.

Completing the layette set is an adorable hat. The hat is designed to keep the baby's head warm and protected from the elements. It is made with the same fabric as the sweater and booties, ensuring a coordinated and stylish look. The hat has a stretchy band, allowing for a comfortable and secure fit on the baby's head. It also features a cute design or pattern, adding a touch of charm to the overall set.

Pattern 13: Baby Layette Set is perfect for both experienced and novice knitters. The pattern provides detailed instructions and diagrams, making it easy to follow along and create the set with precision. It also includes various size options, allowing you to customize the set to fit different baby ages and sizes.

Whether you are knitting this layette set for your own baby or as a thoughtful gift for someone else, Pattern 13: Baby Layette Set is a wonderful choice. It combines functionality, style, and comfort, ensuring that the baby will be cozy and adorable in their new outfit.

One important aspect of designing clothing is adjusting sizes for different ages. As children grow, their bodies change in size and proportion, so it is crucial to create garments that fit them properly at each stage of their development.

When it comes to adjusting sizes for different ages, designers take into consideration various factors. First and foremost, they consider the average measurements and proportions of children at different ages. This involves studying growth charts and understanding how the body changes over time. For example, a designer may find that the average waist size of a 5-year-old is smaller than that of a 10-year-old, so they would adjust the waist measurement accordingly.

In addition to average measurements, designers also consider the specific needs and preferences of different age groups. For instance, younger children may require clothing with more room for movement and play, while older children may prefer more fitted styles. Designers take these factors into account when determining the overall fit and silhouette of the garment.

Another important aspect of adjusting sizes for different ages is considering the functionality and practicality of the clothing. For example, clothing for infants and toddlers often includes features such as snap closures or elastic waistbands to make dressing and diaper changes easier. As children get older, these features may be replaced with more traditional closures like buttons or zippers.

Furthermore, designers also consider the growth potential of the garment. Children grow at different rates, so it is important to create clothing that can accommodate growth spurts. This can be achieved through adjustable features such as elastic waistbands or adjustable straps. By incorporating these elements, designers ensure that the clothing can be worn for a longer period of time, saving parents from having to constantly buy new clothes as their child grows.

Overall, adjusting sizes for different ages is a crucial aspect of clothing design. It involves considering average measurements, specific needs and preferences, functionality, and growth potential. By taking all of these factors into account, designers can create garments that fit children properly at each stage of their development, ensuring both comfort and style.

One important step in the process of knitting or crocheting a project is weaving in ends. When you work on a project, you typically have loose ends of yarn that need to be secured and hidden within the fabric. Weaving in ends is the process of neatly tucking these loose ends into the stitches of your project, ensuring that they are secure and won't unravel over time.

To begin weaving in ends, you will need a yarn needle or a tapestry needle. These needles have a large eye that can accommodate the thickness of yarn and a blunt tip that won't split the fibers of your project. Thread the loose end of yarn through the eye of the needle, leaving a small tail.

Next, identify a stitch or a group of stitches near the loose end. Insert the needle under the stitches, going in the same direction as the yarn. Be careful not to pull too tightly, as this can cause the fabric to pucker or distort. Instead, aim for a snug fit that blends seamlessly with the surrounding stitches.

Once you have inserted the needle, bring it back up through the fabric a short distance away. This creates a loop of yarn that is anchored within the stitches. Repeat this process a few times, always going in a different direction each time, to ensure that the end is securely woven in.

After weaving in the ends, trim any excess yarn close to the fabric, being careful not to cut any of the stitches. The goal is to have the ends completely hidden within the fabric, with no loose or dangling threads.

Weaving in ends is an essential step in completing a knitting or crochet project. It not only ensures that your work looks neat and professional, but it also prevents the ends from coming undone and potentially unraveling your entire project. Taking the time to properly weave in ends will result in a finished piece that is durable and long-lasting.

When it comes to washing and cleaning crocheted baby items, it is important to handle them with care to ensure their longevity and maintain their softness. Crocheted baby items, such as blankets, hats, and booties, are often delicate and require special attention during the cleaning process.

Firstly, it is crucial to read the care instructions provided by the manufacturer or the person who made the item. These instructions may vary depending on the type of yarn used and the specific crochet pattern. If there are no specific instructions available, it is best to err on the side of caution and follow general guidelines for washing delicate fabrics.

Before washing, it is advisable to check the item for any stains or spots. If there are any visible stains, it is recommended to treat them before washing. However, it is important to use gentle stain removers that are suitable for delicate fabrics. Harsh chemicals or bleach should be avoided as they can damage the yarn and affect the overall quality of the item.

When it comes to choosing the right washing method, hand washing is generally the safest option for crocheted baby items. Fill a basin or sink with lukewarm water and add a mild detergent specifically designed for delicate fabrics. Gently agitate the water to create suds, but avoid any vigorous rubbing or twisting that could cause the item to stretch or lose its shape.

Place the crocheted baby item into the soapy water and let it soak for a few minutes. Gently swish the item around to ensure that the detergent reaches all areas. Avoid wringing or twisting the item as this can cause it to lose its shape or stretch out. Instead, carefully lift the item out of the water and gently squeeze out the excess water.

Rinsing is an important step to remove any remaining detergent from the item. Fill another basin or sink with clean lukewarm water and place the item in it. Gently swish the item around to rinse off the soap. Repeat this process if necessary until the water runs clear and there are no traces of detergent left.

After rinsing, it is important to remove excess water from the item before drying. Avoid wringing or twisting the item as this can damage the delicate fibers. Instead, gently squeeze out the water or roll the item in a clean towel to absorb the moisture.

After conducting extensive research and considering various factors such as quality, affordability, and popularity among knitting enthusiasts, we have compiled a comprehensive list of recommended yarn brands. These brands have consistently proven their excellence in providing top-notch yarns that cater to the diverse needs and preferences of knitters worldwide.

1. Lion Brand Yarn: Lion Brand Yarn is a well-established and highly regarded brand known for its wide range of yarns suitable for all types of projects. They offer a variety of fibers, including acrylic, wool, cotton, and blends, ensuring that knitters can find the perfect yarn for their creations. Lion Brand Yarn is known for its durability, softness, and vibrant color options, making it a favorite among both beginners and experienced knitters.

2. Red Heart Yarn: Red Heart Yarn is another popular brand that offers an extensive selection of yarns at affordable prices. They are known for their consistent quality and wide range of colors, making it easy for knitters to find the perfect shade for their projects. Red Heart Yarn offers a variety of fibers, including acrylic, wool, and blends, ensuring that knitters have plenty of options to choose from.

3. Cascade Yarns: Cascade Yarns is a brand that is highly regarded for its high-quality yarns, particularly their wool and wool-blend options. They offer a wide range of weights and colors, allowing knitters to create projects with different textures and aesthetics. Cascade Yarns are known for their

excellent stitch definition and durability, making them a favorite among knitters who value both functionality and aesthetics.

4. Malabrigo Yarn: Malabrigo Yarn is a luxury brand that is highly sought after by knitters who appreciate the finest quality fibers. They specialize in hand-dyed yarns, which are known for their stunning color variations and unique visual appeal. Malabrigo Yarn offers a variety of fibers, including merino wool, silk, and alpaca, ensuring that knitters can indulge in luxurious and soft yarns for their projects.

5. Berroco Yarn: Berroco Yarn is a brand that offers a wide range of yarns suitable for various knitting projects. They are known for their innovative blends and unique textures, allowing knitters to create visually interesting and textured garments. Berroco Yarn offers a variety of fibers, including acrylic, wool, cotton, and blends, ensuring that knitters have plenty of options to choose from based on

Creating handmade baby items can bring a deep sense of satisfaction and fulfillment. The process of crafting these items with love and care allows individuals to tap into their creativity and express their unique style. From knitting adorable baby booties to sewing soft and cozy blankets, the act of creating something by hand for a precious little one can be incredibly rewarding.

One of the main reasons why creating handmade baby items is so satisfying is the joy it brings to both the creator and the recipient. Handmade items are often cherished and treasured, as they are imbued with the time, effort, and thoughtfulness that went into making them. Knowing that a handmade baby item will be used and appreciated by a baby and their parents can bring a sense of pride and accomplishment.

Additionally, creating handmade baby items allows individuals to personalize and customize their creations. They have the freedom to choose the colors, patterns, and materials that best suit their vision and the baby's personality. This level of customization adds a special touch to the item, making it truly one-of-a-kind. It also allows the creator to tailor the item to the specific needs and preferences of the baby and their parents, ensuring that it will be both functional and aesthetically pleasing.

The process of creating handmade baby items can also be a form of therapy and relaxation. Engaging in a creative activity such as knitting, crocheting, or sewing can help individuals unwind and reduce stress. The repetitive motions and focus required in these crafts can have a calming effect on the mind and body. This can be particularly beneficial for new parents or individuals who are looking for a way to relax and unwind amidst the busyness of daily life.

Furthermore, creating handmade baby items can be a way to connect with others who share the same passion. Joining crafting communities or attending workshops and classes can provide opportunities to meet like-minded individuals and exchange ideas and techniques. This sense of community and camaraderie can enhance the overall satisfaction of creating handmade baby items, as individuals can learn from and inspire one another.

In conclusion, the satisfaction of creating handmade baby items is multifaceted. It encompasses the joy of bringing happiness to others, the ability to personalize and customize creations, the therapeutic benefits of engaging in a creative activity, and the sense of community that comes with sharing a passion. Whether it's knitting, sewing, or any other craft, the act of creating something by hand for a baby is a truly fulfilling experience.

Getting Started

Before you begin it's important to have the right materials and tools to achieve the best results. Fortunately, you won't need much, but I encourage you to pay attention to the details – not all yarns are great, so choose wisely, and getting the right hook size and sorting out your gauge (tension) are vital, too.

TOOLS AND MATERIALS

To complete most of the projects in this book you will need only yarn and a crochet hook. While you really don't need any fancy crochet hooks to achieve great results, yarn choice is essential.

YARN

The most important thing for a successful project is a good yarn. I always suggest you use natural fibers – wool, alpaca, yak, cashmere, or cotton. Yes, some babies are allergic to animal-based yarns, which means you'll need to choose synthetic fibers. In this case yarn with polyamide is my favorite as it is much softer than acrylic. You could also try blended yarns, which are usually much softer, and less irritating even for very sensitive skin.

When choosing yarn, the second most important consideration is its thickness, or 'yarn weight'. This varies from #0 up to #6. Most of the projects in this book will call for #2, #3 and #4 yarns, which I find are the best for crochet garments. Bear in mind that within the same yarn weight category you will come across significant variations, and some yarns might be thinner or thicker than you want. For this reason it's extremely important to check the gauge (tension). Each pattern calls for a specific gauge and you need to make a swatch and check it before you start. Very often you can fix the gauge by using a bigger or smaller crochet hook, but sometimes some yarns just will not work for the indicated gauge. I suggest in this case you just accept that, and choose another yarn to avoid any disappointment later.

HOOKS

There's such a wide variety of hooks on the market right now, made in so many different materials. Which one is the best? The simple answer is: the one you feel most comfortable working with. You do need to try them to understand that. For me the simplest aluminum ones are the best. Plastic, wood, or any fancy shapes just slow me down. There are some very pretty hooks out there to add to your collection, but you definitely don't need them to achieve great results in crochet.

OTHER MATERIALS

Some patterns will call for stitch markers, a tapestry needle and buttons.

Stitch markers are useful but can be easily substituted with a strand of yarn, a pin or anything else that you can insert into a stitch without damaging it. I find that for crochet the plastic stitch markers are the best, and usually I use the ones without a closure as they are easy and quick to move around.

A tapestry needle needs to have a pretty large eye for comfortable use. As well as assembling a garment, you can use it to weave in all yarn ends, too.

What kind of buttons you use is up to you. Size is always mentioned in the pattern, but material is usually a personal preference. The most important thing is that they need to be very well attached to the garment. Never put a garment on a baby or toddler with poorly sewn on buttons to avoid a choking risk!

SPECIAL TECHNIQUES

There are a few techniques in my patterns that you might find unusual. One of them is pulling the first chain to the height of dc or hdc, and working dc or hdc into the first stitch. Normally you would work ch3 or ch2 to reach the height of dc or hdc, and would count it as a first stitch – working dc or hdc into the next stitch. I find that avoiding it and working dc or hdc directly into the first st creates a much neater edge. It's also great for side edgings as you avoid unnecessary holes.

To avoid moving the joining line in some patterns you might need to work the first stitch of the round backwards, to the right. If this is the case, it is always mentioned in the pattern. It's important to follow these instructions even if they might seem awkward at first.

For top down sweaters and dresses it is very important to work the foundation chain loosely. Chains are not very elastic, especially worked with cotton yarn. For this reason foundation chains need to be pulled longer than you would normally do. If possible, check if the foundation chain is long enough to pass comfortably over the child's head. It will be impossible to make it larger later, but you can always make it tighter when working the ribbing or with a round of single crochet stitches.

TERMINOLOGY

The patterns are written using US crochet terms. If you're used to working with UK terms, here's a guide to the relevant conversions for the stitch names:

US TERM	UK TERM
Single crochet	Double crochet
Half double crochet	Half treble crochet
Double crochet	Treble crochet
Treble crochet	Double treble crochet

ABBREVIATIONS

The following abbreviations are used in this book:

2-dc CL: two double crochet cluster

bo: bobble

BPdc: back post double crochet

BPdc2tog: back post double crochet two together

BPsc: back post single crochet

CC: contrasting color

ch: chain stitch

CL: cluster

crossed CL: crossed cluster

crossed dc: crossed double crochet

dc: double crochet

dc2tog: double crochet two stitches together

FPdc: front post double crochet

FPdc2tog: front post double crochet two together

FPdc3tog: front post double crochet three together

FPsc: front post single crochet

FPtr: front post treble crochet

FPtr3tog: front post treble crochet three together

2-dc CL: two double crochet cluster

hdc: half double crochet

MC: main color

puff: puff stitch

rnd(s): round(s)

RS: right side

sc: single crochet

sl st: slip stitch

sp: space

st(s): stitch(es)

tr: treble crochet

v-st: v stitch

WS: wrong side

yo: yarn over

BOBBLE ROMPER

~ ★★☆ ~

Rompers are the cutest garments to add to your little one's wardrobe. They can be worn just as they are or over a t-shirt, and this one has a handy button opening for easy diaper (nappy) changing. The Bobble Romper is worked top down from the waist. The straps can be adjusted for a better fit – you can shorten them or make them longer.

SIZES AND MEASUREMENTS OF FINISHED GARMENT

Size	Hips	Length from shoulders to bottom
0–6m	46cm/18¼in	34cm/13¼in
6–12m	50cm/19¾in	40cm/15¾in
12–18m	54cm/21¼in	46cm/18¼in

GAUGE (TENSION)

19 sts and 19 rows in sc to measure 10 x 10cm (4 x 4in) using 3.5mm (E/4) hook (or size required to obtain gauge)

SPECIAL STITCHES

FPdc, BPdc, puff (see Special Stitches)

MATERIALS

3 LIGHT

- 325 (375, 450) meters or 355 (411, 493) yards of any DK weight or light worsted weight yarn
  Suggested yarn: Laines du Nord Dolly 125, 100% wool, shade 411, 50g (1¾oz), 125m (136yd)
- 3.5mm (E/4) crochet hook (or size required to obtain gauge)
- 2 buttons, approximately 2cm (¾in) diameter
- Tapestry needle
- 2 stitch markers (optional)

Pattern is written for size 0–6m, changes for 6–12m and 12–18m are in (…).

Ch1 at the beginning of each round doesn't count as a stitch.

WAIST

Foundation chain: work quite loosely to make the waist as elastic as possible, ch66 (72, 80), join with sl st into first ch.

Rnd 1: ch1, dc in first ch, dc in each following ch, join with sl st in first dc; 66 (72, 80) dc A

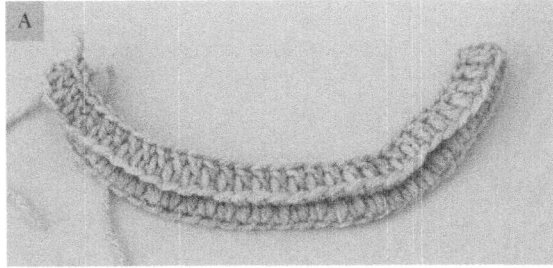

BOTTOM PART

Turn after each rnd and work on both RS and WS.

For sizes 0–6m and 12–18m

Rnd 1 (RS): ch1, sc in first st, sc in next 1 (9)sts, *2sc in next st, sc in each of next 2sts; repeat from * to last st, 2sc in last st, join with sl st in first st, turn; 88 (104) sts B

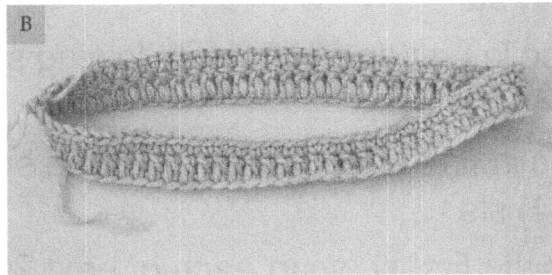

Rnd 2 (WS): ch1, sc in first and in each following st, join with sl st in first st, turn; 88 (104) sts

Rnd 3 (RS): ch1, sc in first and in each following st, join with sl st in first st, turn; 88 (104) sts

Rnd 4 (WS): ch1, sc in first st, sc in each of next 6sts, *puff in next st, sc in each of next 7sts; repeat from * to last st, puff in last st, join with sl st in first sc, turn; 88 (104) sts C

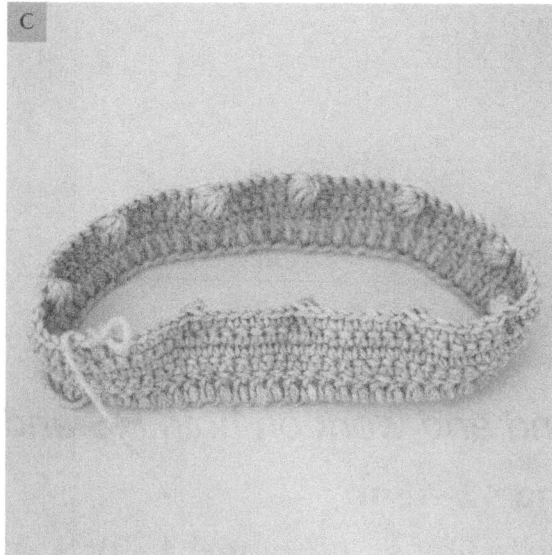

Rnd 5 (RS): ch1, sc in first and in each following st, join with sl st in first st, turn; 88 (104) sts

Rnd 6 (WS): ch1, sc in first and in each following st, join with sl st in first st, turn; 88 (104) sts

Rnd 7 (RS): ch1, sc in first and in each following st, join with sl st in first st, turn; 88 (104) sts

Rnd 8 (WS): ch1, sc in first st, sc in each of next 2sts, *puff in next st, sc in each of next 7sts; repeat from * to end, but in last repeat work sc in each of next 4sts, join with sl st in first st, turn; 88 (104) sts D

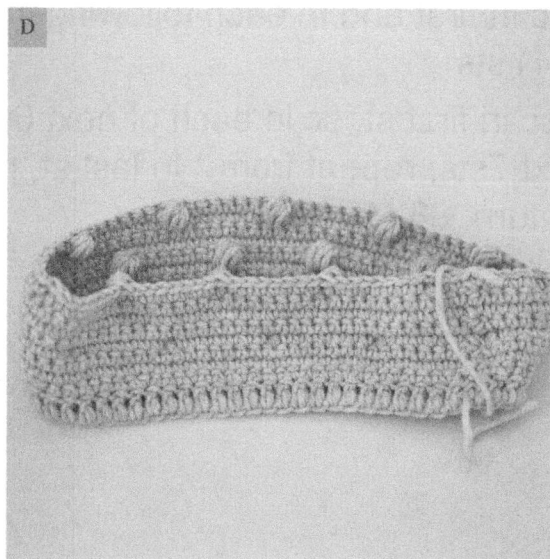

Rnds 9–11: repeat Rnds 5 through 7 E

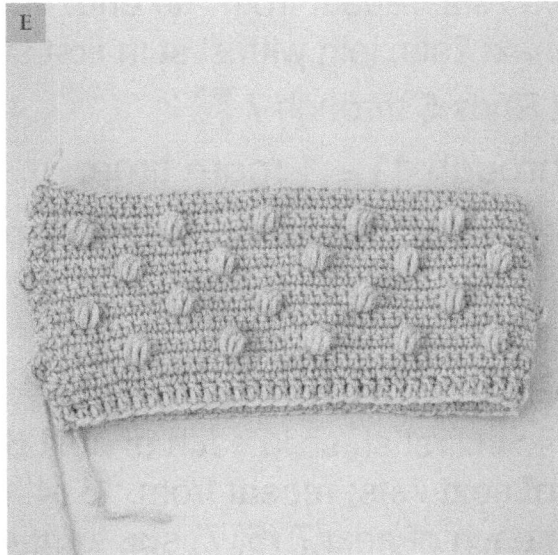

Repeat Rnds 4 through 11 – 1 (2) more times, continue with Back Decreasing.

For size 6–12m

Rnd 1 (RS): ch1, sc in first st, sc in next st, *2sc in next st, sc in each of next 2sts; repeat from * to last st, 2sc in last st, join with sl st in first st, turn; 96 sts B

Rnd 2 (WS): ch1, sc in first and in each following st, join with sl st in first st, turn; 96 sts

Rnd 3 (RS): ch1, sc in first and in each following st, join with sl st in first st, turn; 96 sts

Rnd 4 (WS): ch1, sc in first st, *puff in next st, sc in each of next 7sts; repeat from * to end, in last repeat work sc in each of next 6sts and join with sl st in first st, turn; 96 sts

Rnd 5 (RS): ch1, sc in first and in each following st, join with sl st in first st, turn; 96 sts

Rnd 6 (WS): ch1, sc in first and in each following st, join with sl st in first st, turn; 96 sts

Rnd 7 (RS): ch1, sc in first and in each following st, join with sl st in first st, turn; 96 sts

Rnd 8 (WS): ch1, sc in first st, sc in each of next 4sts, *puff in next st, sc in each of next 7sts; repeat from * to end, but in last repeat work sc in each of next 2sts, join with sl st in first st, turn; 96 sts D

Rnds 9–11: repeat Rnds 5 through 7 E

Repeat Rnds 4 through 11 – 1 more time.

Repeat Rnds 4 through 7 once more and continue with Back Decreasing.

BACK DECREASING

Row 1 (WS): ch1, sc in first st, sc in each of next 6 (4, 6) sts, *puff in next st, sc in each of next 7sts; repeat from * 3 (4, 4) more times, puff in next st, sc in each of next 7 (5, 7) sts, turn; 47 (51, 55) sts

Row 2 (RS): ch1, sc in first st, skip next st, sc in each following st to last 2sts, skip next st, sc in last st, turn; 45 (49, 53) sts

Row 3 (WS): ch1, sc in first st, skip next st, sc in each following st to last 2sts, skip next st, sc in last st, turn; 43 (47, 51) sts F

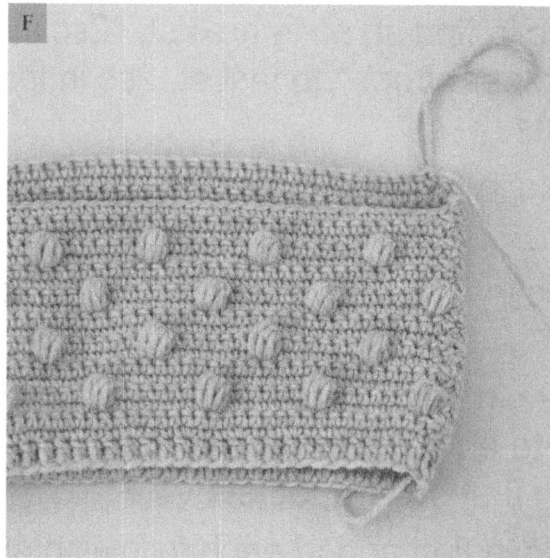

Row 4 (RS): ch1, sc in first st, skip next st, sc in each following st to last 2sts, skip next st, sc in last st, turn; 41 (45, 49) sts

Row 5 (WS): ch1, sc in first st, skip next st, sc in each of next 6 (4, 6) sts, *puff in next st, sc in each of next 7sts; repeat from * 2 (3, 3)

more times, puff in next st, sc in each of next 6 (4, 6) sts, skip next st, sc in last st, turn; 39 (43, 47) sts

Row 6 (RS): ch1, sc in first st, skip next st, sc in each following st to last 2sts, skip next st, sc in last st, turn; 37 (41, 45) sts

Row 7 (WS): ch1, sc in first st, skip next st, sc in each following st to last 2sts, skip next st, sc in last st, turn; 35 (39, 43) sts

Row 8 (RS): ch1, sc in first st, skip next st, sc in each following st to last 2sts, skip next st, sc in last st, turn; 33 (37, 41) sts

Row 9 (WS): ch1, sc in first st, skip next st, sc in each of next 6 (4, 6) sts, *puff in next st, sc in each of next 7sts; repeat from * 1 (2, 2) more times, puff in next st, sc in each of next 6 (4, 6) sts, skip next st, sc in last st, turn; 31 (35, 39) sts

Row 10 (RS): ch1, sc in first st, skip next st, sc in each following st to last 2sts, skip next st, sc in last st, turn; 29 (33, 37) sts

Row 11 (WS): ch1, sc in first st, skip next st, sc in each following st to last 2sts, skip next st, sc in last st, turn; 27 (31, 35) sts

Row 12 (RS): ch1, sc in first st, skip next st, sc in each following st to last 2sts, skip next st, sc in last st, turn; 25 (29, 33) sts

Row 13 (WS): ch1, sc in first st, skip next st, sc in each of next 6 (4, 6) sts, *puff in next st, sc in each of next 7sts; repeat from * 0 (1, 1) more time, puff in next st, sc in each of next 6 (4, 6) sts, skip next st, sc in last st, turn; 23 (27, 31) sts

Row 14 (RS): ch1, sc in first st, skip next st, sc in each following st to last 2sts, skip next st, sc in last st, turn; 21 (25, 29) sts

Row 15 (WS): ch1, sc in first st, skip next st, sc in each following st to last 2sts, skip next st, sc in last st, turn; 19 (23, 27) sts

Row 16 (RS): ch1, sc in first st, skip next st, sc in each following st to last 2sts, skip next st, sc in last st, turn; 17 (21, 25) sts

For size 0–6m

Row 17 (WS): ch1, sc in first st, skip next st, sc in each of next 6sts, puff in next st, sc in each of next 6sts, skip next st, sc in last st, turn; 15 sts

For sizes 6–12m and 12–18m

Row 17 (WS): ch1, sc in first st, skip next st, sc in each of next (4, 6) sts, puff in next st, sc in each of next 7sts, puff in next st, sc in each of next (4, 6) sts, skip next st, sc in last st, turn; (19, 23) sts

For all sizes

Row 18 (RS): ch1, sc in first st, skip next st, sc in each following st to last 2sts, skip next st, sc in last st, turn; 13 (17, 21) sts

Row 19 (WS): ch1, sc in first st, skip next st, sc in each following st to last 2sts, skip next st, sc in last st, turn; 11 (15, 19) sts

Row 20 (RS): ch1, sc in first st, skip next st, sc in each following st to last 2sts, skip next st, sc in last st, turn; 9 (13, 17) sts G

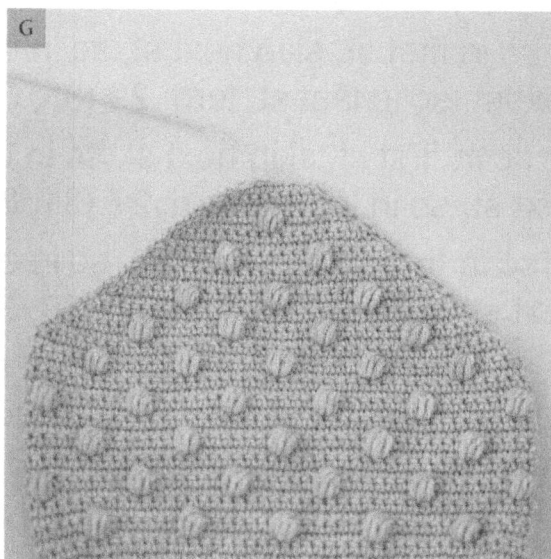

For size 0–6m

Fasten off and continue with Front Decreasing.

For size 6–12m

Row 21 (WS): ch1, sc in first st and in each following st to end, turn; 13 sts

Row 22 (RS): ch1, sc in first st and in each following st to end, turn; 13 sts, fasten off and continue with Front Decreasing.

For size 12–18m

Row 21 (WS): ch1, sc in first st, skip next st, sc in each of next 6sts, puff in next st, sc in each of next 6sts, skip next st, sc in last st, turn; 15 sts

Row 22 (RS): ch1, sc in first st, skip next st, sc in each following st to last 2sts, skip next st, sc in last st, turn; 13 sts

Row 23 (WS): ch1, sc in first st and in each following st to end, turn; 13 sts

Row 24 (RS): ch1, sc in first st and in each following st to end, turn; 13 sts

Rows 25–26: repeat Rows 23 and 24, fasten off and continue with Front Decreasing.

FRONT DECREASING

On WS, skip one st from the Back, join yarn into next st and work H

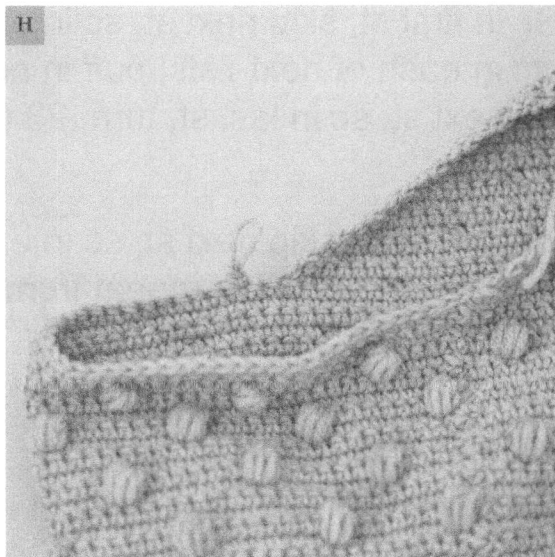

Row 1 (WS): ch1, sc in first st, sc in each of next 6 (8, 6) sts, *puff in next st, sc in each of next 7sts; repeat from * 2 (2, 3) more times, puff in next st, sc in each of next 7 (9, 7) sts, turn; 39 (43, 47) sts

Row 2 (RS): ch1, sc in first st, skip next st, sc in each following st to last 2sts, skip next st, sc in last st, turn; 37 (41, 45) sts

Row 3 (WS): ch1, sc in first st, skip next st, sc in each following st to last 2sts, skip next st, sc in last st, turn; 35 (39, 43) sts

Row 4 (RS): ch1, sc in first st, skip next st, sc in each following st to last 2sts, skip next st, sc in last st, turn; 33 (37, 41) sts

Row 5 (WS): ch1, sc in first st, skip next st, sc in each of next 6 (8, 6) sts, *puff in next st, sc in each of next 7sts; repeat from * 1 (1, 2) more times, puff in next st, sc in each of next 6 (8, 6) sts, skip next st, sc in last st, turn; 31 (35, 39) sts

Row 6 (RS): ch1, sc in first st, skip next st, sc in each following st to last 2sts, skip next st, sc in last st, turn; 29 (33, 37) sts

Row 7 (WS): ch1, sc in first st, skip next st, sc in each following st to last 2sts, skip next st, sc in last st, turn; 27 (31, 35) sts

Row 8 (RS): ch1, sc in first st, skip next st, sc in each following st to last 2sts, skip next st, sc in last st, turn; 25 (29, 33) sts

For sizes 0–6m and 6–12m

Row 9 (WS): ch1, sc in first st, skip next st, sc in each of next 6 (8) sts, puff in next st, sc in each of next 7sts, puff in next st, sc in each of next 6 (8) sts, skip next st, sc in last st, turn; 23 (27) sts

For size 12–18m

Row 9 (WS): ch1, sc in first st, skip next st, sc in each of next 6sts, *puff in next st, sc in each of next 7sts; repeat from * 1 more time, puff in next st, sc in each of next 6sts, skip next st, sc in last st, turn; 31 sts

For all sizes

Row 10 (RS): ch1, sc in first st, skip next st, sc in each following st to last 2sts, skip next st, sc in last st, turn; 21 (25, 29) sts

Row 11 (WS): ch1, sc in first st, skip next st, sc in each following st to last 2sts, skip next st, sc in last st, turn; 19 (23, 27) sts

Row 12 (RS): ch1, sc in first st, skip next st, sc in each following st to last 2sts, skip next st, sc in last st, turn; 17 (21, 25) sts

For sizes 0–6m and 6–12m

Row 13 (WS): ch1, sc in first st, skip next st, sc in each of next 6 (8) sts, puff in next st, sc in each of next 6 (8) sts, skip next st, sc in last st, turn; 15 (19) sts

For size 12–18m

Row 13 (WS): ch1, sc in first st, skip next st, sc in each of next 6sts, puff in next st, sc in each of next 7sts, puff in next st, sc in each of next 6sts, skip next st, sc in last st, turn; 23 sts

For all sizes

Row 14 (RS): ch1, sc in first st, skip next st, sc in each following st to last 2sts, skip next st, sc in last st, turn; 13 (17, 21) sts

Row 15 (WS): ch1, sc in first st, skip next st, sc in each following st to last 2sts, skip next st, sc in last st, turn; 11 (15, 19) sts

Row 16 (RS): ch1, sc in first st, skip next st, sc in each following st to last 2sts, skip next st, sc in last st, turn; 9 (13, 17) sts

For sizes 0–6m and 6–12m

Don't fasten off but work Edging.

For size 12–18m

Row 17 (WS): ch1, sc in first st, skip next st, sc in each of next 6sts, puff in next st, sc in each of next 6sts, skip next st, sc in last st, turn; 15 sts

Row 18 (RS): ch1, sc in first st, skip next st, sc in each following st to last 2sts, skip next st, sc in last st, turn; 13 sts

Row 19 (WS): ch1, sc in first st and in each following st to end, turn; 13 sts

Row 20 (RS): ch1, sc in first st and in each following st to end; 13 sts, don't fasten off but work Edging.

EDGING

Rnd 1 (RS): ch1, but pull it to the height of dc here and throughout, 3dc in first st, work dc evenly across the Front and the Back, on corners work 3dc twice in one st, at the end of the rnd work 3dc only once in one st as you started the rnd with 3dc, join with sl st in first st (number of sts is not important here but it has to be an even number and make sure right and left leg opening have same amount of sts) J

Rnd 2 (RS): ch1, FPdc around first dc, *BPdc around next dc, FPdc around next dc; repeat from * to last dc, BPdc around last dc, join with sl st in first st.

Rnd 3 (RS): on the back piece mark the sts for buttonholes K , for sizes 0–6m and 6–12m make two buttonholes, for sizes 12–18m – three buttonholes; repeat Rnd 2, working FPdc around each FPdc, and BPdc around each BPdc, but skip marked sts and work ch1 instead, join with sl st in first st L

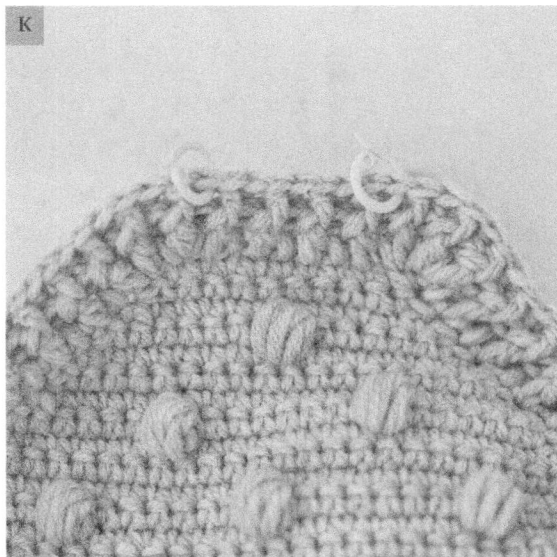

Rnd 4 (RS): ch1, work FPdc around each FPdc and BPdc around each BPdc, work sc into each ch1sp, join with sl st in first st, fasten off M

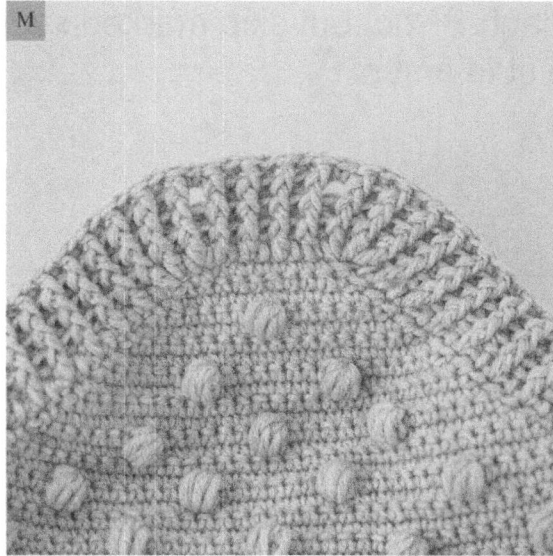

WAIST RIBBING

Join yarn into the remaining loop of foundation chain at joining line and work:

Rnd 1 (RS): ch1, FPdc around first dc, *BPdc around next dc, FPdc around next dc; repeat from * to last dc, BPdc around next dc, join with sl st in first st; 66 (72, 80) dc N

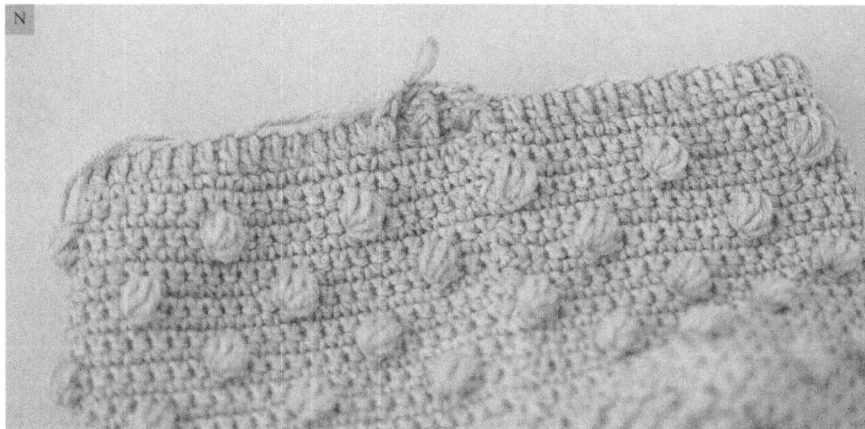

Rnd 2 (RS): ch1, work FPdc around each FPdc and BPdc around each BPdc, join with sl st in first st

Repeat Rnd 2 – 2 more times, fasten off and continue with Front Bib.

The button opening makes diaper changes easy, or at least a bit easier!

FRONT BIB

Mark 27 (29, 31) sts in the middle of the Front, as shown in photo O , first and last st has to be BPdc, and work:

Row 1 (RS): ch1, sc in first BPdc, FPdc around next FPdc, sc in each following 3sts, FPdc around next FPdc, sc in next 15 (17, 19) sts, FPdc around next FPdc, sc in each following 3sts, FPdc around next FPdc, sc in next st, turn; 27 (29, 31) sts P

Row 2 (WS): ch1, sc in first st, sc in each following 2sts, puff in next st, sc in next 19 (21, 23) sts, puff in next st, sc in each following 3sts, turn; 27 (29, 31) sts

Row 3 (RS): ch1, sc in first st, FPdc around next FPdc two rows below, sc in each following 3sts, FPdc around next FPdc two rows below, sc in next 15 (17, 19) sts, FPdc around next FPdc two rows below, sc in each following 3sts, FPdc around next FPdc two rows below, sc in next st, turn; 27 (29, 31) sts

Row 4 (WS): ch1, sc in first st, sc in next st, puff in next st, sc in next st, puff in next st, sc in next 17 (19, 21) sts, puff in next st, sc in next st, puff in next st, sc in each of next 2sts, turn; 27 (29, 31) sts

Row 5 (RS): ch1, sc in first st, FPdc around next FPdc two rows below, sc in each of next 3sts, FPdc around next FPdc two rows below, sc in next 15 (17, 19) sts, FPdc around next FPdc two rows below, sc in each of next 3sts, FPdc around next FPdc two rows below, sc in next st, turn; 27 (29, 31) sts R

Repeat Rows 2 through 5 – 3 (4, 5) more times, continue with Straps S

STRAPS

Row 1 (WS): ch1, sc in first st, sc in each of next 2sts, puff in next st, sc in next 3sts, turn; 7 sts

Row 2 (RS): ch1, sc in first st, FPdc around next FPdc two rows below, sc in each of next 3sts, FPdc around next FPdc two rows below, sc in next st, turn; 7 sts

Row 3 (WS): ch1, sc in first st, sc in next st, puff in next st, sc in next st, puff in next st, sc in each of next 2sts, turn; 7 sts

Row 4 (RS): ch1, sc in first st, FPdc around next FPdc two rows below, sc in each following 3sts, FPdc around next FPdc two rows below, sc in next st, turn; 7 sts

Repeat Rows 1 through 4 – 8 (9, 10) more times T , don't fasten off, but turn the romper inside out and join the strap to the waist working sl sts across through both layers U V . You can choose placement of the strap – it may be closer to the center of the back or just behind the Front. Turn and work sl sts across the strap on the right side to prevent it from stretching out, fasten off W X

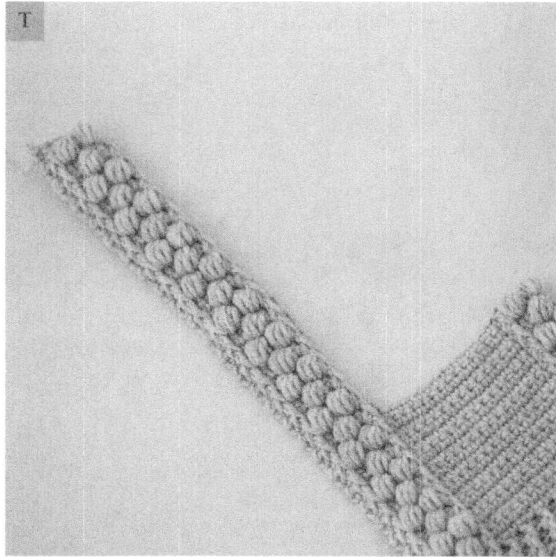

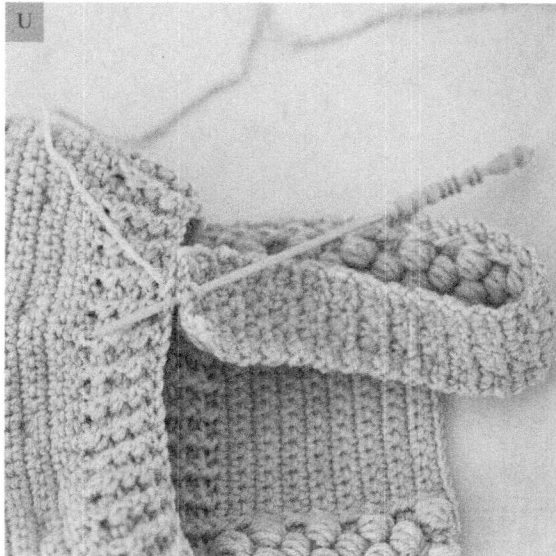

Second Strap

On the WS, join yarn into the 7th st from the side edge Y and repeat Rows 1 through 4 – 9 (10, 11) times, join in the same way as first strap Z . It's important that both straps are placed symmetrically. Fasten off.

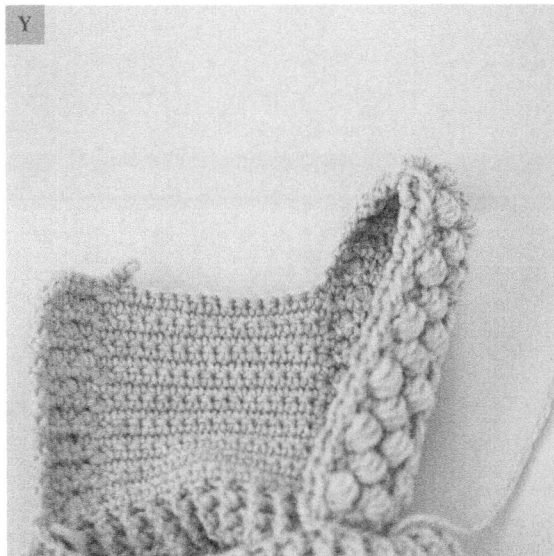

FINISHING

Weave in all ends (see Finishing Techniques).

Sew on the buttons (see Finishing Techniques) on the front, opposite the buttonholes.

RUFFLE SWEATER

~ ★★☆ ~

The Ruffle Sweater is worked from the top down
without seams, and comes together really quickly.
The ruffle is optional but I strongly suggest you
don't omit it. It adds that extra touch that makes this
sweater really special.

SIZES AND MEASUREMENTS OF FINISHED GARMENT

Size	Chest	Length	Sleeve length to underarm
0–6m	48cm/19in	28cm/11in	15cm/6in
6–12m	54cm/21¼in	31cm/12¼in	18cm/7in
1–2y	60cm/23½in	35cm/13¾in	22cm/8½in
3–4y	64cm/25¼in	39cm/15¼in	26cm/10¼in

GAUGE (TENSION)

18 sts and 10 rows in dc to measure 10 x 10cm (4 x 4in) using 4mm (G/6) hook (or size required to obtain gauge)

SPECIAL STITCHES

FPdc, BPdc, CL, Crossed CL, dc2tog (see Special Stitches)

MATERIALS

3 LIGHT

- 500 (550, 625, 750) meters or 547 (602, 684, 820) yards of any DK weight or light worsted weight yarn
  Suggested yarn: Laines du Nord Dolly 125, 100% wool, shade 213, 50g (1¾oz), 125m (136yd)
- 4mm (G/6) crochet hook (or size required to obtain gauge)

Pattern is written for size 0–6m, changes for 6–12m, 1–2y and 3–4y are in (…).

Ch1 at the beginning of each round doesn't count as a stitch.

YOKE

Foundation chain: work loosely, pull each ch longer, it has to pass over child's head, ch56 (58, 60, 64), join with sl st in first st.

Rnd 1 (RS): ch1, but pull it to the height of dc here and throughout where next st is dc, dc in first and in each following ch to end, join with sl st in first st; 56 (58, 60, 64) sts

Rnd 2 (RS): ch1, dc in first st, *2dc in next st, dc in next st; repeat from * to last st, 2 (1, 2, 2) dc in last st, join with sl st in first st; 84 (86, 90, 96) sts A

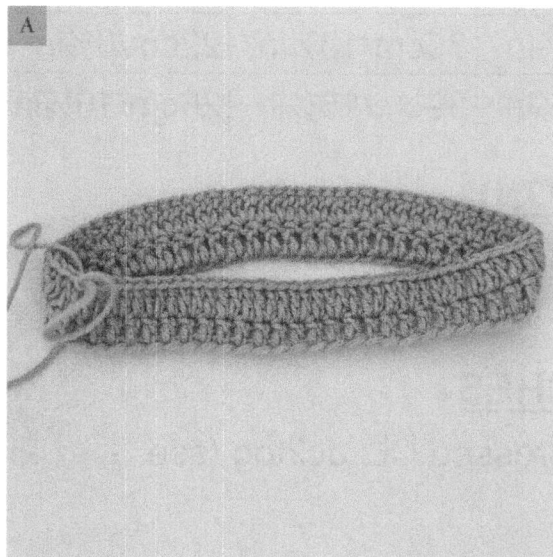

Rnd 3 (RS): ch1, sc in first st, *ch2, skip next st, sc in next st; repeat from * to end, instead of last sc join with sl st in first st; 42 (43, 45, 48) ch2sp made B

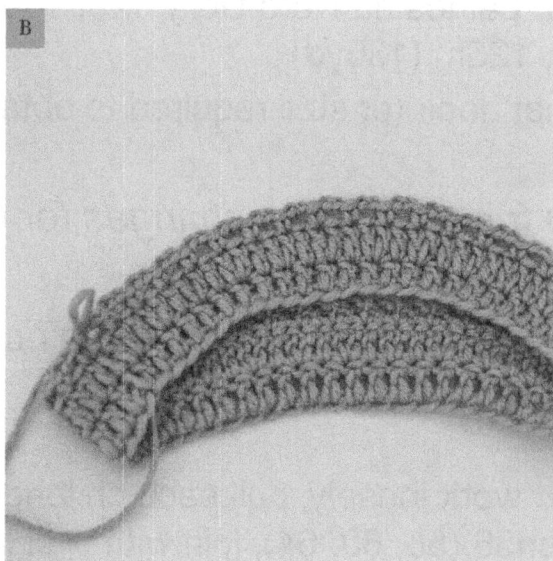

Rnd 4 (RS): ch1, sc in ch2sp to the right, *ch2, skip next sc, sc in next ch2sp; repeat from * to end, instead of last sc join with sl st in first st; 42 (43, 45, 48) ch2sp made C

Rnd 5 (RS): ch1, skip first st, *3dc in next ch2sp, skip next sc; repeat from * to end, for sizes 6–12m and 1–2y in last repeat work 2dc in last ch2sp, join with sl st in first st; 126 (128, 134, 144) sts D

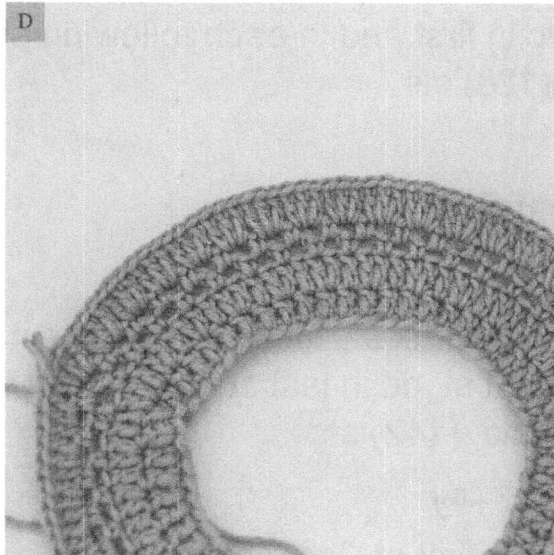

Rnd 6 (RS): ch1, sc in first st, *ch2, skip next st, sc in next st; repeat from * to end, instead of last sc join with sl st in first st; 63 (64, 67, 72) ch2sp made

Rnd 7 (RS): ch1, sc in ch2sp to the right, *ch2, skip next sc, sc in next ch2sp; repeat from * to end, instead of last sc join with sl st in first st; 63 (64, 67, 72) ch2sp made

Rnd 8 (RS): ch1, skip first st, *2dc in next ch2sp, skip next sc; repeat from * to end, join with sl st in first st; 126 (128, 134, 144) sts E

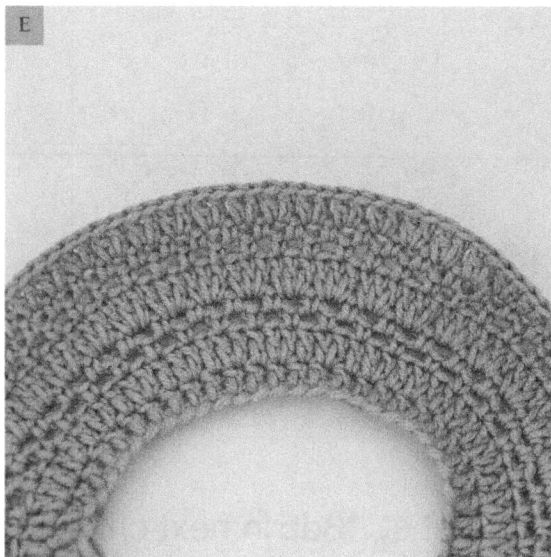

For sizes 0–6m and 6–12m

Rnd 9 (RS): ch1, dc in first and in each following st to end, join with sl st in first st; 126 (128) sts

For size 0–6m

Continue with Last Rnd.

For size 6–12m

Rnd 10 (RS): ch1, dc in first st, *dc in each of next 8sts, 2dc in next st; repeat from * to last st, dc in last st, join with sl st in first st and continue with Last Rnd; (142) sts

For sizes 1–2y and 3–4y

Rnd 9 (RS): ch1, sc in first st, *ch2, skip next st, sc in next st; repeat from * to end, instead of last sc join with sl st in first st; (67, 72) ch2sp made

Rnd 10 (RS): ch1, sc in ch2sp to the right, *ch2, skip next sc, sc in next ch2sp; repeat from * to end, instead of last sc join with sl st in first st; (67, 72) ch2sp made

Rnd 11 (RS): ch1, skip first st, *2dc in next ch2sp, skip next sc; repeat from * to end, join with sl st in first st; (134, 144) sts

Rnd 12 (RS): ch1, dc in first st, *dc in each of next (5, 6) sts, 2dc in next st; repeat from * to last (13, 3) sts, dc in each of next (13, 3) sts, join with sl st in first st and continue with Last Rnd; (154, 164) sts

For all sizes

Last Rnd (RS): ch1, BPdc around first and around each st to end, join with sl st in first st; 126 (142, 154, 164) sts, continue with Divide for Body and Sleeves F

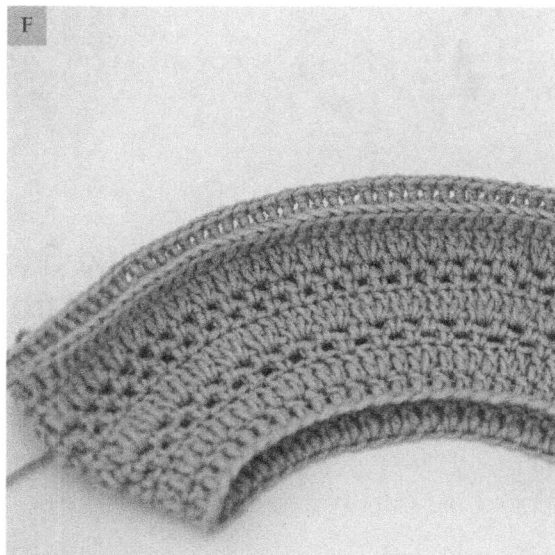

DIVIDE FOR BODY AND SLEEVES

Rnd 1 (RS): ch1, dc in first st, ch5 (6, 7, 8), skip next 26 (28, 30, 32) sts for an armhole, dc in each of next 37 (43, 47, 50) sts, ch5 (6, 7, 8), skip next 26 (28, 30, 32) sts for an armhole, dc in each following st to end, join with sl st in first st; 84 (98, 108, 116) sts including all ch G

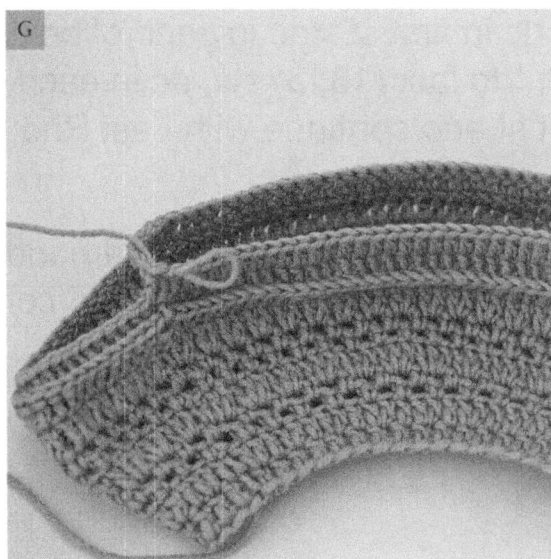

Rnd 2 (RS): ch1, dc in first and in each of next 5 (5, 7, 6) sts, *2dc in next st, dc in each of next 6 (6, 8, 8) sts; repeat from * to last st, 2 (2, 2, 1) sts, dc in last st, join with sl st in first st, turn and work on WS; 96 (112, 120, 128) sts H

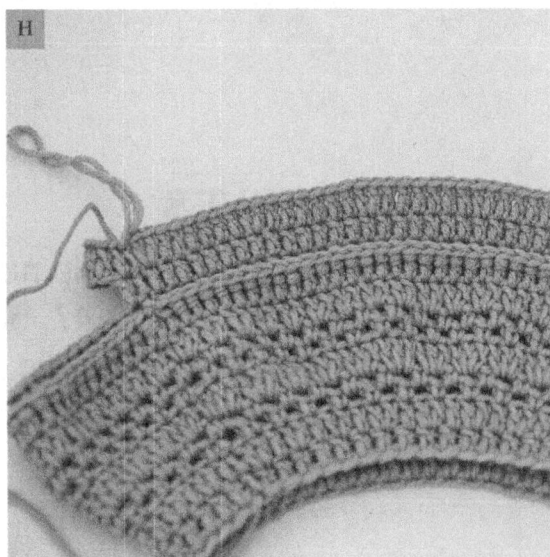

Rnd 3 (WS): ch1, dc in first st, *crossed CL worked over next 2sts, dc in each of next 6sts; I repeat from * to end, in last repeat work dc in each of next 5sts and join with sl st in first st, turn and work on RS; 96 (112, 120, 128) sts

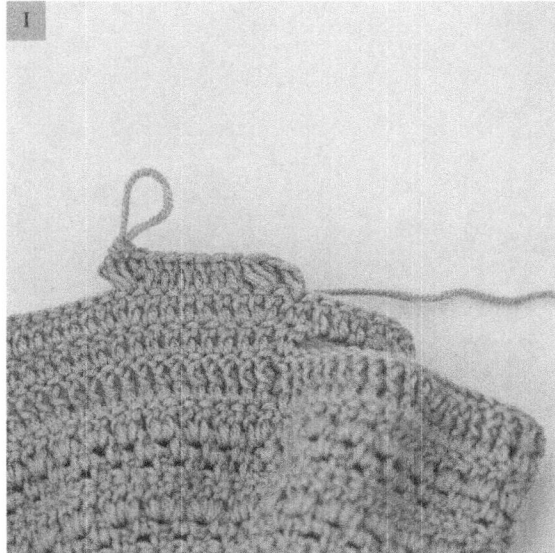

Rnd 4 (RS): ch1, dc in first and in each following st to end, join with sl st in first st; turn and work on WS; 96 (112, 120, 128) sts J

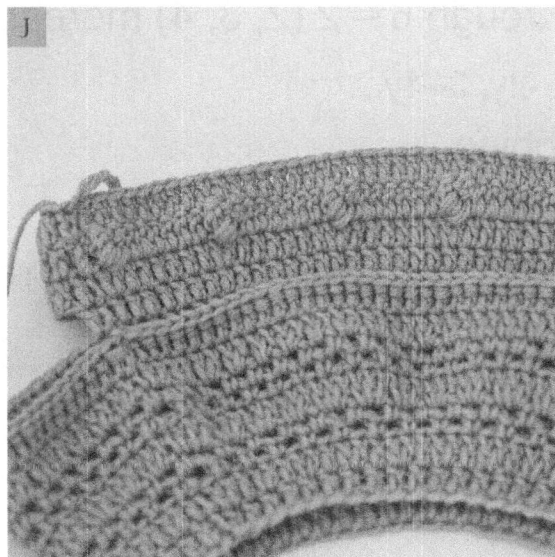

Rnd 5 (WS): ch1, dc in first st, dc in each of next 4sts, *crossed CL worked over next 2sts, dc in each of next 6sts; repeat from * to end, in last repeat work dc in last st and join with sl st in first st, turn and work on RS; 96 (112, 120, 128) sts K

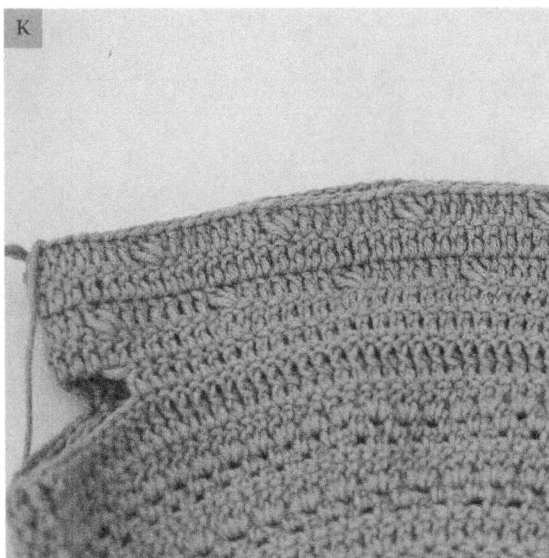

Rnd 6 (RS): ch1, dc in first and in each following st to end, join with sl st in first st; turn and work on WS; 96 (112, 120, 128) sts

Repeat Rnds 3 through 6 – 2 (2, 3, 4) more times.

For sizes 0–6m, 1–2y, 3–4y

Continue with Ribbing.

For size 6–12m

Repeat Rnds 3 and 4 once more and continue with Ribbing.

The texture created on the body of the sweater is continued on the sleeves.

RIBBING

Rnd 1 (RS): ch1, FPdc around first dc, *BPdc around next dc, FPdc around next dc; repeat from * to last dc, BPdc around last dc, join with sl st in first st; 96 (112, 120, 128) sts

Rnd 2 (RS): ch1, FPdc around first FPdc, *BPdc around next BPdc, FPdc around next FPdc; repeat from * to last st, BPdc around last BPdc, join with sl st in first st; 96 (112, 120, 128) sts

Repeat Rnd 2 once more and fasten off.

SLEEVES

On RS, join yarn in the middle of the underarm L , turn after each round and work on both RS and WS.

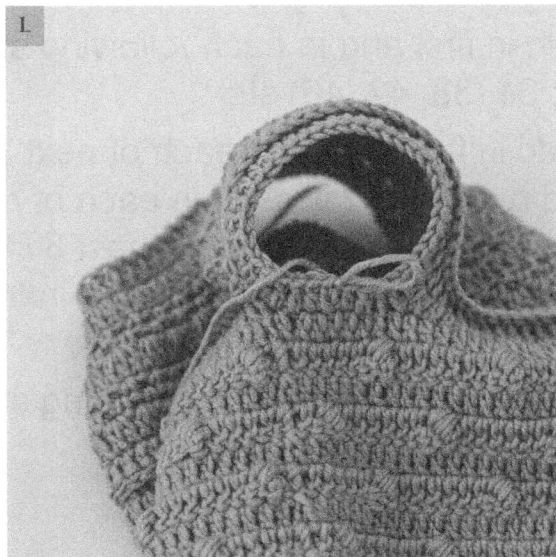

For larger sizes under the arms there will be no CL, that's part of the design to avoid extra bulk.

Rnd 1 (RS): ch1, dc in first st, work evenly 37 (41, 45, 49) dc, join with sl st in first st, turn; 38 (42, 46, 50) sts

Rnd 2 (WS): ch1, dc in first and in each of next 5 (7, 9, 11) sts, crossed CL worked over next 2sts, *dc in each of next 6sts, crossed CL worked over next 2sts; repeat from * to last 6 (8, 10, 12) sts, dc in each st to end, join with sl st in first st, turn; 38 (42, 46, 50) sts

Rnd 3 (RS): ch1, dc in first st, dc2tog, dc in each following st to last 2sts, dc2tog, join with sl st in first st; turn; 36 (40, 44, 48) sts

Rnd 4 (WS): ch1, dc in first st and in each of next 0 (2, 4, 6) sts, *crossed CL worked over next 2sts, dc in each of next 6sts; repeat from * to last 3 (5, 7, 9) sts, crossed CL worked over next 2sts, dc each of next 1 (3, 5, 7) sts, join with sl st in first st, turn; 36 (40, 44, 48) sts

Rnd 5 (RS): ch1, dc in first st, dc2tog, dc in each following st to last 2sts, dc2tog, join with sl st in first st; turn; 34 (38, 42, 46) sts

Rnd 6 (WS): ch1, dc in first st and in each of next 3 (5, 7, 9) sts, *crossed CL worked over next 2 sts, dc in each of next 6sts; repeat from * to end, in last repeat work dc in each of next 4 (6, 8, 10) sts and join with sl st in first st, turn; 34 (38, 42, 46) sts

Rnd 7 (RS): ch1, dc in first and in each following st to end, join with sl st in first st; turn; 34 (38, 42, 46) sts

Rnd 8 (WS): ch1, dc in first st and in each of next 7 (9, 11, 13) sts, crossed CL worked over next 2sts, *dc in each of next 6sts, crossed CL worked over next 2sts; repeat from * to last 8 (10, 12, 14) sts, dc in each of next 8 (10, 12, 14) sts, join with sl st in first st, turn; 34 (38, 42, 46) sts

Rnd 9 (RS): ch1, dc in first and in each following st to end, join with sl st in first st; turn; 34 (38, 42, 46) sts

For size 0–6m

Repeat Rnds 6 and 7 once more or until desired length, don't turn and continue with Cuff.

For size 6–12m

Repeat Rnds 6 through 9 once more or until desired length, don't turn and continue with Cuff.

For size 1–2y

Repeat Rnds 6 through 9 – 2 more times or until desired length, don't turn and continue with Cuff.

For size 3–4y

Repeat Rnds 6 through 9 – 3 more times or until desired length, don't turn and continue with Cuff.

Second Sleeve

Work in exactly the same way as first sleeve.

CUFF

Rnd 1 (RS): ch1, FPdc around first dc, *BPdc around next dc, FPdc around next dc; repeat from * to last st, BPdc around last dc, join with sl st in first st; 34 (38, 42, 46) sts

Rnd 2 (RS): ch1, FPdc around first FPdc, *BPdc around next BPdc, FPdc around next FPdc; repeat from * to last st, BPdc around last BPdc, join with sl st in first st; 34 (38, 42, 46) sts

Repeat Rnd 2 – one more time, fasten off.

Second Cuff

Work in exactly the same way on second sleeve.

COLLAR

Rnd 1 (RS): join yarn into the first st of collar, into the remaining loop and work ch1, FPdc around first dc M , *BPdc around next dc, FPdc around next dc* repeat from * to last st, BPdc around next st, join with sl st in first st; 56 (58, 60, 64) sts

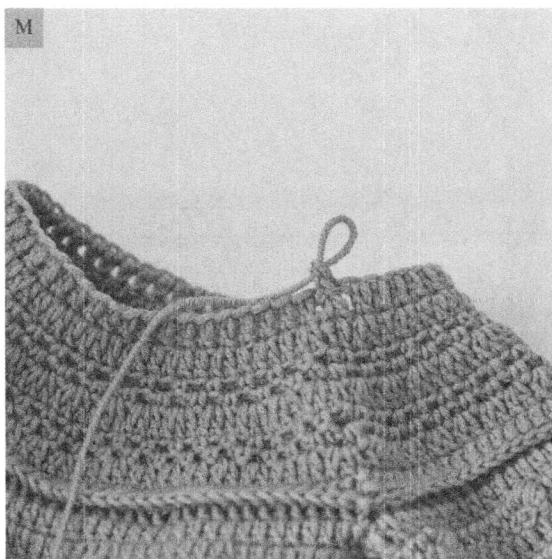

Rnd 2 (RS): ch1, FPdc around first FPdc, *BPdc around next BPdc, FPdc around next FPdc; repeat from * to last st, BPdc around last BPdc, join with sl st in first st; 56 (58, 60, 64) sts

Repeat Rnd 2 – one more time, fasten off N

RUFFLE

Join yarn into the remaining loop of dc on yoke on shoulder and work

Rnd 1 (RS): ch1, 2dc in first st, *3dc in next st, 2dc in next st; repeat from * to end, join with sl st in first st; stitch count is not important but it has to be an even number

Rnd 2 (RS): ch1, dc in first and in each following st, join with sl st in first st

Rnd 3 (RS): ch1, sc in first st, *ch2, skip next st, sc in next st; repeat from * to end, in last repeat instead of last sc join with sl st in first st, fasten off P

The ruffle is optional but I suggest you don't omit it.

FINISHING

Weave in ends, wash and block (see Finishing Techniques).

YAK SWEATER

~ ★★☆ ~

Crochet for boys can be tricky as not all patterns strike the right balance between cute but not too frilly, but that doesn't mean that they have to be boring. This sweater is the perfect gender-neutral pattern. It is worked top down and is completely seamless. The body and sleeve length are easy to adjust, and it works up really quickly too!

SIZES AND MEASUREMENTS OF FINISHED GARMENT

Size	Chest	Length	Sleeve length to underarm	Yoke
0–6m	48cm/19in	28cm/11in	15cm/6in	11cm/4¼in
6–12m	53cm/21in	31cm/12¼in	17cm/6¾in	12cm/4¾in
1–2y	58cm/22¾in	35cm/13¾in	20cm/7¾in	13cm/5in
3–4y	61cm/24in	40cm/15¾in	23cm/9in	15cm/6in

GAUGE (TENSION)

18 sts and 10 rows in dc to measure 10 x 10cm (4 x 4in) using 3.75mm (F/5) hook (or size required to obtain gauge)

SPECIAL STITCHES

BPdc, FPdc, dc2tog (see Special Stitches)

MATERIALS

3 LIGHT

- 345 (414, 506, 575) meters or 378 (453, 554, 630) yards of any DK weight or light worsted weight yarn
  Suggested yarn: Laines du Nord Merino Yak, 70% wool, 15% alpaca, 15% yak, shade 02, 50g (1¾oz), 115m (125yd)
- 3.75mm (F/5) crochet hook (or size required to obtain gauge)

Pattern is written for size 0–6m, changes for 6–12m, 1–2y and 3–4y are in (…).

Ch1 at the beginning of each round doesn't count as a stitch.

YOKE

Foundation chain: working loosely (it has to pass comfortably over child's head), ch 60 (64, 68, 72), join with sl st in first ch.

Rnd 1 (RS): ch1, but pull it to the height of dc here and throughout where next st is dc or tr, dc in first and in each following ch, join with sl st in first st; 60 (64, 68, 72) sts A

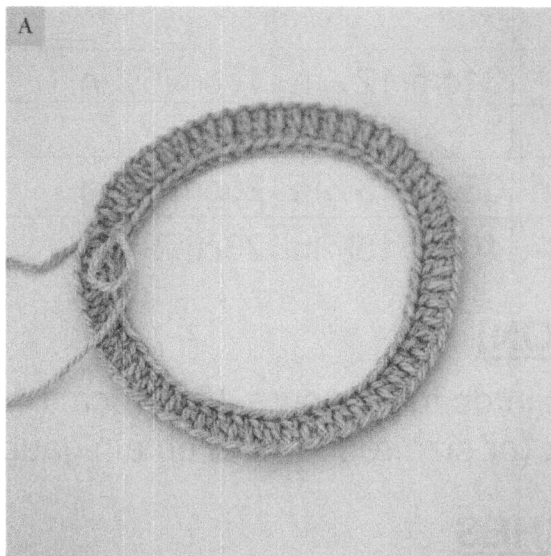

Rnd 2 (RS): ch1, skip first st, tr in next st, 3dc in skipped st working behind tr just made, B *skip next st, 3dc in next st, C tr in skipped st working in front of 3dc just made, D skip next st, tr in next st, 3dc in skipped st working behind tr just made; E repeat from * to last 2 sts, skip next st, 3dc in next st, tr in skipped st working in front of 3dc just made, join with sl st in first st; 120 (128, 136, 144) sts F

Rnd 3 (RS): ch1, sc in first and in each following st, join with sl st in first st; 120 (128, 136, 144) sts G

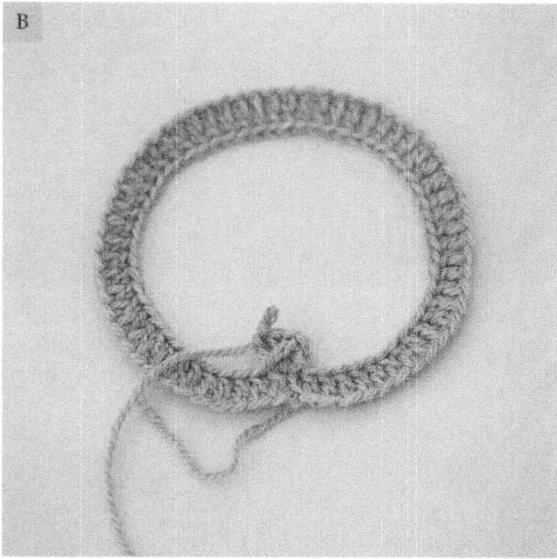

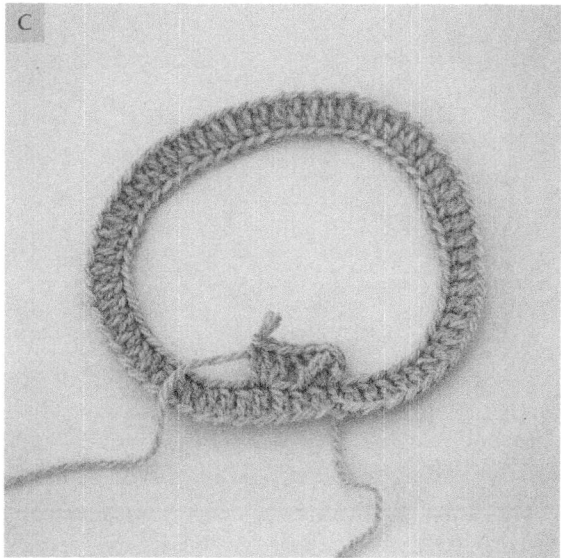

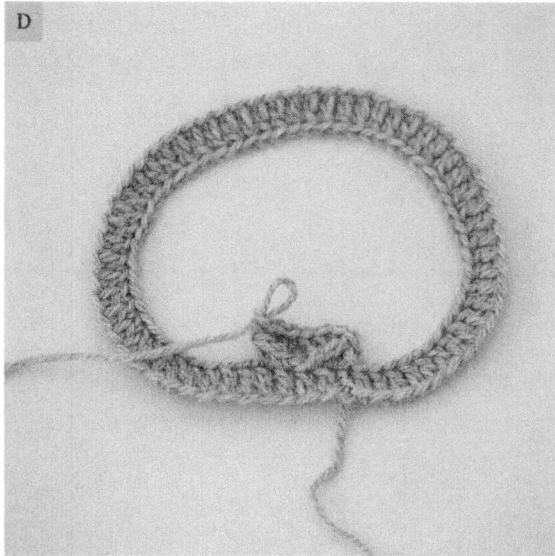

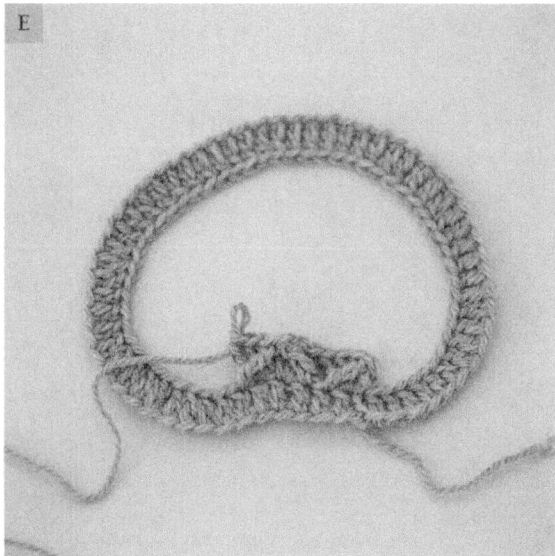

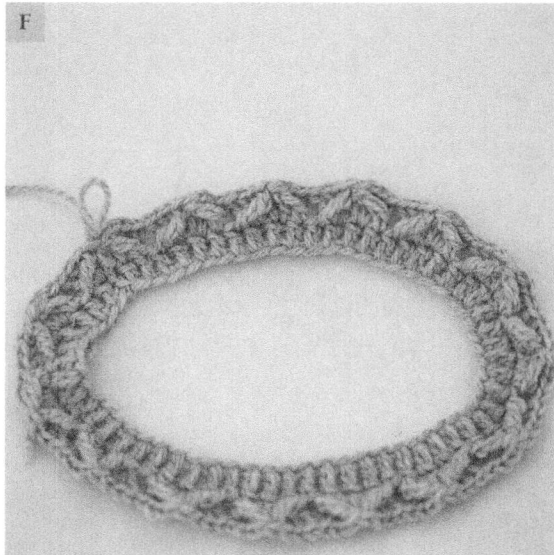

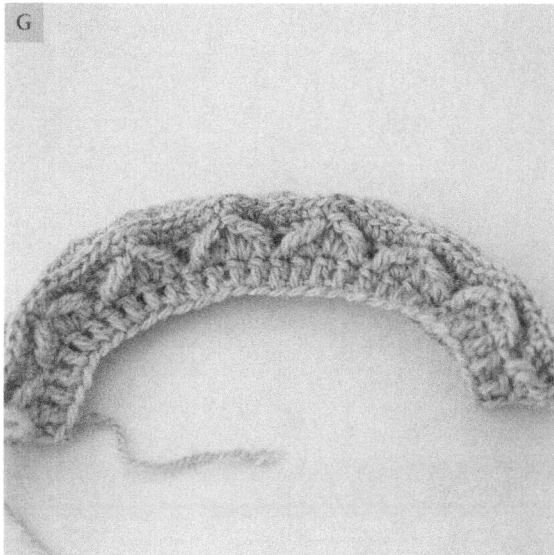

Rnd 4 (RS): ch1, skip first and next 2sts, tr in next st `H` , dc in each of 3 skipped sts working behind tr just made `I` , *skip next st, dc in each of next 3sts, tr in skipped st working in front of 3dc just made, skip next 3sts, tr in next st, dc in each of 3 skipped sts working behind tr just made; repeat from * to last 4sts, skip next st, dc in each of next 3sts, tr in skipped st working in front of 3dc just made, join with sl st in first st; 120 (128, 136, 144) sts `J`

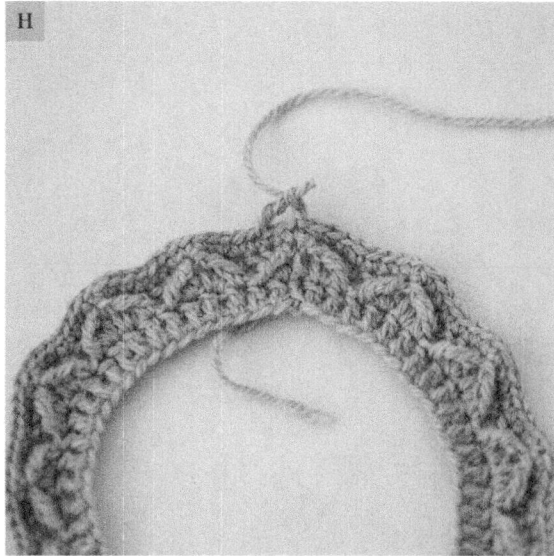

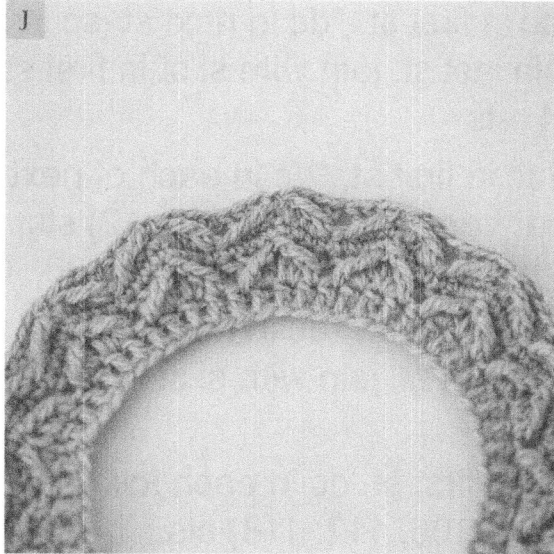

Repeat Rnds 3 and 4 – 2 (3, 4, 5) more times.

Repeat Rnd 3 once more.

DIVIDE FOR SLEEVES AND BODY

Rnd 1 (RS): ch1, dc in first and in each of next 33 (36, 39, 42) sts, ch5 (7, 8, 9), skip 26 (27, 28, 29) sts for first armhole, dc in each of next 34 (37, 40, 43) sts, ch5 (7, 8, 9), skip 26 (27, 28, 29) sts for second armhole, join with sl st in first st, turn and work on WS; 78 (88, 96, 104) sts K

Rnd 2 (WS): ch1, sc in first st, *dc in next st, sc in next st; repeat from * to last st, dc in last st, join with sl st in first st, turn and work on RS; 78 (88, 96, 104) sts

Rnd 3 (RS): ch1, 2dc in first st, *dc in each of next 3 (4, 5, 6) sts, 2dc in next st; repeat from * to last 1 (2, 5, 12) sts, dc in each following st, join with sl st in first st, turn; 98 (106, 112, 118) sts

Rnd 4 (WS): ch1, sc in first st, *dc in next st, sc in next st; repeat from * to last st, dc in last st, join with sl st in first st, turn; 98 (106, 112, 118) sts

Rnd 5 (RS): ch1, dc in first st, dc in each following st to end, join with sl st in first st, turn; 98 (106, 112, 118) sts

Repeat Rnds 4 and 5 – 5 (6, 7, 8) more times or until 3 (3, 4, 4)cm/1¼ (1¼, 1½, 1½)in short of desired length; continue with Ribbing.

RIBBING

Rnd 1 (RS): ch1, FPdc around first dc, *BPdc around next dc, FPdc around next dc; repeat from * to last st, BPdc around last dc, join with sl st in first st; 98 (106, 112, 118) sts

Rnd 2 (RS): ch1, FPdc around first FPdc, *BPdc around next BPdc, FPdc around next FPdc; repeat from * to last st, BPdc around last BPdc, join with sl st in first st; 98 (106, 112, 118) sts L

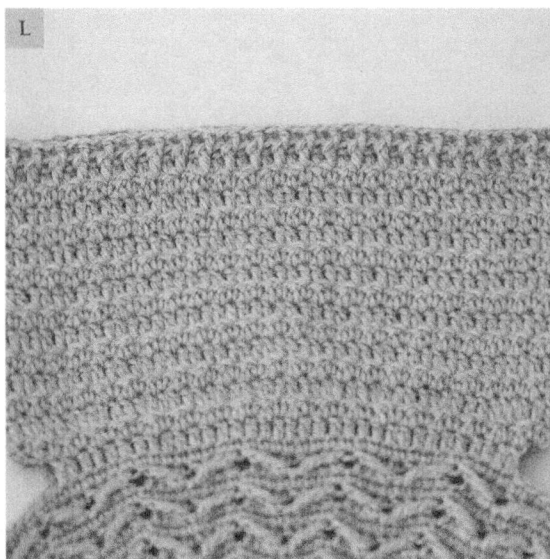

Repeat Rnd 2 – 1 (1, 2, 2) more times, and fasten off.

SLEEVES

On RS, join yarn in the middle of the underarm M

Rnd 1 (RS): ch1, evenly work 36 (38, 40, 42) dc around the armhole, join with sl st in first st, turn; 36 (38, 40, 42) sts N

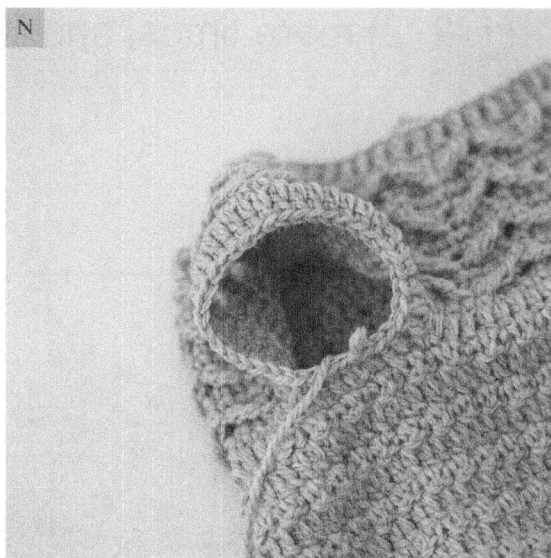

Rnd 2 (WS): ch1, sc in first st, *dc in next st, sc in next st; repeat from * to last st, dc in last st, join with sl st in first st, turn; 36 (38, 40, 42) sts

Rnd 3 (RS): ch1, dc in first st, dc2tog, dc in each following st to last 2sts, dc2tog, join with sl st in first st, turn; 34 (36, 38, 40) sts

Rnd 4 (WS): ch1, sc in first st, *dc in next st, sc in next st; repeat from * to last st, dc in last st, join with sl st in first st, turn; 34 (36, 38, 40) sts

Rnd 5 (RS): ch1, dc in first st, dc2tog, dc in each following st to last 2 sts, dc2tog, join with sl st in first st, turn; 32 (34, 36, 38) sts

Rnd 6 (WS): ch1, sc in first st, *dc in next st, sc in next st; repeat from * to last st, dc in last st, join with sl st in first st, turn; 32 (34, 36, 38) sts

Rnd 7 (RS): ch1, dc in first st and in each following st to end, join with sl st in first st, turn; 32 (34, 36, 38) sts

Repeat Rnds 6 and 7 – 3 (5, 7, 8) more times or until 3 (3, 4, 4)cm/1¼ (1¼, 1½, 1½)in short of desired length; continue with Cuff.

Second Sleeve

Work in exactly the same way as first sleeve.

CUFF

Rnd 1 (RS): ch1, FPdc around first dc, *BPdc around next dc, FPdc around next dc; repeat from * to last st, BPdc around last dc, join with sl st in first st; 32 (34, 36, 38) sts

Rnd 2 (RS): ch1, FPdc around first FPdc, *BPdc around next BPdc, FPdc around next FPdc; repeat from * to last st, BPdc around last BPdc, join with sl st in first st; 32 (34, 36, 38) sts

Repeat Rnd 2 – 1 (1, 2, 2) more times, and fasten off.

Second Cuff

Work in exactly same way on second sleeve.

COLLAR

Rnd 1 (RS): join yarn into the remaining loop of your foundation ch and ch1, FPdc around first dc, O *BPdc around next dc, FPdc around next dc; repeat from * to last st, BPdc around last dc, join with sl st in first st; 60 (64, 68, 72) sts

Rnd 2 (RS): ch1, FPdc around first FPdc, *BPdc around next BPdc, FPdc around next FPdc; repeat from * to last st, BPdc around last BPdc, join with sl st in first st; 60 (64, 68, 72) sts

Repeat Rnd 2 – 1 (1, 2, 2) more times, and fasten off.

FINISHING

Weave in all ends, wash and dry flat (see Finishing Techniques).

HEAVENLY SWEATER

~ ★★★ ~

When I designed the yoke for this sweater my first thought was that the pattern in the stitches looked like angels flying down, probably on some important mission. This seamless sweater is worked top down and is made with DK weight yarn so that it drapes beautifully and is really soft and comfortable to wear.

SIZES AND MEASUREMENTS OF FINISHED GARMENT

Size	Chest	Length	Sleeve length to underarm
0–6m	48cm/19in	27cm/10½in	14cm/5½in
6–12m	54cm/21¼in	31cm/12¼in	18cm/7in
1–2y	58cm/22¾in	35cm/13¾in	22cm/8½in
3–4y	66cm/26in	39cm/15¼in	26cm/10¼in

GAUGE (TENSION)

18 sts and 10 rows in dc to measure 10 x 10cm (4 x 4in) using 3.75mm (F/5) hook (or size required to obtain gauge)

SPECIAL STITCHES

BPdc, FPdc, FPdc3tog, bo (4-dc bobble)(see Special Stitches)

MATERIALS

3 LIGHT

- 325 (370, 460, 550) meters or 355 (405, 500, 602) yards of any DK weight or light worsted weight yarn
  Suggested yarn: Lana Gatto Royal Alpaca, 70% baby alpaca, 30% nylon, shade 9164, 50g (1¾oz), 115m (125yd)
- 3.75mm (F/5) crochet hook (or size required to obtain gauge)

Pattern is written for size 0–6m, changes for 6–12m, 1–2y and 3–4y are in (…).

Ch1 at the beginning of each round doesn't count as a stitch.

YOKE

Foundation chain: work loosely, pull each ch longer (it has to pass comfortably over child's head), ch60 (60, 66, 72), join with sl st in first ch.

Rnd 1 (RS): ch1, but pull it to the height of dc here and throughout where next st is dc, dc in first and in each next ch, join with sl st in first st; 60 (60, 66, 72) sts

Rnd 2 (RS): ch1, 2dc in first st, *skip next 2sts, (3tr, ch1, dc, ch1, 3tr) in next st, skip next 2sts, 2dc in next st A ; repeat from * to end, but in last repeat instead of last 2dc join with sl st in first st; 10 (10, 11, 12) shells made B

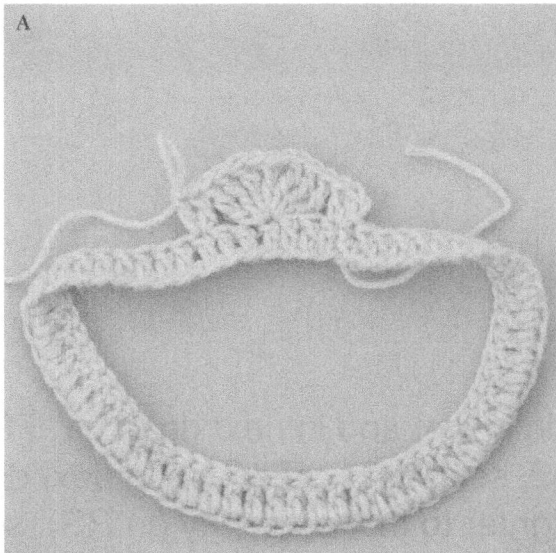

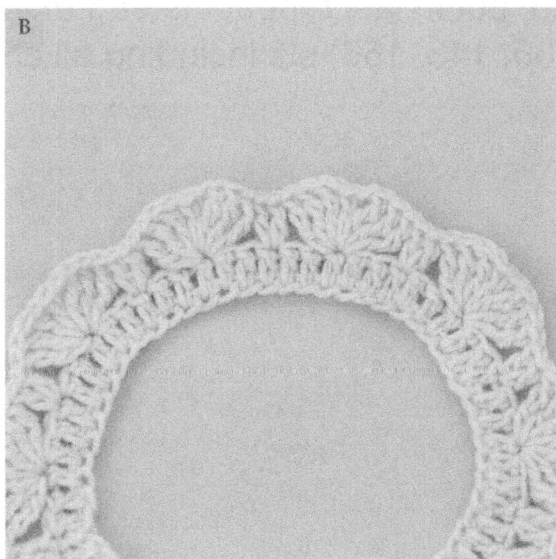

Rnd 3 (RS): ch1, dc in first and in next dc, *FPdc around each of next 3tr, ch2, skip ch1, dc in next dc, ch2, skip ch1, FPdc around each of next 3tr, dc in each of next 2dc; repeat from * to end, but in last repeat instead of last 2dc join with sl st in first st; 130 (130, 143, 156) sts including all ch C

Rnd 4 (RS): ch1, dc in first and in next dc, *ch1, FPdc3tog working around next 3tr, ch2, sc in next ch2sp, bo in next dc (pull it to the RS and work next sc tighter to make bo stay on RS), sc in next ch2sp, ch2, FPdc3tog working around next 3tr, ch1, dc in each of next 2dc; repeat from * to end, but in last repeat instead of last 2dc join with sl st in first st; 130 (130, 143, 156) sts including all ch D

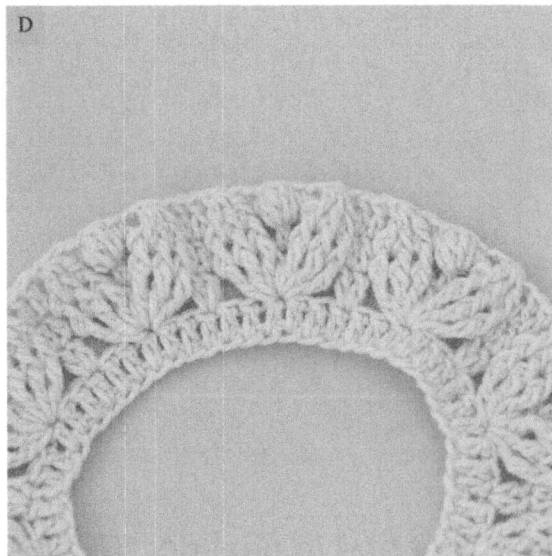

For size 0–6m

Rnd 5 (RS): (for this size work sc instead of dc to make the yoke shorter) ch1, sc in first and in each next st, sc in each dc, sc in each ch1sp, sc in each sc, 1 sc in each ch2sp, sc in each bo, sc in top of each FPdc3tog to end, join with sl st in first st; 110 sts

For sizes 6–12m, 1–2y and 3–4y

Rnd 5 (RS): ch1, dc in first and in each next st, dc in each dc, dc in each ch1sp, dc in each sc, 1dc in each ch2sp, dc in each bo, dc in top of each FPdc3tog to end, join with sl st in first st; (110, 121, 132) sts E

For all sizes

Rnd 6 (RS): ch1, dc in first and in each of next 2sts, *skip next 3sts, (3tr, ch1, dc, ch1, 3tr) in next st, skip next 3sts, dc in each of next 4sts; repeat from * to end, but in last repeat work dc in each remaining st and join with sl st in first st; 130 (130, 143, 156) sts including all ch F

Rnd 7 (RS): ch1, dc in first and in each of next 2sts, *FPdc around each of next 3tr, ch2, skip ch1, dc in next dc, ch2, skip ch1, FPdc around each of next 3tr, dc in each of next 4dc; repeat from * to end, but in last repeat work dc in last st and join with sl st in first st; 150 (150, 165, 180) sts including all ch [G]

Rnd 8 (RS): ch1, dc in first and in each of next 2sts, *ch1, FPdc3tog working around next 3tr, ch2, sc in next ch2sp, bo in next dc (pull it to the RS and work next sc tighter to make bo stay on RS), sc in next ch2sp, ch2, FPdc3tog working around next 3tr, ch1, dc in each of

next 4dc; repeat from * to end, but in last repeat work dc in last st and join with sl st in first st; 150 (150, 165, 180) sts including all ch H

Rnd 9 (RS): ch1, dc in first and in each next st, dc in each dc, dc in each ch1sp, dc in each sc, 1 (2, 2, 2) dc in each ch2sp, dc in top of each FPdc3tog to end, (for size 1–2y work 1dc in ch2sp once), join with sl st in first st; 130 (150, 164, 180) sts I

For sizes 0–6m and 6–12m

Work Last Rnd.

For sizes 1–2y and 3-4y

Rnd 10 (RS): ch1, dc in first and in each next st, join with sl st in first st; (164, 180) sts

For size 1–2y

Work Last Rnd.

For size 3–4y

Repeat Rnd 10 once more and continue with Last Rnd.

For all sizes

Last Rnd (RS): ch1, BPdc around each next dc, join with sl st in first st; 130 (150, 164, 180) sts J

Continue with Divide for Sleeves and Body.

DIVIDE FOR SLEEVES AND BODY

Rnd 1 (RS): ch1, 1 (1, 2, 2) dc in first st, ch4 (5, 5, 6), skip next 27 (31, 35, 37) sts for an armhole, dc in each of next 38 (44, 47, 53) sts, ch4 (5, 5, 6), skip next 27 (31, 35, 37) sts for an armhole, dc in each next st to end, join with sl st in first st; 84 (98, 105, 119) sts including all ch K

Rnd 2 (RS): ch1, 2dc in first st, *skip next 2sts, sc in next st, ch3, sc in next st, skip next 2sts, (2dc, ch2, 2dc) in next st; repeat from * to end, but in last repeat work (2dc, ch2) in same st as first 2dc and join with sl st in first st, turn and work on WS; 12 (14, 15, 17) shells and 12 (14, 15, 17) sets of (sc, ch3, sc) made L

Rnd 3 (WS): ch1, *(sc, ch3, sc) in next ch2sp, skip next 3sts, (2dc, ch2, 2dc) in next ch3sp, skip next 3sts; repeat from * to end, join with sl st in first st, turn and work on RS; 12 (14, 15, 17) shells and 12 (14, 15, 17) sets of (sc, ch3, sc) made M

Rnd 4 (RS): ch1, 2dc in ch3sp to the right, *skip next 3sts, (sc, ch3, sc) in next ch2sp N , skip next 3sts, (2dc, ch2, 2dc) in next ch3sp; repeat from * to end, but in last repeat work (2dc, ch2) in same ch3sp as first 2dc and join with sl st in first st, turn; 12 (14, 15, 17) shells and 12 (14, 15, 17) sets of (sc, ch3, sc) made

Repeat Rnds 3 and 4 – 6 (8, 9, 10) more times or until desired length, fasten off O

SLEEVES

On RS, join yarn in the middle of the underarm P , turn after each round and work on both RS and WS.

Rnd 1 (RS): ch1, 2dc in first st, skip 2sts (or sp equal to 2sts), sc in next st Q , ch3, skip next st, sc in next st, skip next 3sts, *(2dc, ch2, 2dc) in next st, skip next 3sts, sc in next st, ch3, skip next st, sc in next st, skip next 3sts; repeat from * 2 (3, 3, 4) more times, work (2dc, ch2) in same st as first 2dc and join with sl st in first st, turn; 4 (5, 5, 6) shells and 4 (5, 5, 6) sets of (sc, ch3, sc) made R

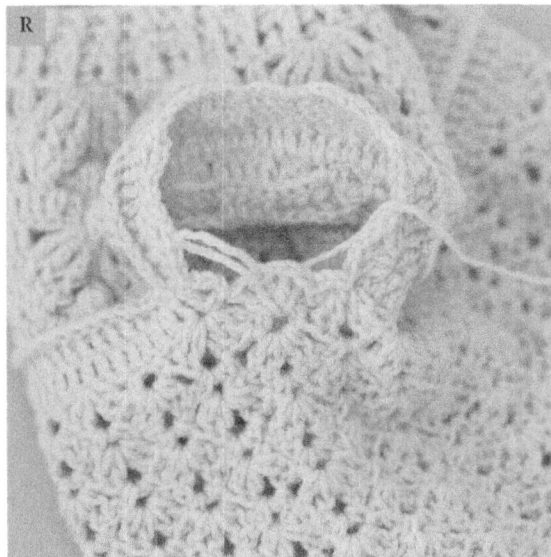

Rnd 2 (WS): ch1, *(sc, ch3, sc) in next ch2sp, skip next 3sts, (2dc, ch2, 2dc) in next ch3sp, skip next 3sts; repeat from * to end, join with sl st in first st, turn; 4 (5, 5, 6) shells and 4 (5, 5, 6) sets of (sc, ch3, sc) made S

Rnd 3 (RS): ch1, 2dc in ch3sp to the right, *skip next 3sts, (sc, ch3, sc) in next ch2sp, skip next 3sts, (2dc, ch2, 2dc) in next ch3sp; repeat from * to end, but in last repeat work (2dc, ch2) in same ch3sp as first 2dc and join with sl st in first st, turn; 4 (5, 5, 6) shells and 4 (5, 5, 6) sets of (sc, ch3, sc) made

Repeat Rnds 2 and 3 – 4 (6, 7, 8) more times or until desired length, fasten off.

Second Sleeve

Work in exactly the same way as first sleeve.

COLLAR

On RS, join yarn into the first st of collar, into the remaining loop and work:

Rnd 1 (RS): ch1, FPdc around first dc T , *BPdc around next dc, FPdc around next dc* repeat from * to last st, BPdc around next st, join with sl st in first st; 60 (60, 66, 72) sts

Rnd 2 (RS): ch1, FPdc around first FPdc, *BPdc around next BPdc, FPdc around next FPdc; repeat from * to last st, BPdc around last BPdc, join with sl st in first st; 60 (60, 66, 72) sts

Repeat Rnd 2 – one more time, fasten off

FINISHING

Weave in ends, wash and block (see Finishing Techniques).

FLUTTERBY SHRUG

~ ★★☆ ~

A shrug is the cutest thing you can make for your little one's wardrobe. It can be worn over a dress as an extra layer, or over a fitted shirt and a skirt to add some texture and extra sweetness to an outfit. It drapes beautifully on the back and could be made with long sleeves too.

SIZES AND MEASUREMENTS OF FINISHED GARMENT

Size	Chest	Length from shoulders
0–6m	47cm/18½in	20cm/7¾in
6–12m	50cm/19¾in	23cm/9in
1–2y	55cm/21½in	26cm/10¼in
3–4y	58cm/22¾in	29cm/11½in

GAUGE (TENSION)

18 sts and 9 rows in dc to measure 10 x 10cm (4 x 4in) using 4mm (G/6) hook (or size required to obtain gauge)

SPECIAL STITCHES

FPsc, 2-dc CL (see Special Stitches)

MATERIALS

3 LIGHT

- 200 (250, 300, 350) meters or 219 (275, 330, 383) yards of any DK weight or light worsted weight yarn
  Suggested yarn: Lana Gatto Flamingo, 90% cotton, 10% cashmere, shade 7860, 50g (1¾oz), 100m (109yd)
- 4mm (G/6) crochet hook (or size required to obtain gauge)
- 1 button, approximately 2cm (¾in) diameter
- Tapestry needle

Pattern is written for size 0–6m, changes for 6–12m, 1–2y and 3–4y are in (…).

YOKE

Row 1: ch23 (27, 31, 37), sc in 2nd ch from hook and in each next ch, turn; 22 (26, 30, 36) sts

Row 2: ch4 (counts as first dc and ch1 here and throughout), 2dc in next st, dc in each of next 3 (4, 5, 7) sts, (2dc, ch1, 2dc) in next st, dc in each of next 10 (12, 14, 16) sts, (2dc, ch1, 2dc) in next st, dc in each of next 3 (4, 5, 7) sts, 2dc in next st, ch1, dc in last st, turn; 34 (38, 42, 48) sts including all ch1 A

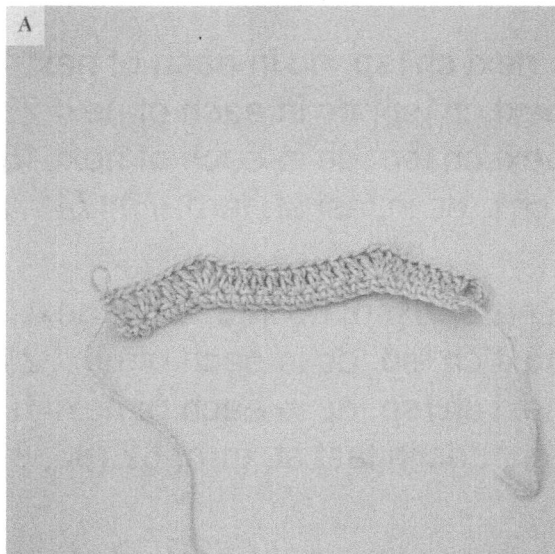

Row 3: ch4, 2dc in next ch1sp, dc in each of next 7 (8, 9, 11) sts, (2dc, ch1, 2dc) in next ch1sp, dc in each of next 14 (16, 18, 20) sts, (2dc, ch1, 2dc) in next ch1sp, dc in each of next 7 (8, 9, 11) sts, 2dc in next ch1sp, ch1, dc in last st, turn; 46 (50, 54, 60) sts including all ch1 B

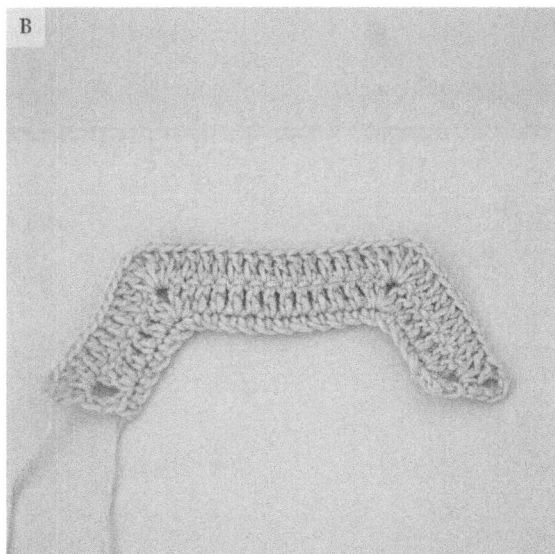

Row 4: ch4, 2dc in next ch1sp, dc in each of next 11 (12, 13, 15) sts, (2dc, ch1, 2dc) in next ch1sp, dc in each of next 18 (20, 22, 24) sts,

(2dc, ch1, 2dc) in next ch1sp, dc in each of next 11 (12, 13, 15) sts, 2dc in next ch1sp, ch1, dc in last st, turn; 58 (62, 66, 72) sts including all ch1

Row 5: ch4, 2dc in next ch1sp, dc in each of next 15 (16, 17, 19) sts, (2dc, ch1, 2dc) in next ch1sp, dc in each of next 22 (24, 26, 28) sts, (2dc, ch1, 2dc) in next ch1sp, dc in each of next 15 (16, 17, 19) sts, 2dc in next ch1sp, ch1, dc in last st, turn; 70 (74, 78, 84) sts including all ch1

Row 6: ch4, 2dc in next ch1sp, dc in each of next 19 (20, 21, 23) sts, (2dc, ch1, 2dc) in next ch1sp, dc in each of next 26 (28, 30, 32) sts, (2dc, ch1, 2dc) in next ch1sp, dc in each of next 19 (20, 21, 23) sts, 2dc in next ch1sp, ch1, dc in last st, turn; 82 (86, 90, 96) sts including all ch1

Row 7: ch4, 2dc in next ch1sp, dc in each of next 23 (24, 25, 27) sts, (2dc, ch1, 2dc) in next ch1sp, dc in each of next 30 (32, 34, 36) sts, (2dc, ch1, 2dc) in next ch1sp, dc in each of next 23 (24, 25, 27) sts, 2dc in next ch1sp, ch1, dc in last st, turn; 94 (98, 102, 108) sts including all ch1 C

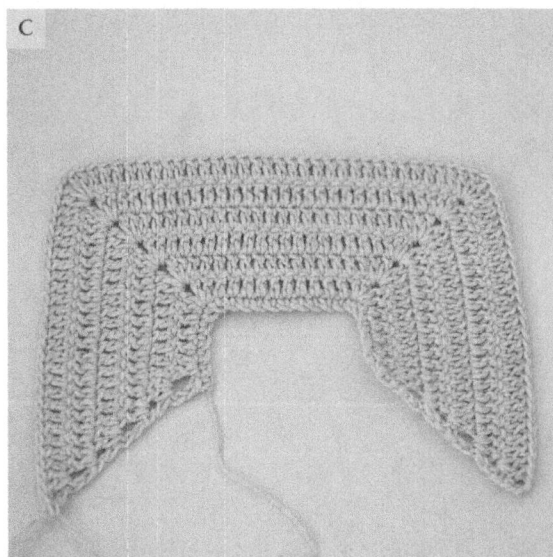

For size 0–6m

Fasten off and continue with Lower Part.

For size 6–12m

106

Row 8: ch4, 2dc in next ch1sp, dc in each of next 28 sts, (2dc, ch1, 2dc) in next ch1sp, dc in each of next 36 sts, (2dc, ch1, 2dc) in next ch1sp, dc in each of next 28 sts, 2dc in next ch1sp, ch1, dc in last st, turn; 110 sts including all ch1

Fasten off and continue with Lower Part.

For sizes 1–2y and 3–4y

Row 8: ch4, 2dc in next ch1sp, dc in each of next (29, 31) sts, (2dc, ch1, 2dc) in next ch1sp, dc in each of next (38, 40) sts, (2dc, ch1, 2dc) in next ch1sp, dc in each of next (29, 31) sts, 2dc in next ch1sp, ch1, dc in last st, turn; (114, 120) sts including all ch1

Row 9: ch4, 2dc in next ch1sp, dc in each of next (33, 35) sts, (2dc, ch1, 2dc) in next ch1sp, dc in each of next (42, 44) sts, (2dc, ch1, 2dc) in next ch1sp, dc in each of next (33, 35) sts, 2dc in next ch1sp, ch1, dc in last st, turn; (126, 132) sts including all ch1

Fasten off and continue with Lower Part.

LOWER PART

WS facing, join yarn into the remaining loop of foundation chain at the collar and work D

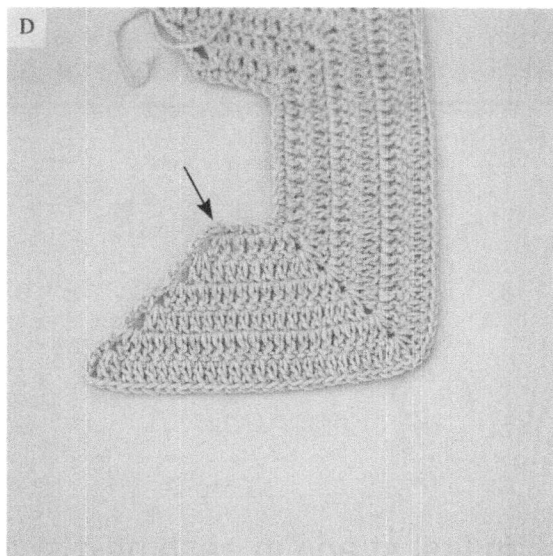

Row 1 (WS): ch1, work evenly 13 (16, 18, 18) sc across the front diagonal line, sc next ch1sp, ch4, skip next 27 (32, 37, 39) dc for an armhole E, sc in next ch1sp, sc in next 34 (40, 46, 48) dc, sc in next ch1sp, ch4, skip next 27 (32, 37, 39) dc for an armhole, sc in next ch1sp and work evenly 13 (16, 18, 18) sc across the diagonal line of other front, turn; 72 (84, 94, 96) sts F

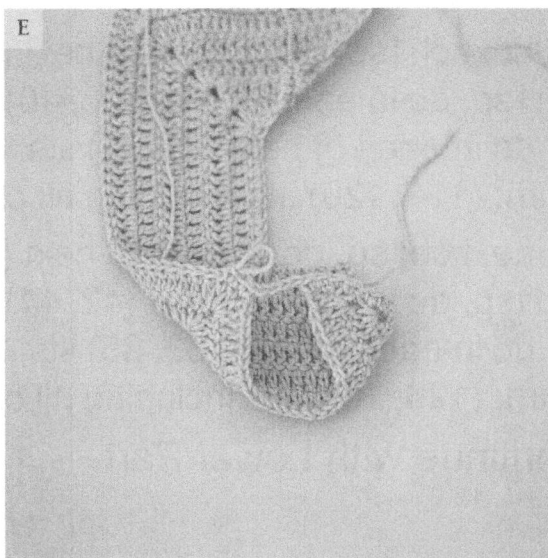

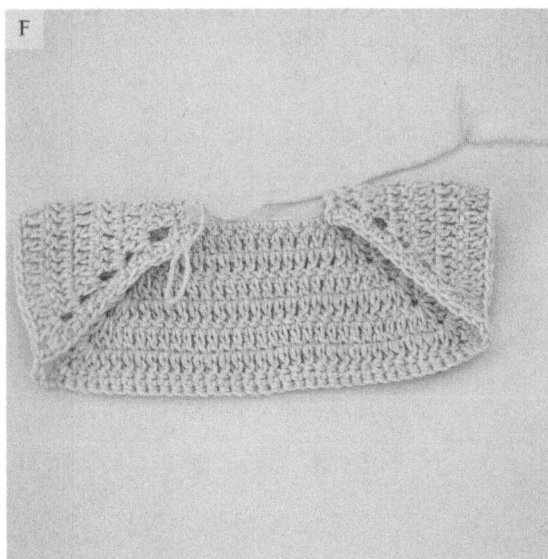

Row 2 (RS): ch1, sc in first st and in each next st, including all chains worked for underarms, turn; 72 (84, 94, 96) sts

Row 3 (WS): ch1, FPsc around each sc, sc in last st, turn; 72 (84, 94, 96) sts G

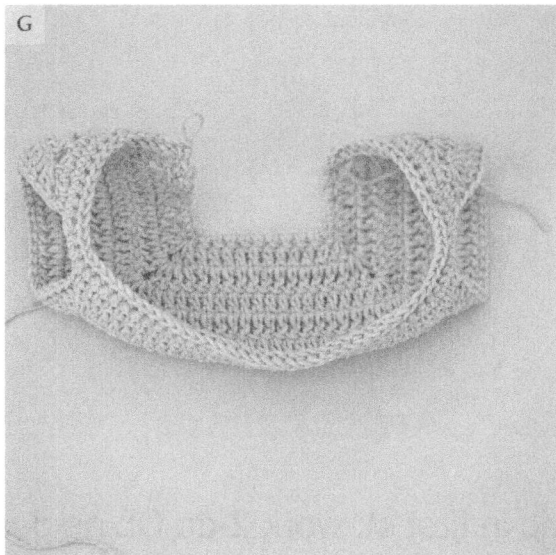

Row 4 (RS): ch1, dc in first st, dc in next 16 (22, 26, 27) sts, 2dc in each of next 38 (38, 40, 40) sts, dc in next 17 (23, 27, 28) sts, turn; 110 (122, 134, 136) sts H

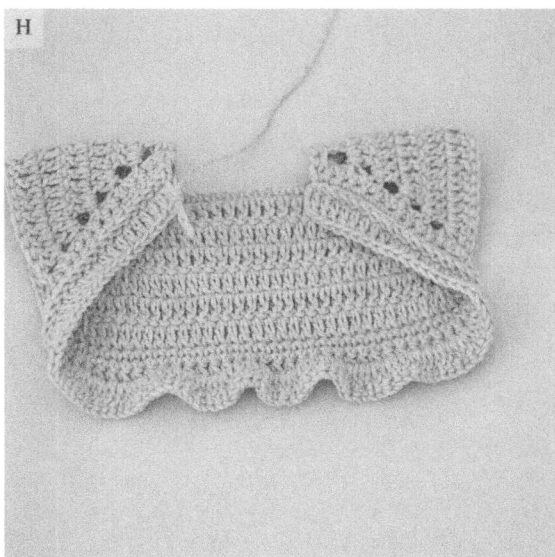

Row 5 (WS): ch1, sc in first st, *(sc, ch3, sc) in next st, skip next st; repeat from * to last st, sc in last st, turn; 54 (60, 66, 67) ch3sp made I

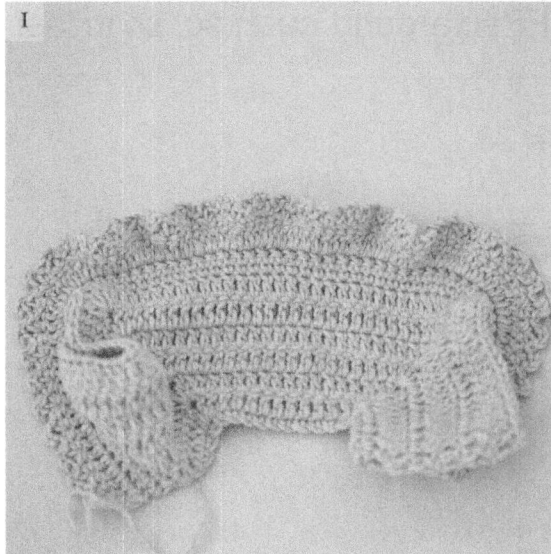

Row 6 (RS): ch1, dc in first st, work 2-dc CL as described in Special Stitches working first half-closed dc in same st as first dc J K, *ch2, 2-dc CL working first half-closed dc in same sc as last dc of last cluster, skip next sc and skip ch3, work second half-closed dc in next sc, complete 2-dc CL L; repeat from * to last st, dc in last st, turn; 54 (60, 66, 67) CL made

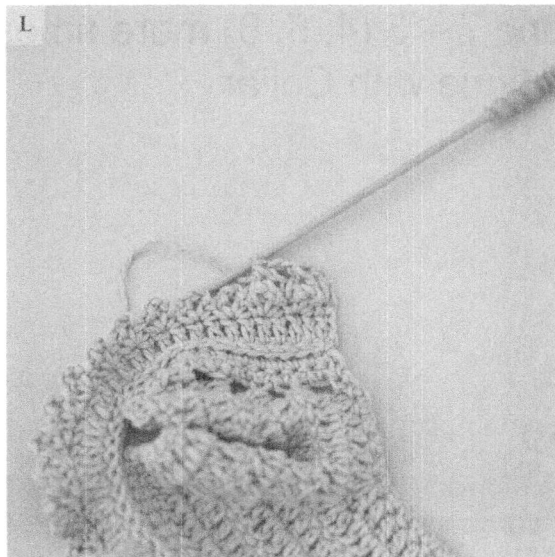

Row 7 (WS): ch1, sc in first st, *(sc, ch3, sc) in top of next cluster, skip next ch2sp; repeat from * to last cluster, sc in last st, turn; 54 (60, 66, 67) ch3sp made M

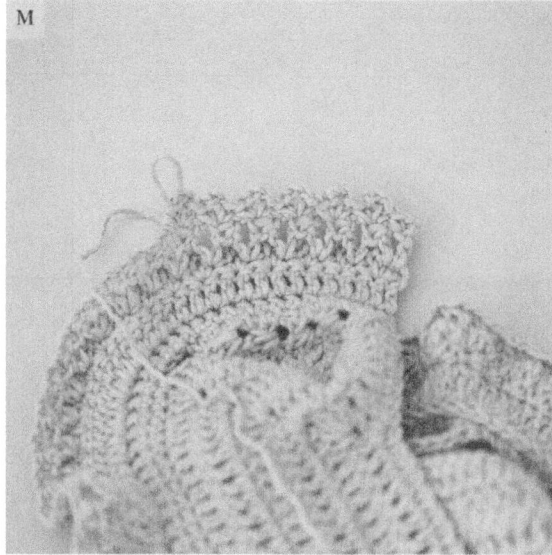

Repeat Rows 6 and 7 – 3 (4, 5, 6) more times N. Don't fasten off, but continue with Collar.

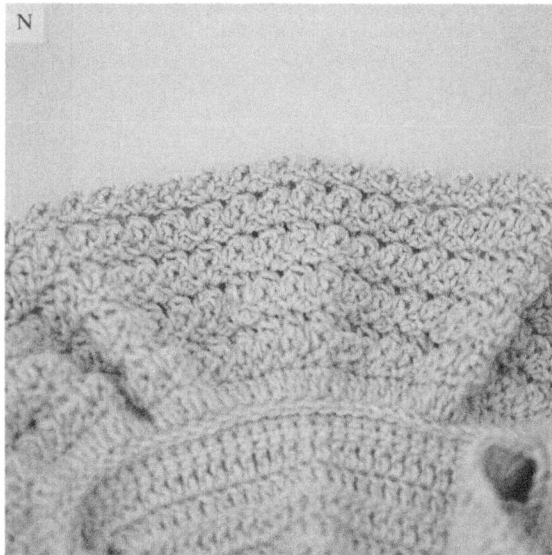

COLLAR

Row 1 (WS): ch1, work evenly sc across the front, collar and other front, turn; stitch count is not important, but work same amount of sts across both fronts

Row 2 (RS): ch1, sc in each st, turn

Row 3 (WS): ch1, sc in each following st to last 3sts, ch2, skip next 2sts, sc in last st, turn

Row 4 (RS): ch1, sc in first st, 2sc in ch2sp, sc in each following st to end, fasten off O

SLEEVES

RS facing, join yarn into the middle of the underarm and work P

Rnd 1 (RS): ch1, work evenly 32 (36, 42, 44) sc around the armhole, join with sl st in first st, turn

Rnd 2 (WS): ch1, sc in first st, *(sc, ch3, sc) in next st, skip next st; repeat from * to end, join with sl st in first st, turn; 16 (18, 21, 22) ch3sp made

Rnd 3 (RS): ch1, dc in first st, 2-dc CL working first half-closed dc in same st as first dc, skip next sc and skip ch3, work second half-closed dc in next sc, complete 2-dc CL, *ch2, 2-dc CL working first half-closed dc in same sc as last dc of last cluster, skip next sc and skip ch3, work second half-closed dc in next sc, complete 2-dc CL; repeat from * to end, join with sl st in first st, turn; 16 (18, 21, 22) CL made

Rnd 4 (WS): ch1, sc in first st, *(sc, ch3, sc) in top of next cluster, skip next ch2sp; repeat from * to end, join with sl st in first st, turn; 16 (18, 21, 22) ch3sp made, fasten off Q

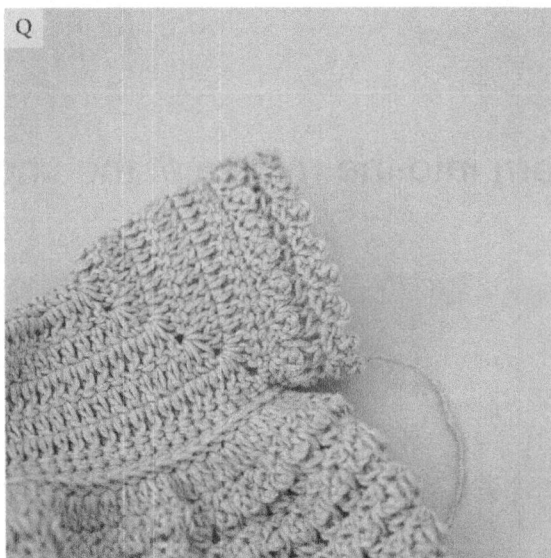

For a Longer Sleeve

Repeat Rnds 3 and 4 until desired length.

Second Sleeve

Work in exactly the same way as first sleeve.

FINISHING

Sew on the button and weave in all ends (see Finishing Techniques).

The construction of the shrug gives it a very pretty drape at the back.

HARVEST CARDIGAN

~ ★★☆ ~

I call this one the Harvest Cardigan because the pattern in the yoke hints of leaves and cherries. Don't work the single crochet stitches in the yoke too tightly, and if it seems a bit uneven when complete, just wash the cardigan and dry it flat. Work from the top down, choosing whether to use two colors or one, and how many buttons to include.

SIZES AND MEASUREMENTS OF FINISHED GARMENT

Size	Chest	Length	Sleeve length to underarm
0–6m	50cm/19¾in	27cm/10½in	14cm/5½in
6–12m	54cm/21¼in	30cm/11¾in	18cm/7in
1–2y	60cm/23½in	33cm/13in	22cm/8½in
3–4y	64cm/25¼in	40cm/15¾in	26cm/10¼in

GAUGE (TENSION)

19 sts and 19 rows in sc to measure 10 x 10cm (4 x 4in) using 4mm (G/6) hook (or size required to obtain gauge)

SPECIAL STITCHES

FPdc, BPdc, FPsc, FPdc2tog, bo (4-dc bobble), v-st, shell (Harvest Cardigan shell), BPsc, BPdc2tog (see Special Stitches)

MATERIALS

3 LIGHT

- 425 (500, 575, 700) meters or 465 (557, 630, 767) yards of any DK weight or light worsted weight yarn; if using two colors you will need 105 (155, 205, 255) meters or 115 (169, 224, 278) yards in CC and 320 (345, 370, 445) meters or 350 (378, 405, 489) yards in MC
  Suggested yarn: Rowan Alpaca Soft DK, 70% virgin wool, 30% alpaca, shades 210 and 211, 50g (1¾oz), 125m (136yd)
- 4mm (G/6) crochet hook (or size required to obtain gauge)
- 2 or more buttons, approximately 2cm (¾in) diameter
- Tapestry needle

Pattern is written for size 0–6m, changes for 6–12m, 1–2y and 3–4y are in (…).

Ch1 at the beginning of each round doesn't count as a stitch.

All color changes are optional.

YOKE

If using two colors, use CC.

Row 1 (RS): ch52 (56, 60, 64), sc in 2nd ch from the hook, sc in each next ch, turn; 51 (55, 59, 63) sc

Row 2 (WS): ch1, sc in first st, sc in each next 3 (2, 4, 6) sts, *v-st in next st, sc in each of next 5sts; repeat from * 6 (7, 7, 7) more times, v-st in next st, sc in each of next 4 (3, 5, 7) sts, turn; 8 (9, 9, 9) v-sts made) A

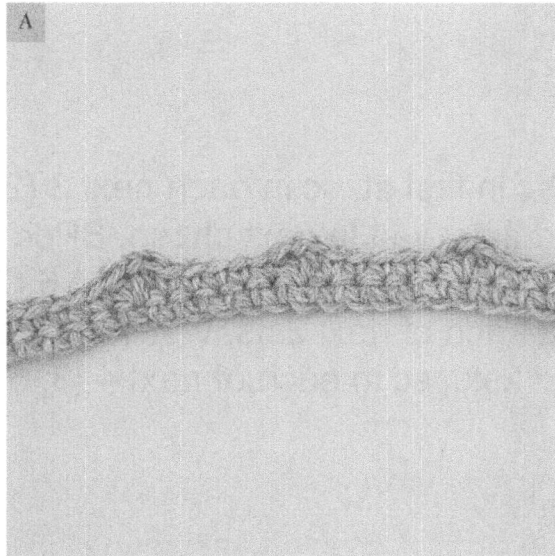

Row 3 (RS): ch1, sc in first st, sc in each next 3 (2, 4, 6) sts, *FPdc around next dc, v-st in next ch1sp, FPdc around next dc, sc in each of next 5sts; repeat from * 6 (7, 7, 7) more times, FPdc around next dc, v-st in next ch1sp, FPdc around next dc, sc in each of next 4 (3, 5, 7) sts, turn; 83 (91, 95, 99) sts including all chs B

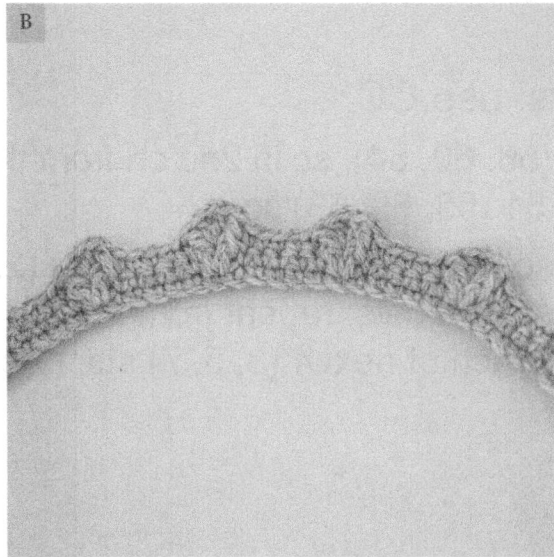

Row 4 (WS): ch1, sc in first st, sc in each next 3 (2, 4, 6) sts, *BPdc around each of next 2sts, v-st in next ch1sp, BPdc around each of next 2sts, sc in each of next 5sts; repeat from * 6 (7, 7, 7) more times, BPdc around each of next 2sts, v-st in next ch1sp, BPdc around each of next 2sts, sc in each of next 4 (3, 5, 7) sts, turn; 99 (109, 113, 117) sts

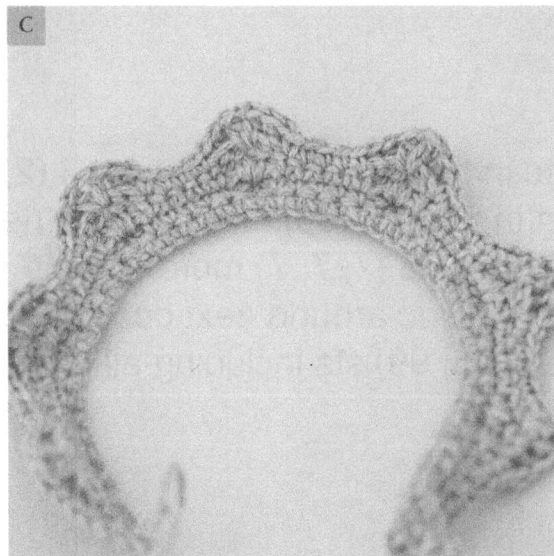

Row 5 (RS): ch1, sc in first st, sc in each next 3 (2, 4, 6) sts, *FPdc around each of next 3sts, v-st in next ch1sp, FPdc around each of next 3sts, sc in each of next 5sts; repeat from * 6 (7, 7, 7) more

times, FPdc around each of next 3sts, v-st in next ch1sp, FPdc around each of next 3sts, sc in each of next 4 (3, 5, 7) sts, turn; 115 (127, 131, 135) sts D

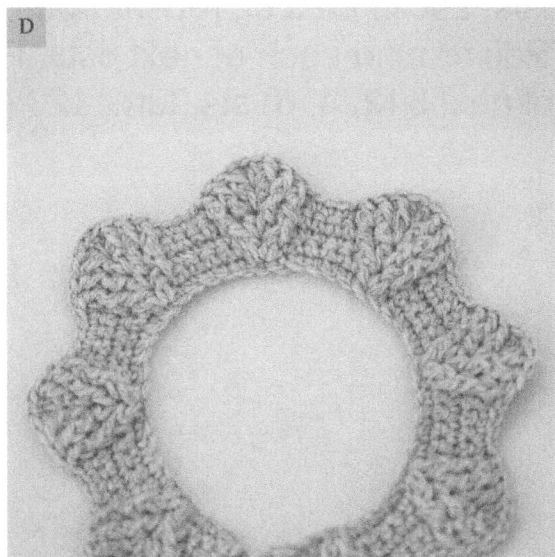

Row 6 (WS): ch1, sc in first st, sc in each of next 3 (2, 4, 6) sts, *BPdc around each of next 4sts, v-st in next ch1sp, BPdc around each of next 4sts, sc in each of next 5sts; repeat from * 6 (7, 7, 7) more times, BPdc around each of next 4sts, v-st in next ch1sp, BPdc around each of next 4sts, sc in each of next 4 (3, 5, 7) sts, turn; 131 (145, 149, 153) sts E

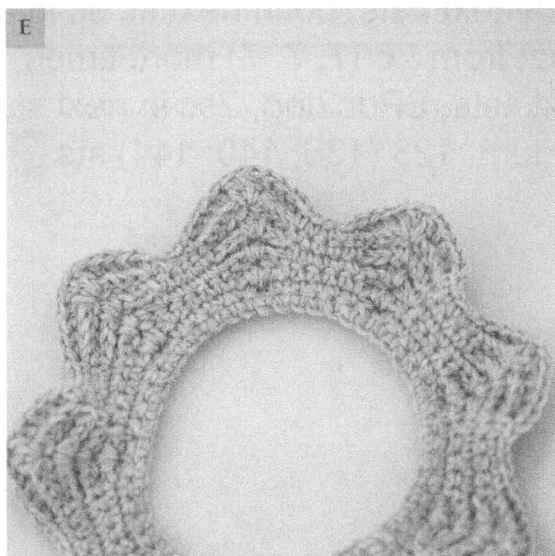

Row 7 (RS): in this row you will have to skip all ch1sp of leaves, ch1, sc in first st, sc in each of next 2 (1, 3, 5) st, 2sc in next st, *FPdc2tog, FPdc around each of next 6sts, FPdc2tog, 2sc in next st, sc in each of next 3sts, 2sc in next st; repeat from * 6 (7, 7, 7) more times, FPdc2tog, FPdc around each of next 6sts, FPdc2tog, 2sc in next st, sc in each of next 3 (2, 4, 6) sts, turn; 123 (136, 140, 144) sts
F

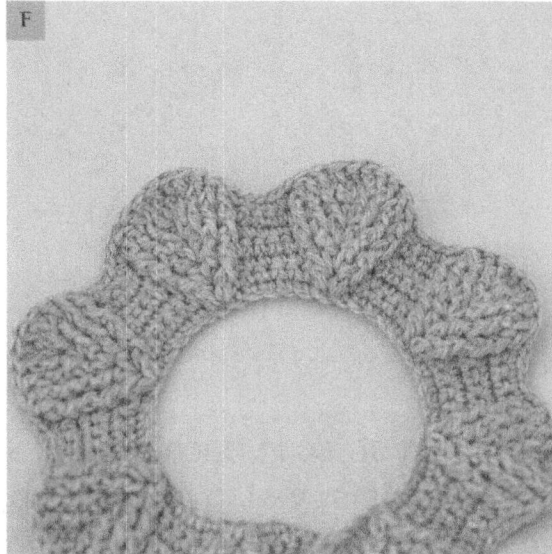

Row 8 (WS): ch1, sc in first st, sc in each of next 3 (2, 4, 6) sts, 2sc in next st, *BPdc2tog, BPdc around each of next 4sts, BPdc2tog, 2sc in next st, sc in each next 2sts, bo in next st, sc in each of next 2sts, 2sc in next st; repeat from * 6 (7, 7, 7) more times, BPdc2tog, BPdc around each of next 4sts, BPdc2tog, 2sc in next st, sc in each of next 4 (3, 5, 7) sts, turn; 123 (136, 140, 144) sts G

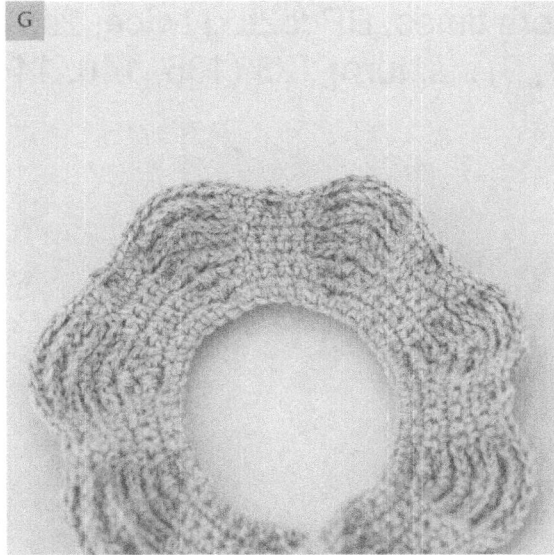

Row 9 (RS): ch1, sc in first st, sc in each of next 4 (3, 5, 7) sts, 2sc in next st, *FPdc2tog, FPdc around each of next 2sts, FPdc2tog, 2sc in next st, sc in each of next 7sts, 2sc in next st; repeat from * 6 (7, 7, 7) more times, FPdc2tog, FPdc around each of next 2sts, FPdc2tog, 2sc in next st, sc in each of next 5 (4, 6, 8) sts, turn; 123 (136, 140, 144) sts

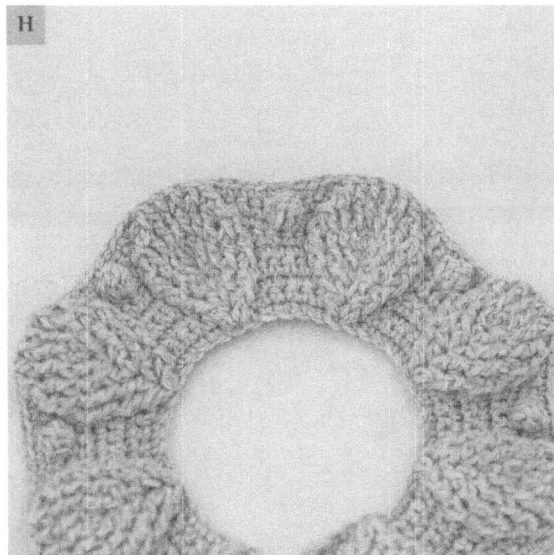

Row 10 (WS): ch1, sc in first st, sc in each next 5 (4, 6, 8) sts, 2sc in next st, *BPdc2tog twice, 2sc in next st, sc in next 2sts, bo in next st, sc in next 3sts, bo in next st, sc in next 2sts, 2sc in next st; repeat

from * 6 (7, 7, 7) more times, BPdc2tog twice, 2sc in next st, sc in each of next 6 (5, 7, 9) sts, turn; 123 (136, 140, 144) sts I

Row 11 (RS): ch1, sc in first st, sc in each next 6 (5, 7, 9) sts, 2sc in next st, *FPdc2tog, 2sc in next st, sc in each of next 11sts, 2sc in next st; repeat from * 6 (7, 7, 7) more times, FPdc2tog, 2sc in next st, sc in each of next 7 (6, 8, 10) sts, turn; 131 (145, 149, 153) sts J

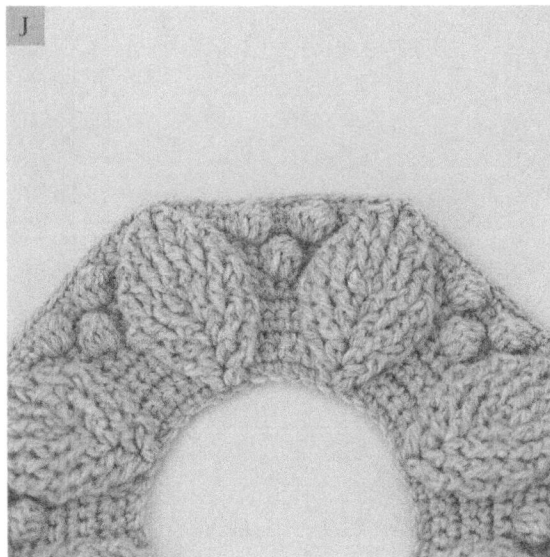

Row 12 (WS): ch1, sc in first st, sc in each of next 12 (11, 13, 15) sts, *bo in next st, sc in next 7sts, bo in next st, sc in next 7sts;

repeat from * 6 (7, 7, 7) more times, sc in each of next 6 (5, 7, 9) sts, turn; 131 (145, 149, 153) sts K

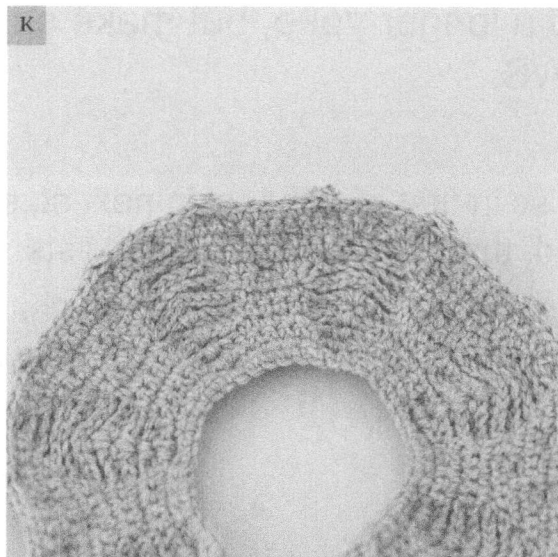

Row 13 (RS): ch1, sc in first st, sc in each of next 10 (4, 4, 12) sts, *2sc in next st, sc in each of next 11 (13, 7, 9) sts; repeat from * to end, turn; 141 (155, 167, 167) sts

You could make this cardigan in just one color rather than two, if you prefer.

For size 0–6m

Continue with Row A.

For sizes 6–12, 1–2y and 3–4y

Row 14 (WS): ch1, sc in first and in each next st, turn; (155, 167, 167) sts

Row 15 (RS): ch1, sc in first and in each next st, turn; (155, 167, 167) sts

Repeat Row 15 – (0, 2, 4) more times; in third rnd for size 3–4y evenly increase by 14sts working 2sc in approximately every 11th st; (155, 167, 181) sts

At this point the yoke has to measure approximately 7 (8, 9, 10)cm/2¾ (3⅛, 31½, 4)in, you can repeat Row 15 more times if you need a longer yoke, but make sure you start next row, Row A, on WS.

For all sizes

Row A (WS): ch1, sc in first st, *ch1, skip next st, sc in next st; repeat from * to end, turn; 141 (155, 167, 181) sts

Row B (RS): ch1, sc in first sc, *ch1, skip next ch, BPdc around next sc; repeat from * to end, but instead of last BPdc work sc in last sc, turn; 141 (155, 167, 181) sts L M

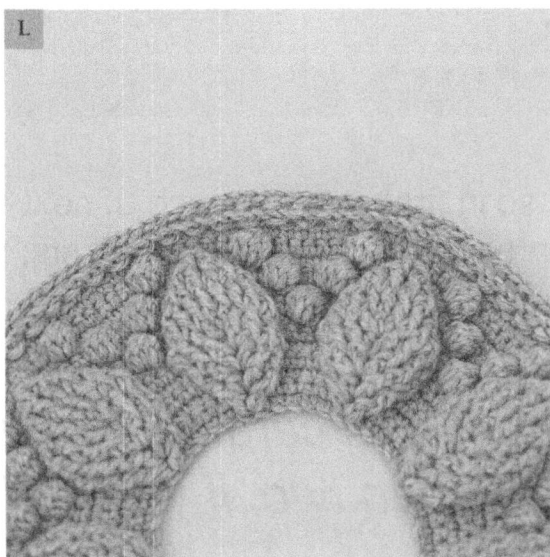

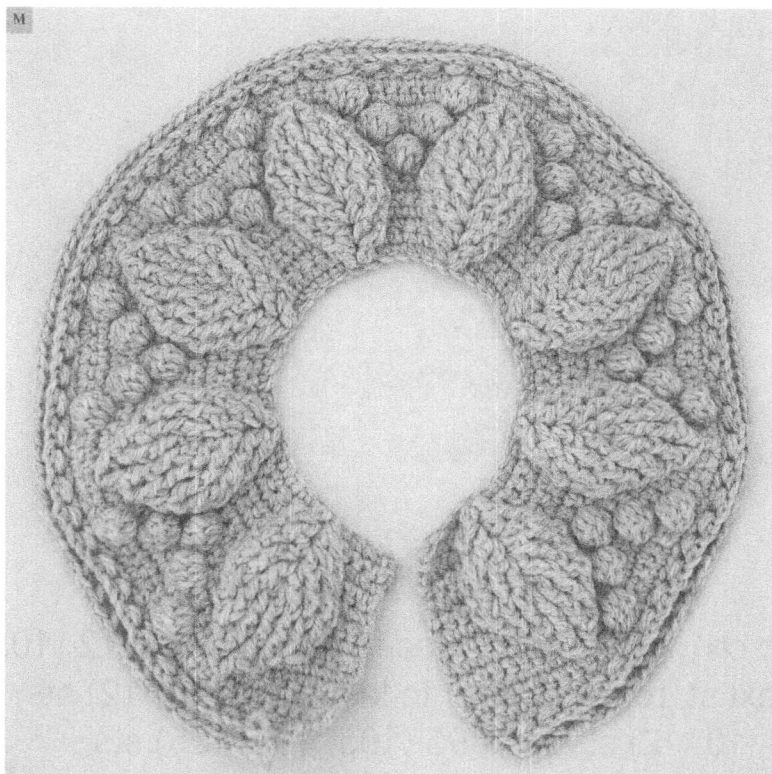

If using two colors, change to MC.

Row C (WS): ch1, dc in first st, dc in each ch1sp and in each BPdc, dc in last sc, turn; 141 (155, 167, 181) sts

Continue with Divide for Sleeves and Body.

DIVIDE FOR SLEEVES AND BODY

Row 1 (RS): ch1, sc in first and in each of next 18 (20, 22, 24) sts, ch4 (4, 5, 6), skip next 30 (33, 35, 38) sts for an armhole, sc in each of next 43 (47, 51, 55) sts, ch4 (4, 5, 6), skip next 30 (33, 35, 38) sts for an armhole, sc in each of next 19 (21, 23, 25) sts, turn; 89 (97, 107, 117) sts made N

Row 2 (WS): ch1, sc in first st, *sc in each of next 12 (10, 11, 12) sts, 2sc in next st; repeat from * to last 10 (8, 10, 12) sts, sc in each of next 10 (8, 10, 12) sts turn; 95 (105, 115, 125) sts

Row 3 (RS): ch1, (dc, ch1, dc) in first st, *skip next st, sc in next st, skip next 2sts, shell in next st; repeat from * to last 4sts, skip next st, sc in next st, skip next st and work (dc, ch1, dc) in last st, turn; 18 (20, 22, 24) shells and 2 half shells made O P

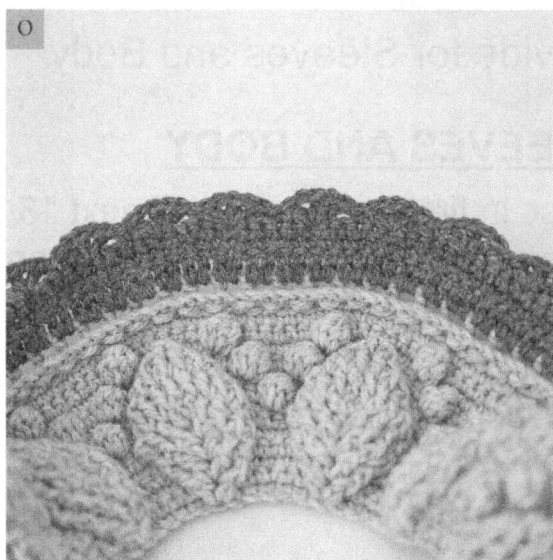

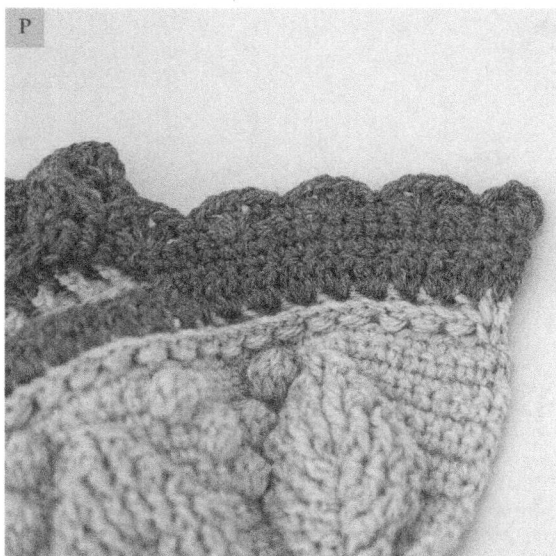

Row 4 (WS): ch1, sc in first dc, *skip next dc, shell in next sc, skip next dc, FPsc around next dc; repeat from * to end, but in last repeat instead of last FPsc work sc in last st, turn; 19 (21, 23, 25) shells made Q

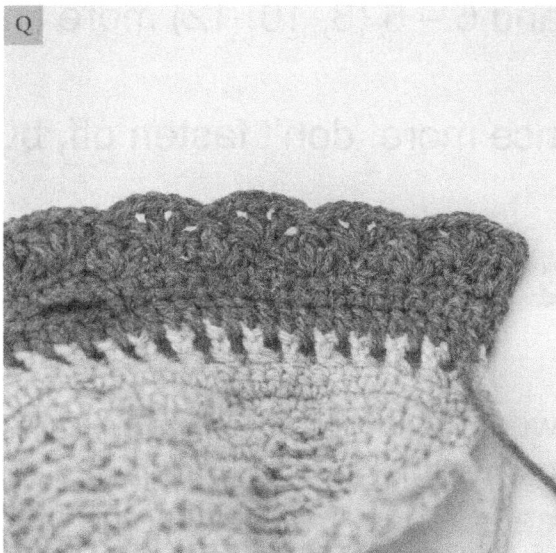

Row 5 (RS): ch1, (dc, ch1, dc) in first st, *skip next dc, BPsc around next dc, skip next dc, shell in next FPsc of previous row; repeat from * to end, but in last repeat instead of last shell work (dc, ch1, dc) in last st and turn; 18 (20, 22, 24) shells and 2 half shells made R

Row 6 (WS): ch1, sc in first dc, *skip next dc, shell in next BPsc of previous row, skip next dc, FPsc around next dc; repeat from * to end, but in last repeat instead of last FPsc work sc in last st, turn; 19 (21, 23, 25) shells made

Repeat Rows 5 and 6 – 6 (8, 10, 12) more times or until desired length.

Repeat Row 5 once more, don't fasten off, but continue with Front Edging.

FRONT EDGING

Right Front

Row 1 (RS): ch1, work evenly 40 (50, 62, 72) dc across the right front, turn; it can be any other even number of sts too, but don't make them too close or too far from each other, then work the same amount of stitches for Left Front S

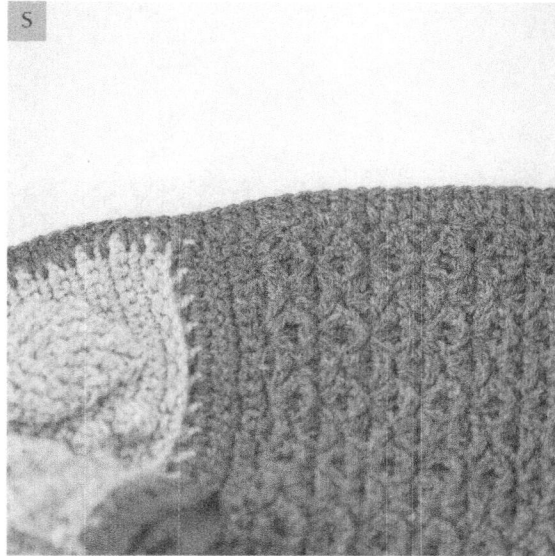

Row 2 (WS): ch1, hdc in first st, *BPdc around next st, FPdc around next st; repeat from * to last st, hdc in last st, turn; 40 (50, 62, 72) sts

On RS, mark BPdc stitches where you would like to make buttonholes, keeping in mind that the first buttonhole will be on the collar; you can decide how many buttonholes you'd like to make.

Row 3 (RS): ch1, hdc in first st, *(BPdc around next BPdc, FPdc around next FPdc) to the next marked st for buttonhole, ch1, skip next BPdc, FPdc around next FPdc; repeat from * as many times as needed, where you don't need to make buttonholes work FPdc around each FPdc, BPdc around each BPdc to last st, hdc in last st, turn; 40 (50, 62, 72) sts T

Row 4 (WS): ch1, hdc in first st, work BPdc around each BPdc, FPdc around each FPdc, sc in each ch1sp, to last st, hdc in last st; 40 (50, 62, 72) sts, fasten off.

Left Front

On RS, join yarn into the first st of the collar and work across the Left Front.

Row 1 (RS): ch1, work evenly 40 (50, 62, 72) dc across the left front, turn

Row 2 (WS): ch1, hdc in first st, *FPdc around next st, BPdc around next st; repeat from * to last st, hdc in last st, turn; 40 (50, 62, 72) sts

Row 3 (RS): ch1, hdc in first st, *FPdc around next FPdc, BPdc around next BPdc; repeat from * to last st, hdc in last st, turn; 40 (50, 62, 72) sts

Row 4 (WS): ch1, hdc in first st, *FPdc around next FPdc, BPdc around next BPdc; repeat from * to last st, hdc in last st; 40 (50, 62, 72) sts

Don't fasten off but continue with Collar.

COLLAR

Row 1 (WS): ch1, work evenly 61 (67, 71, 75) dc in each st across the collar, including front edgings, don't work into the remaining loops of foundation chain, but into sc of the first row [U] , turn

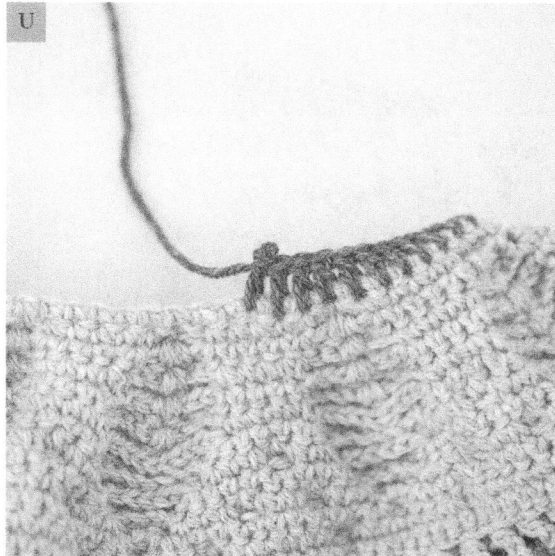

Row 2 (RS): ch1, hdc in first st, FPdc around first dc, *BPdc around next dc, FPdc around next dc; repeat from * to last st, hdc in last st, turn; 61 (67, 71, 75) sts

Row 3 (WS): ch1, hdc in first st, BPdc around first BPdc, *FPdc around next FPdc, BPdc around next BPdc; repeat from * to last 3sts, ch1, skip next FPdc (for a buttonhole), BPdc around next BPdc, hdc in last st, turn; 61 (67, 71, 75) sts

Row 4 (RS): ch1, hdc in first st, work FPdc around each FPdc, BPdc around each BPdc, sc in ch1sp, to last st, hdc in last st, fasten off [V]

SLEEVES

If using two colors work with MC; on RS, join yarn in the middle of the underarm W

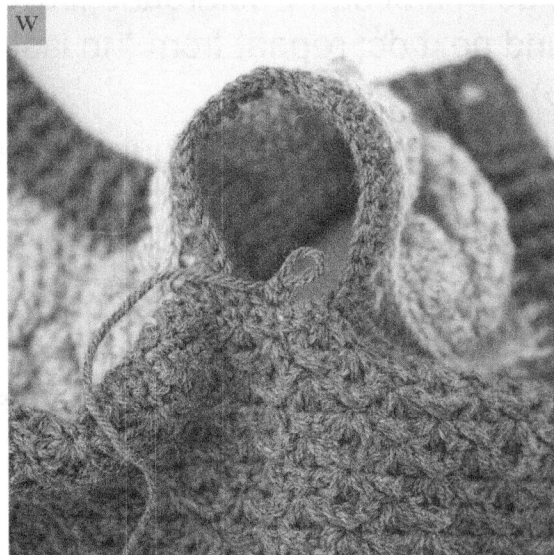

Rnd 1 (RS): ch1, sc in first st, *skip next 2sts, shell in next st, skip next 2sts, sc in next st; repeat from * 6 (6, 7, 8) more times, but in last repeat instead of last sc join with sl st in first sc, turn; where you don't have sts skip sp equivalent to 2sts; 7 (7, 8, 9) shells made X

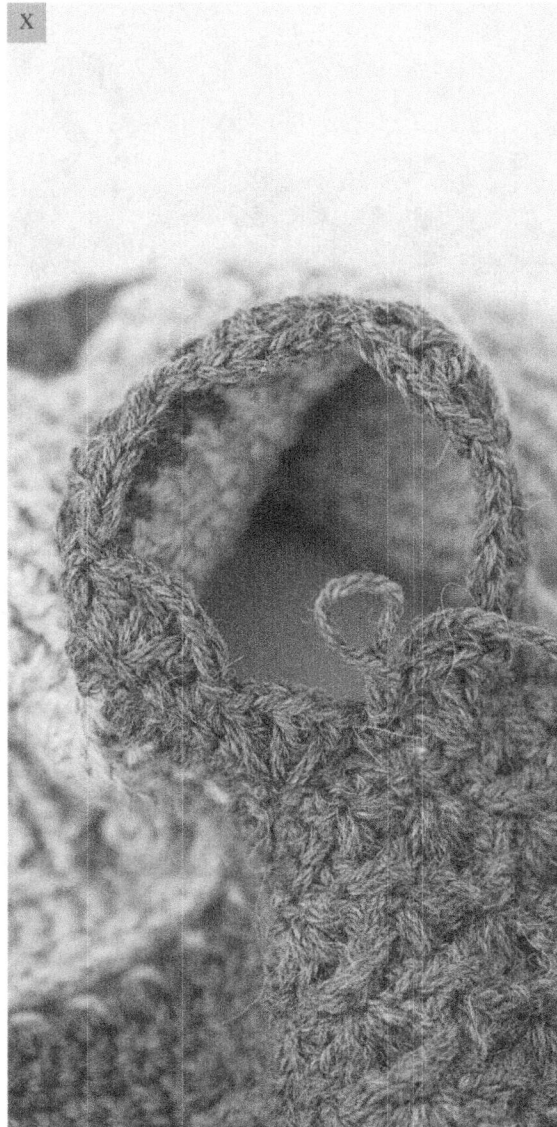

Rnd 2 (WS): ch1, (dc, ch1, dc) in first st, *skip next dc, FPsc around next dc, skip next dc, shell in next sc; repeat from * to end, but in last repeat instead of last shell work dc in same st as first 2dc, ch1 and join with sl st in first st, turn; 7 (7, 8, 9) shells made

Rnd 3 (RS): ch1, BPsc around first dc, *skip next dc, shell in next FPsc of previous rnd, skip next dc, BPsc around next dc; repeat from * to end, but in last repeat instead of last BPsc join with sl st in first BPsc, turn; 7 (7, 8, 9) shells made Y

135

Repeat Rnds 2 and 3 – 6 (8, 10, 12) more times or until desired length and continue with Cuff.

Second Sleeve

Work in exactly the same way as first sleeve.

CUFF

Rnd 1: (RS) ch1, dc in each BPsc and in each dc, skip all ch1, join with sl st in first st; 28 (28 (32, 36) sts; stitch count doesn't change throughout the Cuff Z

Rnd 2 (RS): ch1, FPdc around first dc, *BPdc around next dc, FPdc around next dc; repeat from * to last st, BPdc around last dc and join with sl st in first st

Rnd 3 (RS): ch1, FPdc around first FPdc, *BPdc around next BPdc, FPdc around next FPdc; repeat from * to last st, BPdc around last BPdc and join with sl st in first st

Repeat Rnd 3 – 1 more time or until desired length, fasten off AA

Second Cuff

Work in exactly the same way on second sleeve.

FINISHING

Weave in all ends. Wash and block (see Finishing Techniques).

You could use anything between one and four buttons on this cardigan.

SEMILLA CARDIGAN

~ ★★☆ ~

The pattern of the lower part of this cardigan is fun to make and creates a wonderful texture. I suggest using sport weight or 5ply yarn, which will create a very flowing and soft fabric. If you decide instead to use DK weight it needs to be a very light yarn that's closer to a sport weight. The Semilla Cardigan is worked from the top down.

SIZES AND MEASUREMENTS OF FINISHED GARMENT

Size	Chest	Length	Sleeve length to underarm
0–6m	51cm/20in	26cm/10¼in	14cm/5½in
6–12m	57cm/22½in	29cm/11½in	16cm/6¼in
1–2y	66cm/26in	33cm/13in	20cm/7¾in
3–4y	69cm/27in	37cm/14½in	24cm/9½in

GAUGE (TENSION)

21 sts and 10 rows in dc to measure 10 x 10cm (4 x 4in) using 3.5mm (E/4) hook (or size required to obtain gauge)

SPECIAL STITCHES

FPdc, BPdc:, FPsc, shell (Semilla Cardigan shell), dc2tog, BPdc2tog (see Special Stitches)

MATERIALS

3 LIGHT

- 375 (495, 600, 750) meters or 411 (541, 656, 820) yards of any sport weight or very light DK weight yarn
  Suggested yarn: Laines du Nord Ciliegia, 100% baby alpaca superfine, shade 03, 50g (1¾oz), 150m (164yd)
- 3.5mm (E/4) crochet hook (or size required to obtain gauge)
- 3–5 buttons, approximately 2cm (¾in) diameter
- Tapestry needle

Pattern is written for size 0–6m, changes for 6–12m, 1–2y and 3–4y are in (…).

Ch1 at the beginning of each round doesn't count as a stitch.

YOKE

Row 1 (WS): work quite loosely, ch49 (53, 57, 61), dc in 4th ch from hook (ch3 counts as first dc), dc in each next ch, turn; 47 (51, 55, 59) dc

Row 2 (RS): ch1, pull it to the height of dc (here and throughout where next st is dc), dc in first st, *2dc in next st, dc in next st; repeat from * to end, turn; 70 (76, 82, 88) dc A

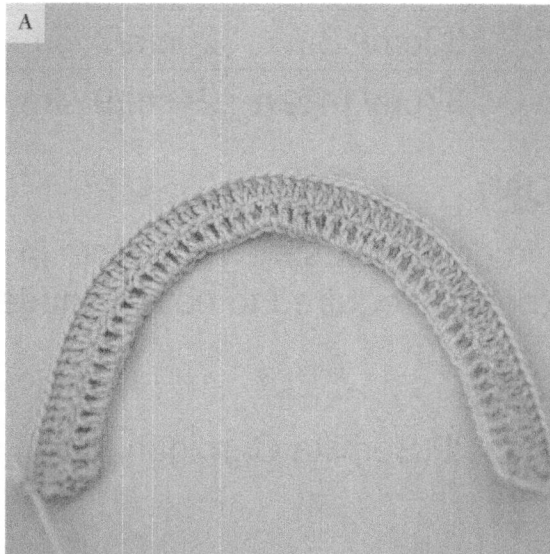

Row 3 (WS): ch1, dc in first and in each next st to end, for sizes 0–6m and 1–2y increase by 1 st, turn; 71 (76, 83, 88) dc

Row 4 (RS): ch1, dc in first st, skip next 2 sts, shell in next st, *skip next 3sts, shell in next st; repeat from * 15 (16, 18, 19) more times, skip next 2 (3, 2, 3) sts, dc in last st, turn; 17 (18, 20, 21) shells made B C

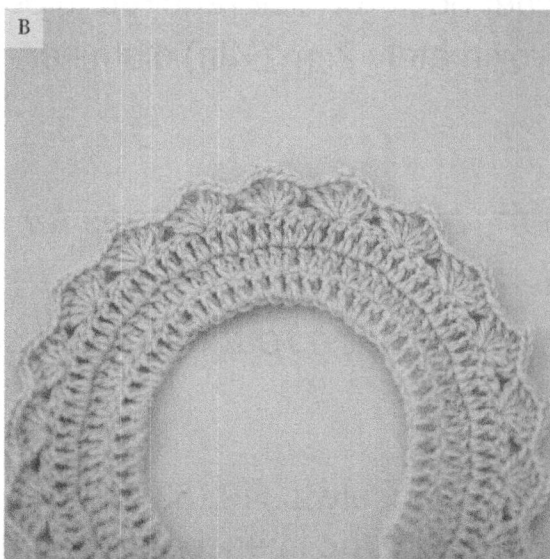

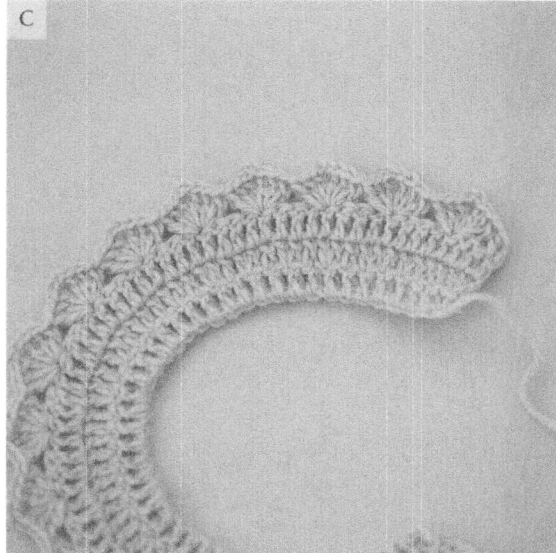

Row 5 (WS): ch1, dc in first st, ch1, skip next dc, *FPsc around each of next 2dc, 2sc in next ch2sp, FPsc around each of next 2dc, ch2, skip next 2dc; repeat from * 15 (16, 18, 19) more times, FPsc around each of next 2dc, 2sc in next ch2sp, FPsc around each of next 2dc, ch1, skip next dc, dc in last st, turn D

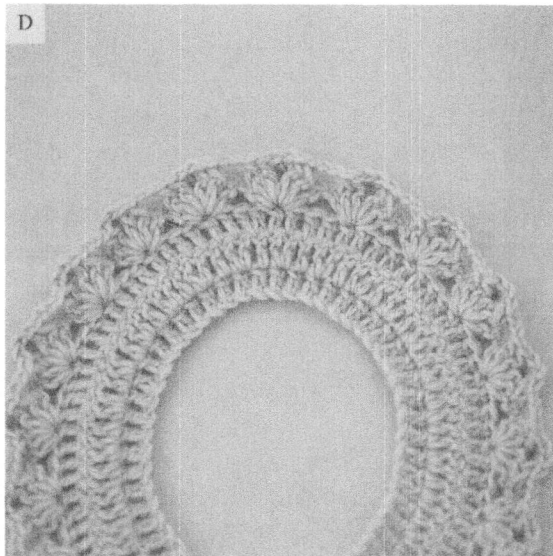

Row 6 (RS): ch1, dc in first st, dc in each st and in each ch1sp, 2dc in each ch2sp, turn; 138 (146, 162, 170) sts E

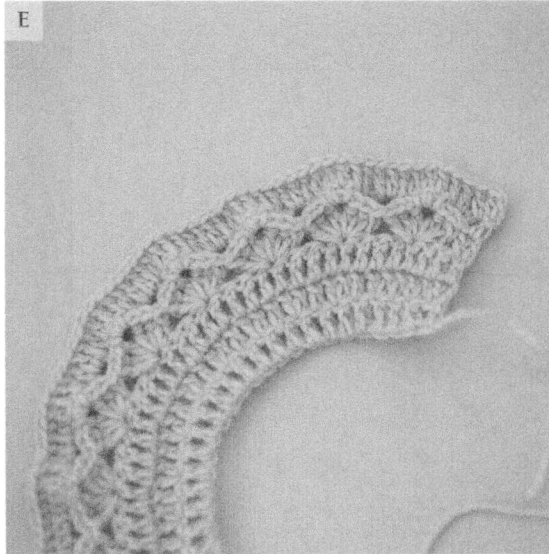

Row 7 (WS): ch1, dc in first st and in each next st to end, for sizes 0–6m and 1–2y increase by 1st, turn; 139 (146, 163, 170) sts

Row 8 (RS): ch1, dc in first st, skip next 2sts, shell in next st, *skip next 5sts, shell in next st; repeat from * to last 3 (4, 3, 4) sts, skip next 2 (3, 2, 3) sts, dc in last st, turn; 23 (24, 27, 28) shells made

Row 9 (WS): ch1, dc in first st, ch1, skip next dc, *FPsc around each of next 2dc, 2sc in next ch2sp, FPsc around each of next 2dc, ch2, skip next 2dc; repeat from * 21 (22, 25, 26) more times, FPsc around

each of next 2dc, 2sc in next ch2sp, FPsc around each of next 2dc, ch1, skip next dc, dc in last st, turn

For size 0–6m

Row 10 (RS): (in this row for this size you work sc instead of dc to shorten the yoke): ch1, sc in first st, sc in next ch1sp, *sc in each of next 6sts, 1sc in next ch2sp; repeat from * 21 more times, in last repeat work 2sc in ch2sp, sc in each of next 6sts, sc in next ch1sp, sc in last st, turn; 165 sts G H

For sizes 6–12m and 3–4y

Row 10 (RS): ch1, dc in first st, dc in next ch1sp, *dc in each of next 6sts, 2dc in next ch2sp, dc in each of next 6sts, 1dc in next ch2sp; repeat from * (11, 13) more times (in last repeat last dc work in ch1sp; for size 3–4y in last repeat work 1dc in both ch2sp), dc in last st, turn; (183, 212) sts

For size 1–2y

Row 10 (RS): ch1, dc in first st, dc in next ch1sp, *dc in each of next 6sts, 2dc in next ch2sp, dc in each of next 6sts, 1dc in next ch2sp; repeat from * 12 more times, dc in each of next 6sts, 1dc in next ch1sp, dc in last st, turn; 205 sts

For sizes 0–6m and 6–12m

Continue with Divide for Sleeves and Body.

For sizes 1–2y and 3–4y

Row 11 (WS): ch1, dc in first st and in each next st to end, turn; (205, 212) sts

Row 12 (RS): ch1, dc in first st, skip next 3sts, shell in next st, *skip next 6sts, shell in next st; repeat from * to last 4sts, skip next 3sts, dc in last st, turn; (29, 30) shells made

Row 13 (WS): ch1, dc in first st, ch1, skip next dc, *FPsc around each of next 2dc, 2sc in next ch2sp, FPsc around each of next 2dc, ch2, skip next 2dc; repeat from * (27, 28) more times, FPsc around each of next 2dc, 2sc in next ch2sp, FPsc around each of next 2dc, ch1, skip next dc, dc in last st, turn

For size 1–2y

Row 14 (RS): (in this row for this size work sc instead of dc to shorten the yoke): ch1, sc in first st, sc in next ch1sp, *sc in each of next 6sts, 1sc in next ch2sp; repeat from * to end, (in last repeat work sc in ch1sp), sc in last st, turn; (206) sts

Continue with Divide for Sleeves and Body.

For size 3–4y

Row 14 (RS): ch1, dc in first st, dc in next ch1sp, *dc in each of next 6sts, 1dc in next ch2sp; repeat from * to end, (in last repeat work dc in ch1sp), dc in last st, turn; (213) sts

Continue with Divide for Sleeves and Body.

Sport weight yarn is lovely and light but still gives you good stitch definition.

DIVIDE FOR SLEEVES AND BODY

Row 1 (WS): ch1, dc in first and in each of next 22 (25, 30, 31) sts, ch4 (5, 6, 6), skip next 33 (36, 38, 39) sts for an armhole, dc in each of next 53 (59, 68, 71) sts, ch4 (5, 6, 6), skip next 33 (36, 38, 39) sts for an armhole, dc in each of next 23 (26, 31, 32) sts, turn; 107 (121, 142, 147) sts

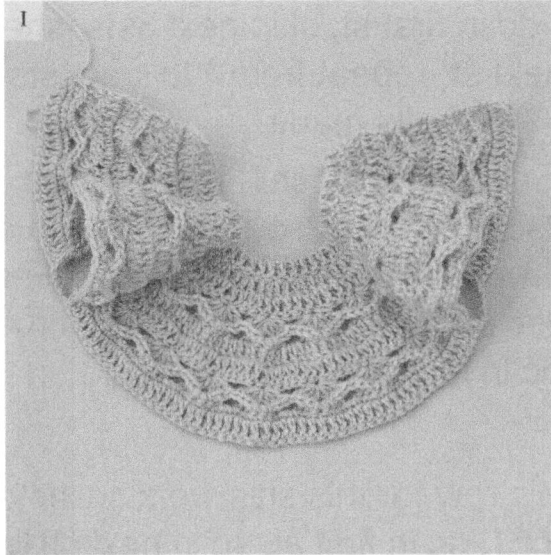

Row 2 (RS): (each ch of underarm counts as st) ch1, dc in first st, skip next 2sts, shell in next st, *skip next 4sts, shell in next st; repeat from * to last 3 (2, 3, 3) sts, skip next 2 (1, 2, 2) sts, dc in last st, turn; 21 (24, 28, 29) shells made

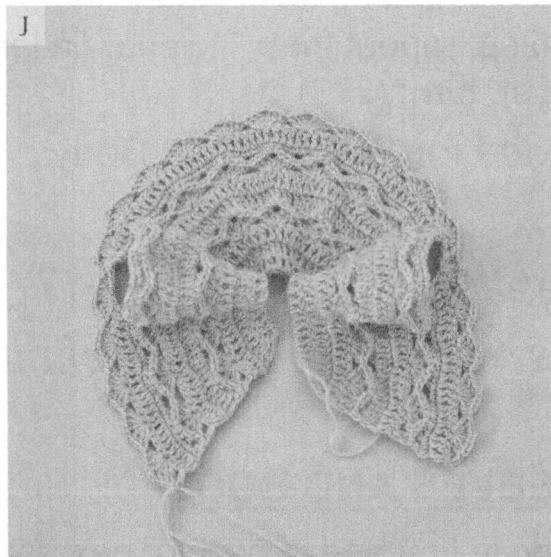

Row 3 (WS): ch1, dc in first st, ch1, skip next dc, *FPsc around each of next 2dc, 2sc in next ch2sp, FPsc around each of next 2dc, ch2, skip next 2dc; repeat from * 19 (22, 26, 27) more times, FPsc around each of next 2dc, 2sc in next ch2sp, FPsc around each of next 2dc, ch1, skip next dc, dc in last st, turn

Row 4 (RS): ch1, dc in first st, 3dc in next ch1sp, *skip next 6sts, shell in next ch2sp; repeat from * 19 (22, 26, 27) more times, skip next 6sts, 3dc in next ch1sp, dc in last st, turn; 20 (23, 27, 28) shells made K

Row 5 (WS): ch1, sc in first st, FPsc around each of next 2dc, *ch2, skip next 2dc, FPsc around each of next 2dc, 2sc in next ch2sp, FPsc around each of next 2dc; repeat from * 19 (22, 26, 27) more times, ch2, skip next 2dc, FPsc around each of next 2dc, sc in last st, turn

Row 6 (RS): ch1, dc in first st, skip next 2sts, shell in next ch2sp, *skip next 6sts, shell in next ch2sp; repeat from * 19 (22, 26, 27) more times, skip next 2sts, dc in last st, turn; 21 (24, 28, 29) shells made

Repeat Rows 3 through 6 – 2 (3, 4, 5) more times, or until desired length.

Repeat Rows 3 through 5 once more, continue with Front Edging.

FRONT EDGING

Left Front

Row 1 (WS): ch1, work evenly 46 (52, 58, 66) dc across the left front, turn L

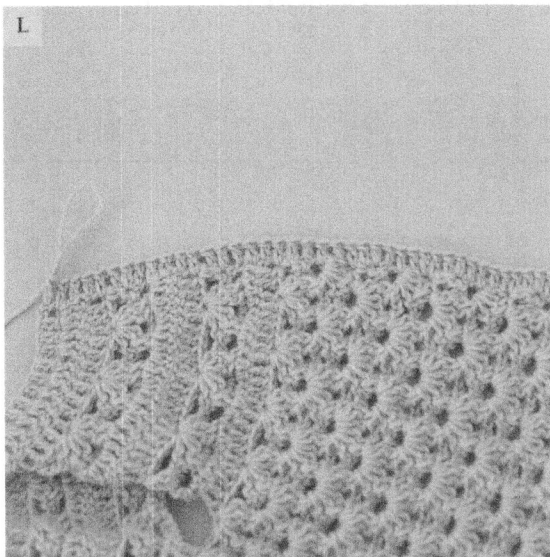

Row 2 (RS): ch1, hdc in first st, *FPdc around next st, BPdc around next st; repeat from * to last st, hdc in last st, turn; 46 (52, 58, 66) sts

Row 3 (WS): ch1, hdc in first st, *FPdc around next FPdc, BPdc around next BPdc; repeat from * to last st, hdc in last st, turn; 46 (52, 58, 66) sts

Row 4 (RS): ch1, hdc in first st, *FPdc around next FPdc, BPdc around next BPdc; repeat from * to last st, hdc in last st, fasten off; 46 (52, 58, 66) sts M

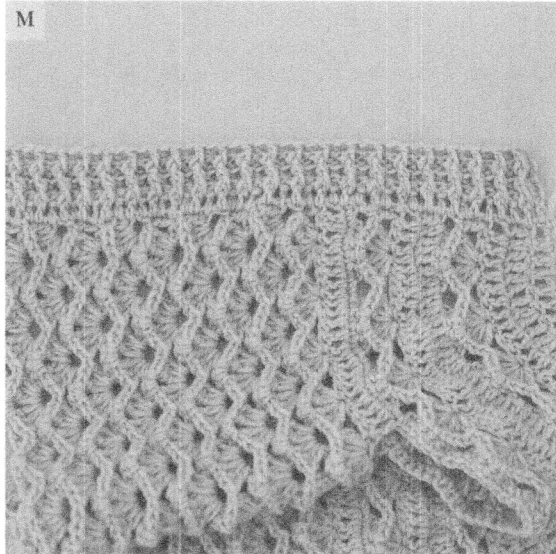

Right Front

On WS, join yarn into the first st of the collar and work across the right front.

Row 1 (WS): ch1, work evenly 46 (52, 58, 66) dc across the right front, turn

Row 2 (RS): ch1, hdc in first st, *BPdc around next st, FPdc around next st; repeat from * to last st, hdc in last st, turn; 46 (52, 58, 66) sts

Row 3 (WS): ch1, hdc in first st, BPdc around next BPdc, *ch1, skip next FPdc, [BPdc around next BPdc, FPdc around next FPdc] 3 times, BPdc around next BPdc; repeat from * 2 (2, 2, 3) more times (or to end if prefer more buttons), continue to work FPdc around next FPdc, BPdc around next BPdc, to last st, hdc in last st, turn; 46 (52, 58, 66) sts

Row 4 (RS): ch1, hdc in first st, work (BPdc around each BPdc and FPdc around each FPdc, hdc in each ch1sp) to last st, hdc in last st; 46 (52, 58, 66) sts N

Work ch1, and work sc evenly across the collar (including both edgings) and fasten off.

SLEEVES

On WS, join yarn in the middle of the underarm [O]

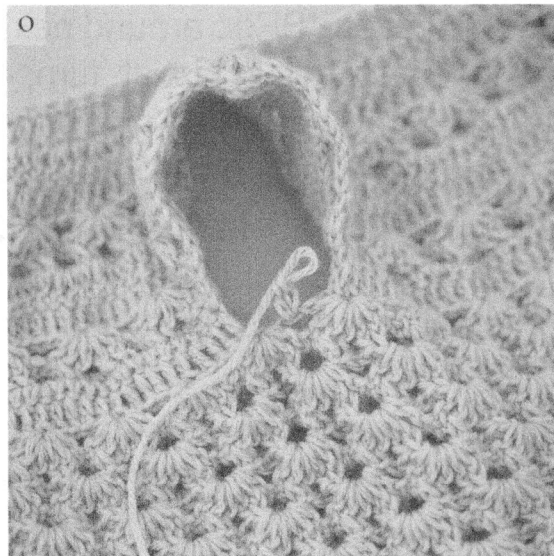

Sleeves are worked in rounds but on both RS and WS, turn after each round.

Rnd 1 (WS): ch1, but pull it to the height of dc (here and throughout), dc in st at the base of ch1, and work 41 (46, 48, 49) dc evenly around the armhole, join with sl st in first st, and turn; 42 (47, 49, 50) dc P

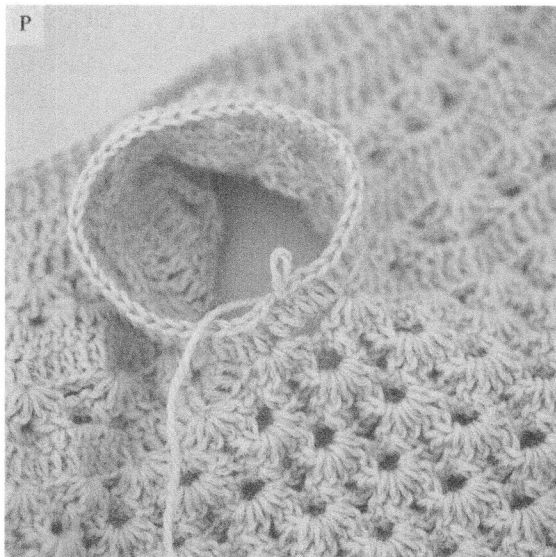

Rnd 2 (RS): ch1, dc in st at the base of ch1, dc2tog, dc in each st to last 2sts, dc2tog, join with sl st in first st, turn; 40 (45, 47, 48) dc

Repeat Rnd 2 – 2 (3, 4, 3) more times or until desired width, turning after each rnd and working on both RS and WS; 36 (39, 39, 42) dc

Next Rnd: ch1, dc in first and in each next st, join with sl st in first st, turn; 36 (39, 39, 42) dc

Repeat Next Rnd – 6 (8, 10, 13) more times or until desired length, turning after each rnd and working on both RS and WS; 36 (39, 39, 42) dc

Continue with Cuff.

Second Sleeve

Work in exactly the same way as first sleeve.

CUFF

Rnd 1 (RS): ch1, FPdc around first st, *BPdc2tog around next 2sts, FPdc around next st; repeat from * to end, but in last repeat instead of last FPdc join with sl st in first FPdc; 24 (26, 26, 28) sts

Rnd 2 (RS): ch1, *FPdc around next FPdc, BPdc around next BPdc; repeat from * to end, join with sl st in first FPdc; 24 (26, 26, 28) sts Q

Repeat Rnd 2 – 2 (3, 3, 3) times, or until desired length, fasten off.

Second Cuff

Work in exactly the same way on second sleeve.

FINISHING

Weave in all ends and sew on buttons (see Finishing Techniques).

WAVES SWEATER

~ ★★☆ ~

This sweater is worked bottom up in rounds, then divided for the back and front. As such it's almost seamless – you'll just have to make small shoulder seams. It looks equally good made from either a chunky or thinner yarn. You could even use sport weight yarn and looser stitches to make a light and lacy summer sweater.

SIZES AND MEASUREMENTS OF FINISHED GARMENT

Size	Chest	Length	Sleeve length to underarm
0–6m	50cm/19¾in	30cm/11¾in	16cm/6¼in
6–12m	56cm/22in	33cm/13in	19cm/7½in
1–2y	61cm/24in	36cm/14in	22cm/8½in
3–4y	67cm/26½in	42cm/16½in	26cm/10¼in

GAUGE (TENSION)

18 sts and 10 rows in dc to measure 10 x 10cm (4 x 4in) using 3.5mm (E/4) hook (or size required to obtain gauge)

SPECIAL STITCHES

bo (4-dc bobble), FPdc, BPdc, BPdc2tog, BPsc (see Special Stitches)

MATERIALS

3 LIGHT

- 450 (550, 625, 750) meters or 493 (602, 684, 820) yards of any DK weight or light worsted weight yarn
  Suggested yarn: Laines du Nord Holiday, 70% wool, 30% acrylic, shade 610, 50g (1¾oz), 125m (136yd)
- 3.5mm (E/4) crochet hook (or size required to obtain gauge)

Pattern is written for size 0–6m, changes for 6–12m, 1–2y and 3–4y are in (…).

Ch1 at the beginning of each round doesn't count as a stitch.

Attention – some rounds are worked on WS, some on RS, follow instructions to turn.

BODY

Foundation chain: ch90 (100, 110, 120), join with sl st in first ch.

Rnd 1 (RS): ch1, but pull it longer (here and throughout when next st is dc), dc in first ch, dc in each next ch, join with sl st in first st, turn and work on WS; 90 (100, 110, 120) sts

Rnd 2 (WS): ch1, sc in first st, *bo in next st, sc in each of next 4sts; repeat from * to end, in last repeat work sc in each of next 3sts, join with sl st in first st, turn and work on RS; 90 (100, 110, 120) sts A

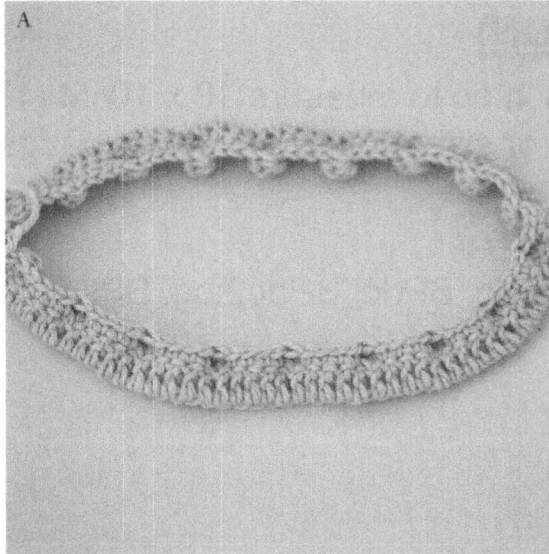

Rnd 3 (RS): ch1, sc in first st, sc in each of next 3sts, *ch2, skip next bo, sc in each of next 4sc; repeat from * to last st, ch2, skip next bo, join with sl st in first st; 18 (20, 22, 24) ch2sp made B

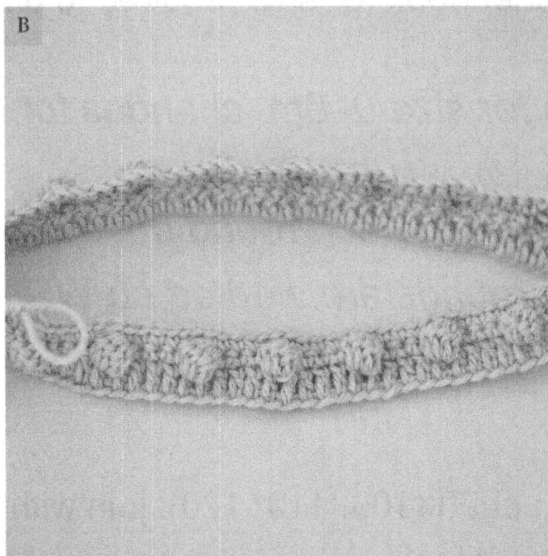

Rnd 4 (RS): ch1, *skip next 4sc, 6dc in next ch2sp; repeat from * to end, join with sl st in first st; 18 (20, 22, 24) 6dc shells made C

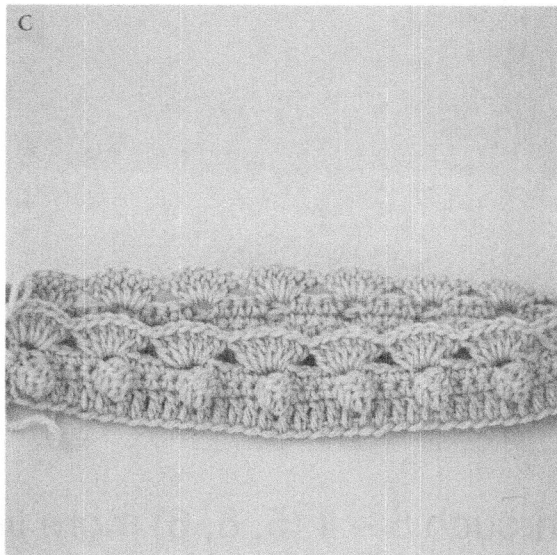

Rnd 5 (RS): ch1, skip first dc, *BPsc around each of next 4dc, ch2, skip next 2dc; repeat from * to end, join with sl st in first st, turn; 18 (20, 22, 24) ch2sp made D

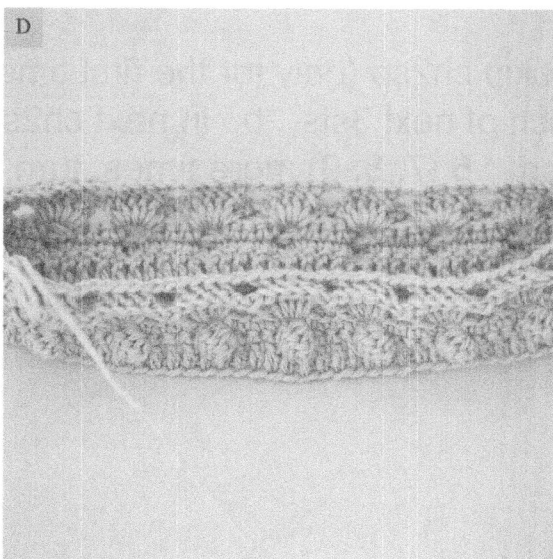

Rnd 6 (WS): ch1, sc in first st, *bo in next ch2sp, sc in each of next 4sc; repeat from * to end, in last repeat work sc in each of next 3sts, join with sl st in first st, turn; 18 (20, 22, 24) bo made E

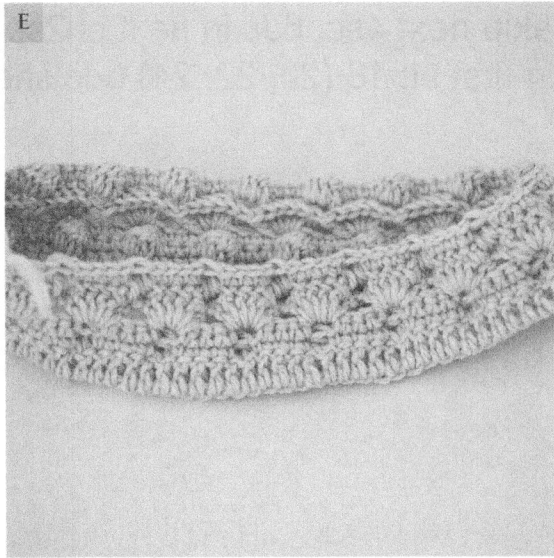

Repeat Rnds 3 through 6 – 4 (5, 6, 6) more times, or until desired length (length to underarm); the joining line will move but it will be practically invisible.

Repeat Rnds 3 through 5 once more and continue with Back.

BACK

Row 1 (WS): ch1, skip ch2sp (only for the first time, not for repeats), sc in first and in each of next 3sts, *bo in next ch2sp, sc in each of next 4sc; repeat from * 6 (7, 8, 9) more times, turn; 7 (8, 9, 10) bo made F

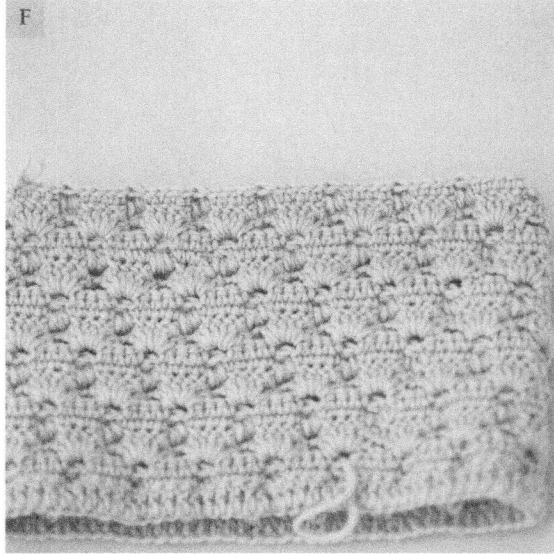

Row 2 (RS): ch1, sc in first and in each of next 3sts, *ch2, skip next bo, sc in each of next 4sc; repeat from * 6 (7, 8, 9) more times, turn; 7 (8, 9, 10) ch2sp made

Row 3 (WS): ch1, dc in first st, skip next 3sc, *6dc in next ch2sp, skip next 4sc; repeat from * 6 (7, 8, 9) more times, in last repeat skip 3sc and work dc in last sc, turn; 7 (8, 9, 10) 6dc shells made G

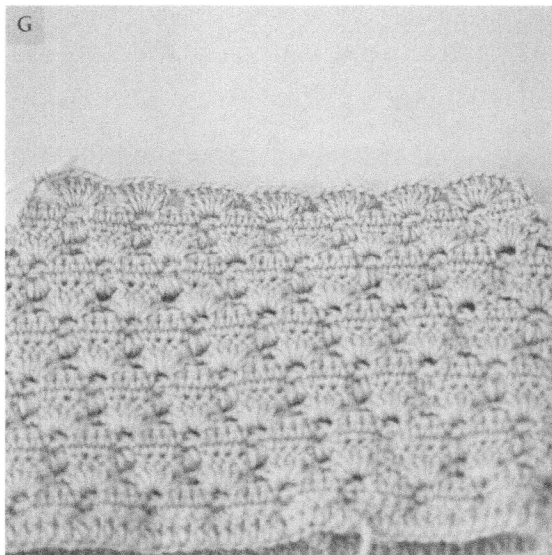

Row 4 (RS): ch1, sc in first st, ch1, skip next dc, *BPsc around each of next 4dc, ch2, skip next 2dc; repeat from * 6 (7, 8, 9) more times, in last repeat skip 1dc, ch1, sc in last dc, turn H

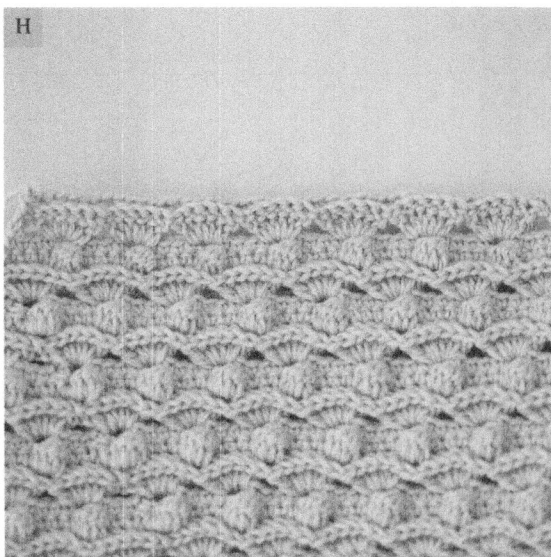

Row 5 (WS): ch1, sc in first st, bo in next ch1sp, *sc in each of next 4sc, bo in next ch2sp; repeat from * to end, but in last repeat work bo in ch1sp, sc in last sc, turn; 8 (9, 10, 11) bo made

Row 6 (RS): ch1, sc in first st, ch1, *skip next bo, sc in each next 4sc, ch2; repeat from * to end, but in last repeat work ch1, skip next bo, sc in last st, turn I

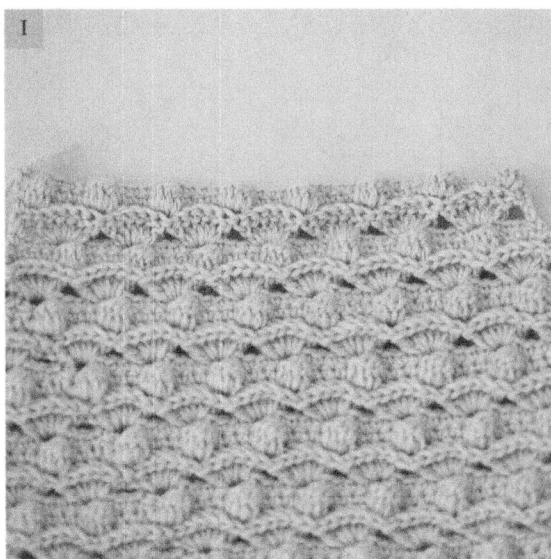

Row 7 (WS): ch1, dc in first st, 4dc in next ch1sp, *skip next 4sc, 6dc in next ch2sp; repeat from * to end, but in last repeat work 4dc in ch1sp, dc in last st, turn J

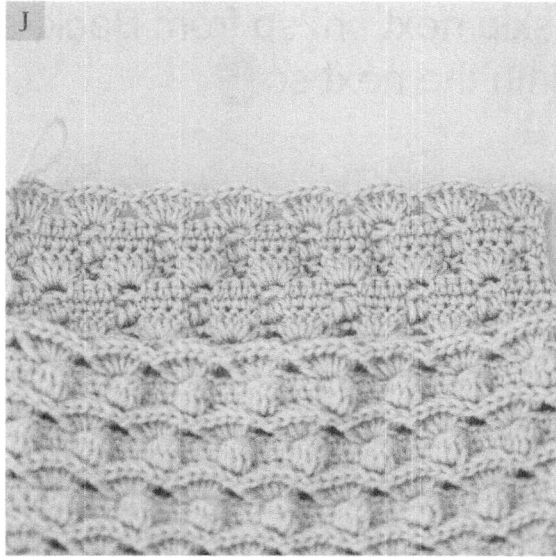

Row 8 (RS): ch1, sc in first st, BPsc around each of next 3dc, *ch2, skip next 2dc, BPsc around each of next 4dc; repeat from * to end, but in last repeat work BPsc around each of next 3dc, sc in last dc, turn; 8 (9, 10, 11) ch2sp made

For sizes 0–6m, 6–12m and 1–2y

Repeat Rows 1 through 7 once more, fasten off K

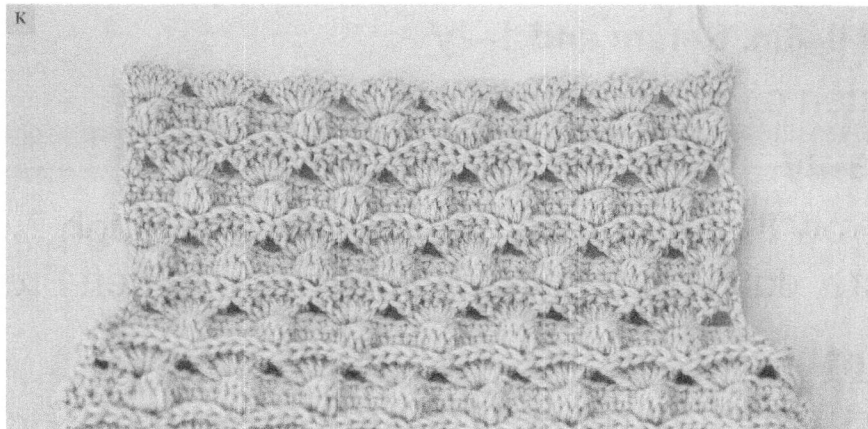

For size 3–4y

Repeat Rows 1 through 8 once more; then repeat Rows 1 through 7 once more, fasten off.

FRONT

With WS facing, skip next ch2sp from Back, skip 4sc and next ch2sp, join into the next sc L

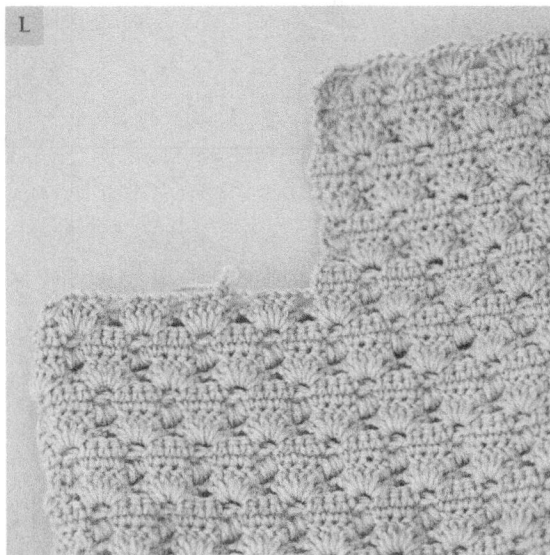

Row 1 (WS): ch1, sc in first and in each of next 3sts, *bo in next ch2sp, sc in each of next 4sc; repeat from * 6 (7, 8, 9) more times, turn; 7 (8, 9, 10) bo made

Repeat Rows 2 through 7 as for Back.

For sizes 0–6m, 6–12m and 1–2y

Don't fasten off, but continue with Left Front.

For size 3–4y

Repeat Row 8 of Back and repeat Rows 1 through 7 of Back once more, don't fasten off, but continue with Left Front.

Left Front

Row 1 (RS): ch1, sc in first st, BPsc around each of next 3dc, *ch2, skip next 2dc, BPsc around each of next 4dc; only for size 3–4y repeat from * once more, turn M

Row 2 (WS): ch1, sc in first and in each of next 3sts, *bo in next ch2sp, sc in each next 4sc; only for size 3–4y repeat from * once more, turn

Row 3 (RS): ch1, sc in first and in each of next 3sts, *ch2, skip next bo, sc in each next 4sc; only for size 3–4y repeat from * once more, turn

For sizes 0–6m, 6–12m and 1–2y

Row 4 (WS): ch1, dc in first st, skip next 3sc, 6dc in next ch2sp, skip next 3sc, dc in last sc, turn

Row 5 (RS): ch1, sc in first st, ch1, skip next dc, BPsc around each of next 4dc, ch1, skip next dc, sc in last dc, turn

Row 6 (WS): ch1, sc in first st, bo in next ch1sp, sc in each of next 4sc, bo in next ch1sp, sc in last sc, turn

Row 7 (RS): ch1, sc in first st, ch1, skip next bo, sc in each next 4sc, ch1, skip next bo, sc in last sc, turn

Row 8 (WS): ch1, dc in first st, 4dc in next ch1sp, skip next 4sc, 4dc in next ch1sp, dc in last sc, turn N

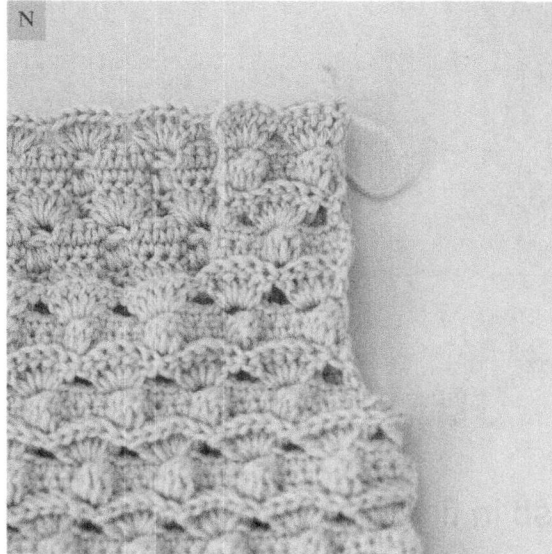

Don't fasten off, but join the Front panel to the Back working on WS sl sts across through both layers O , fasten off.

For size 3–4y

Row 4 (WS): ch1, dc in first st, skip next 3sc, *6dc in next ch2sp, skip next 4sc; repeat from * once more but in last repeat skip 3sc and work dc in last sc, turn

Row 5 (RS): ch1, sc in first st, ch1, skip next dc, *BPsc around each of next 4dc, ch2, skip 2dc; repeat from * once more, but in last repeat work ch1, skip next dc, sc in last dc, turn

Row 6 (WS): ch1, sc in first st, bo in next ch1sp, *sc in each of next 4sc, bo in next ch2sp; repeat from * once more, but in last repeat

166

work bo in ch1sp, sc in last sc, turn

Row 7 (RS): ch1, sc in first st, ch1, skip next bo, *sc in each of next 4sc, ch2, skip next bo; repeat from * once more, but in last repeat work ch1, skip next bo, sc in last sc, turn

Row 8 (WS): ch1, dc in first st, 4dc in next ch1sp, *skip next 4sc, 6dc in next ch2sp; repeat from * once more, but in last repeat work 4dc in ch1sp, dc in last sc, turn N

Don't fasten off, but join the Front panel to the Back working on WS sl sts across through both layers O , fasten off.

Right Front

On RS, skip next 4 (5, 6, 5) shells, skip next dc, join into next dc P and repeat Rows 1 through 8 as for Left Front Q

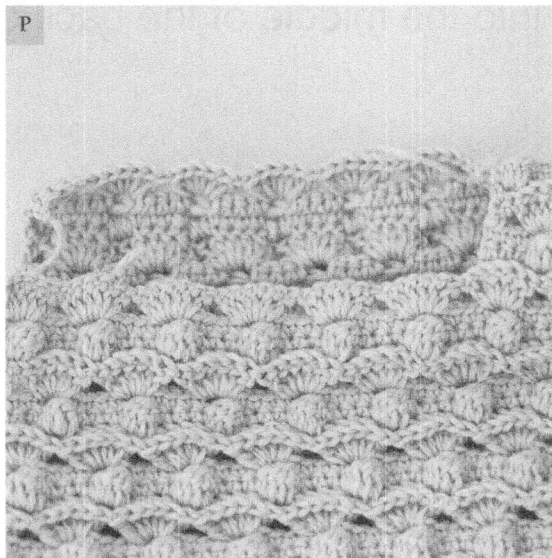

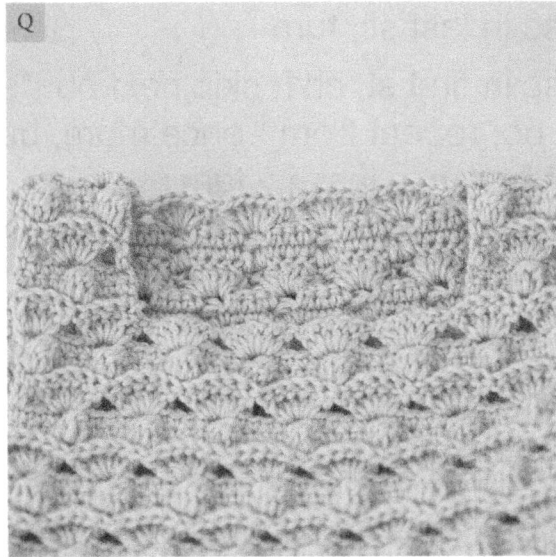

COLLAR

On RS, join yarn into the middle of the back of the neck R and work:

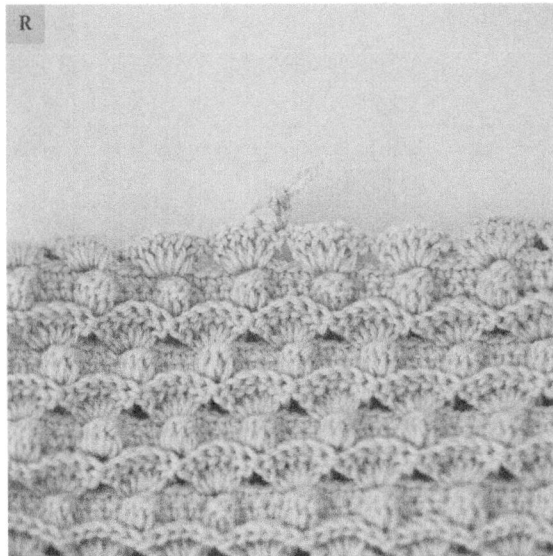

Rnd 1 (RS): ch1, work evenly dc around the collar, join with sl st in first st (number is not important, but it has to be multiple of 3; don't make them too far from each other, and not too close; it might seem wide at this point but we will be decreasing number of sts in next rnd) S

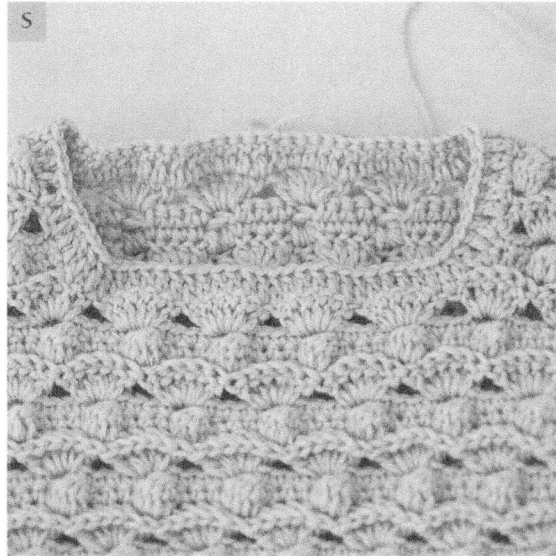

Rnd 2 (RS): ch1, FPdc around first dc, *BPdc2tog, FPdc around next dc; repeat from * to end, join with sl st in first st

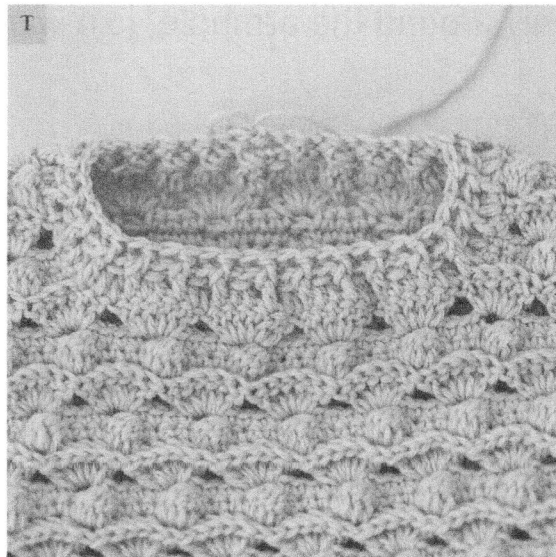

Rnd 3 (RS): ch1, FPdc around first FPdc, *BPdc around next BPdc, FPdc around next FPdc; repeat from * to last st, BPdc around next BPdc, join with sl st in first st

Repeat Rnd 3 – one more time, fasten off.

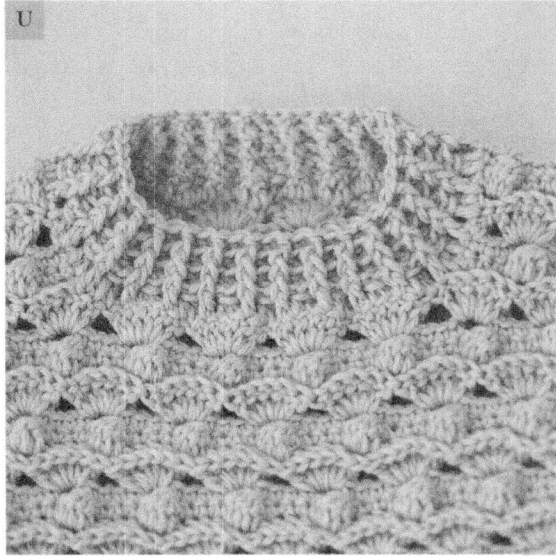

SLEEVES

Rnd 1 (RS): join yarn into the first ch2sp of underarm and work 42 (48, 54, 60) sc evenly around the armhole, join with sl st in first st

Rnd 2 (RS): ch1, sc in first and each of next 3sc, *ch2, skip next 2sc, sc in next 4sc; repeat from * to last 2sts, ch2, skip next 2sts, join with sl st in first st, turn and work on WS; 7 (8, 9, 10) ch2sp made

Rnd 3 (WS): ch1, sc in first st, *bo in next ch2sp, sc in each next 4sc; repeat from * to end, in last repeat work sc in each of next 3sts, join with sl st in first st, turn and work on RS; 7 (8, 9, 10) bo made

Rnd 4 (RS): ch1, sc in first and in each of next 3sts, *ch2, skip next bo, sc in each next 4sc; repeat from * to last st, ch2, skip next bo, join with sl st in first st; 7 (8, 9, 10) ch2sp made

Rnd 5 (RS): ch1, *skip next 4sc, 6dc in next ch2sp; repeat from * to end, join with sl st in first st; 7 (8, 9, 10) shells made

Rnd 6 (RS): ch1, skip first dc, *BPsc around each of next 4dc, ch2, skip next 2dc; repeat from * to end, join with sl st in first st, turn and work on WS; 7 (8, 9, 10) ch2sp made X

For sizes 0–6m, 6–12m and 1–2y

Repeat Rnds 3 through 6 – 4 (5, 6) more times or until desired length; last repeat end with Rnd 5 and continue with Cuff.

For size 3–4y

Repeat Rnds 3 through 6 once more; then repeat Rnds 3 and 4 once again and continue with Cuff.

Second Sleeve

Work in exactly the same way as first sleeve.

CUFF

Rnd 1 (RS): ch1, FPdc around next dc, *BPdc2tog, FPdc around next dc; repeat from * to last 2sts, BPdc2tog, join with sl st in first st; 28 (32, 36, 40) sts Y

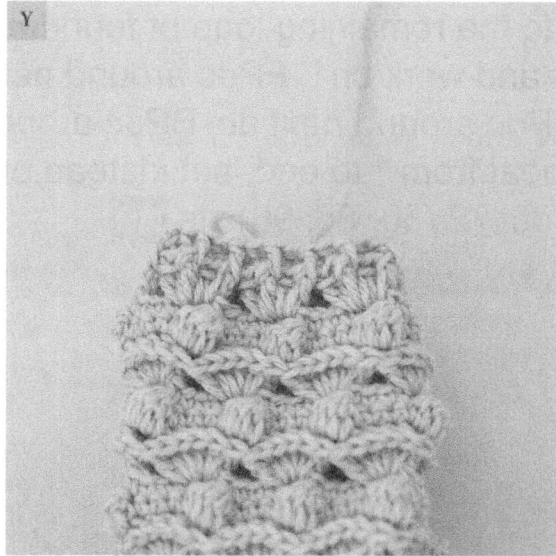

Rnd 2 (RS): ch1, FPdc around first FPdc, *BPdc around next BPdc, FPdc around next FPdc; repeat from * to last st, BPdc around next BPdc, join with sl st in first st 28 (32, 36, 40) sts

Repeat Rnd 2 – 2 more times, fasten off Z

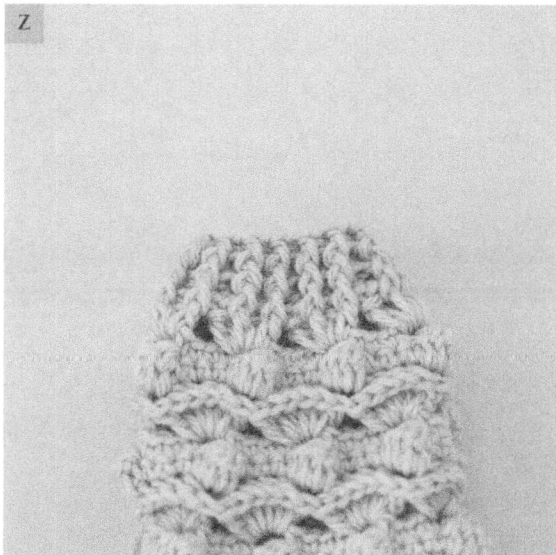

Second Cuff

Work in exactly the same way on second sleeve.

BOTTOM RIBBING

Rnd 1 (RS): join into the remaining loop of foundation chain on the side of the sweater and work ch1, FPdc around next dc `AA` , *BPdc around next 2dc, FPdc around next dc, BPdc around next dc, FPdc around next dc; repeat from * to end, but instead of last FPdc join with sl st in first FPdc; 72 (80, 88, 96) sts `AB`

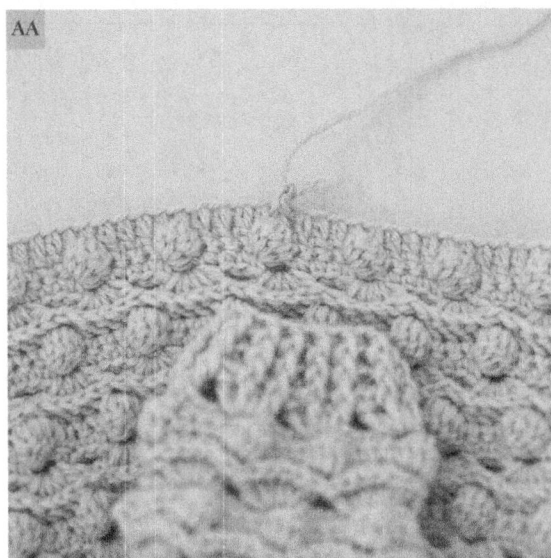

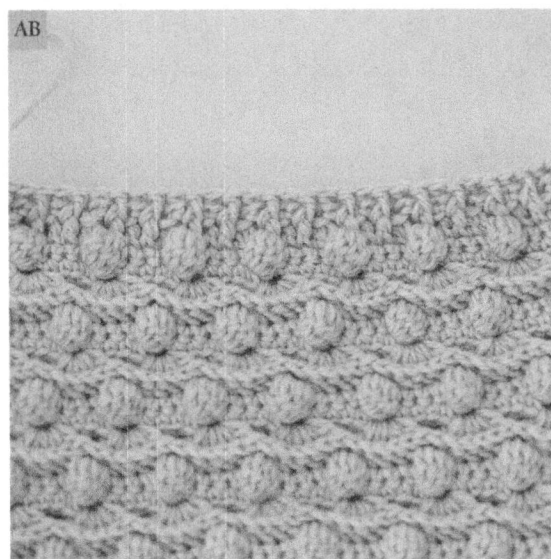

Rnd 2 (RS): ch1, FPdc around first FPdc, *BPdc around next BPdc, FPdc around next FPdc; repeat from * to last st, BPdc around next BPdc, join with sl st in first FPdc; (72 (80, 88, 96) sts

Repeat Rnd 2 – 2 more times, fasten off.

FINISHING

Weave in all ends (see Finishing Techniques).

ANGEL ROMPER

~ ★★☆ ~

Rompers are great not only for cute photo shoots, but to keep your little one warm and comfy. This one can be worn over a long-sleeve bodysuit for colder days or even as a swimsuit in hot weather. If you are making a summer version I suggest choosing a cotton-blend yarn, as it will tend to be more comfortable and stretchy than 100% cotton.

SIZES AND MEASUREMENTS OF FINISHED GARMENT

Size	Chest	Length from shoulders to bottom
0–6m	44cm/17¼in	35cm/13¾in
6–12m	47cm/18½in	41cm/16¼in
12–18m	51cm/20in	43cm/17in
18–24m	53cm/21in	45cm/17¾in

GAUGE (TENSION)

19 sts and 10 rows in dc to measure 10 x 10cm (4 x 4in) using 3.5mm (E/4)hook (or size required to obtain gauge)

SPECIAL STITCHES

FPdc, BPdc, FPtr, FPtr3tog, bo (4-dc bobble), dc2tog (see Special Stitches)

MATERIALS

3 LIGHT

- 360 (420, 480, 540) meters or 394 (460, 525, 590) yards of any DK weight or light worsted weight yarn
  Suggested yarn: Lana Gatto Super Soft DK, 100% merino wool, shade 14393, 50g (1¾oz), 125m (136yd)
- 3.5mm (E/4) crochet hook (or size required to obtain gauge)
- Stitch markers
- 4 buttons, approximately 2cm (¾in) diameter

Pattern is written for size 0–6m, changes for 6–12m, 12–18m and 18–24m are in (…).

Ch1 at the beginning of each round doesn't count as a stitch.

FRONT BIB

Row 1 (RS): ch21 (21, 23, 23), dc in 4th ch from hook (ch3 counts as first dc) and in each next ch, turn; 19 (19, 21, 21) sts

Row 2 (WS): ch1, but pull it to the height of dc (here and throughout where first st is dc), dc in first and in each of next 6 (6, 7, 7) sts, skip next 2sts, (3tr, ch1, dc, ch1, 3tr) in next st, skip next 2sts, dc in each of next 7 (7, 8, 8) sts, turn; 23 (23, 25, 25) sts including all ch here and throughout

Row 3 (RS): ch1, dc in first and in each of next 2 (2, 3, 3) sts, FPdc around next dc, dc in each of next 2sts, skip next dc, FPdc around each of next 3tr, ch2, skip next ch, sc in next dc, ch2, skip next ch, FPdc around each of next 3tr, skip next dc, dc in each of next 2sts, FPdc around next dc, dc in each of next 3 (3, 4, 4) sts, turn; 23 (23, 25, 25) sts A

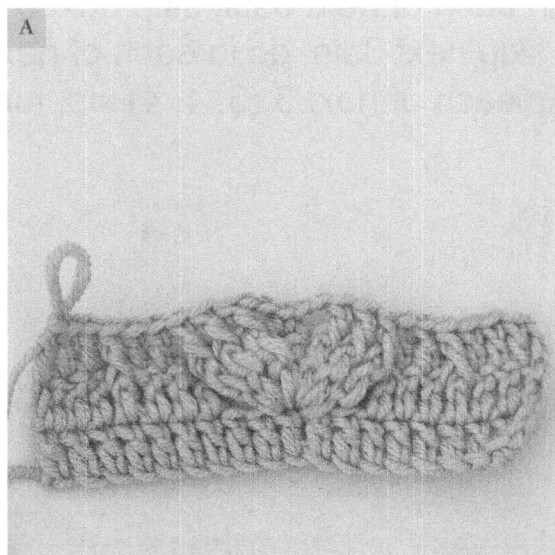

Row 4 (WS): ch1, sc in first st and in each of next 8 (8, 9, 9) sts, sc in next ch2sp, bo in next st, sc in next ch2sp, sc in each of next 9 (9, 10, 10) sts, turn; 21 (21, 23, 23) sts

Row 5 (RS): ch1, dc in first and in each of next 2 (2, 3, 3) sts, FPtr around next FPdc one row below, dc in each of next 2sts, FPtr3tog working around next 3FPdc one row below, dc in each of next 7sts, FPtr3tog working around next 3FPdc one row below, dc in each of next 2sts, FPtr around next FPdc one row below, dc in each of next 3 (3, 4, 4) sts, turn; 21 (21, 23, 23) sts B

Row 6 (WS): ch1, dc in first and in each of next 2 (2, 3, 3) sts, BPdc around next st, dc in each of next 3sts, skip next 3sts, (3tr, ch1, dc, ch1, 3tr) in next st, skip next 3sts, dc in each of next 3sts, BPdc around next st, dc in each of next 3 (3, 4, 4) sts, turn; 23 (23, 25, 25) sts

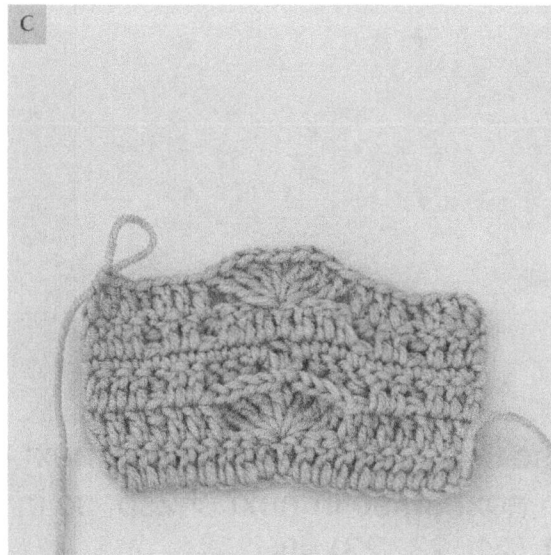

Row 7 (RS): ch1, dc in first and in each of next 2 (2, 3, 3) sts, FPdc around next FPdc, dc in each of next 2sts, skip next dc, FPdc around each of next 3tr, ch2, skip next ch, sc in next dc, ch2, skip next ch, FPdc around each of next 3tr, skip next dc, dc in each of next 2sts, FPdc around next FPdc, dc in each of next 3 (3, 4, 4) sts, turn; 23 (23, 25, 25) sts

For sizes 0–6m and 6–12m

Repeat Rows 4 and 5 – once more and continue with Body.

For sizes 12–18m and 18–24m

Repeat Rows 4 through 7 once more, repeat Rows 4 and 5 once more and continue with Body.

BODY

Rnd 1 (RS): work loosely, ch 44 (48, 52, 54) and join with sl st in first dc of last row of Front Bib; 65 (69, 75, 77) sts including sts of the Front Bib D

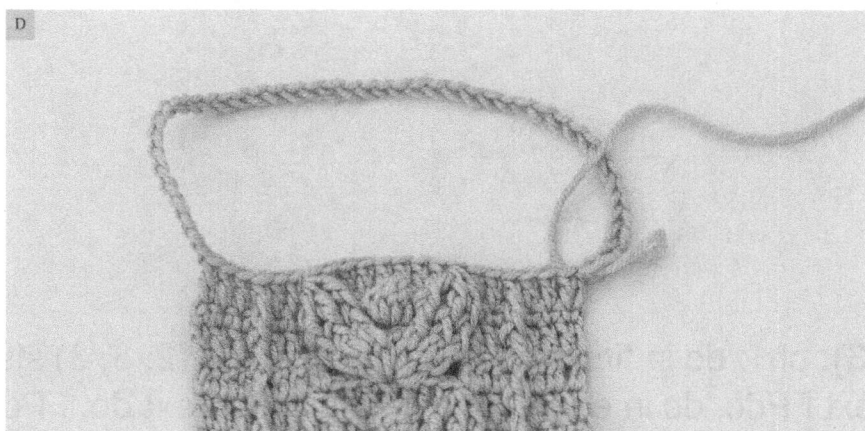

Rnd 2 (RS): ch1, dc in first and in each of next 2 (2, 3, 3) sts, FPdc around next FPtr, dc in each of next 3sts, skip next 3sts, (3tr, ch1, dc, ch1, 3tr) in next st, skip next 3sts, dc in each of next 3sts, FPdc around next FPtr, dc in each of next 47 (51, 56, 58) sts, join with sl st in first st; 67 (71, 77, 79) sts E

Rnd 3 (RS): ch1, dc in first and in each of next 2 (2, 3, 3) sts, FPdc around next FPdc, dc in each of next 2sts, skip next dc, FPdc around each of next 3tr, ch2, skip next ch, sc in next dc, ch2, skip next ch, FPdc around each of next 3tr, skip next dc, dc in each of next 2sts, FPdc around next FPdc, dc in each of next 3 (3, 4, 4) sts, *2dc in next st, dc in next st; repeat from * to end, join with sl st in first st, turn; 89 (95, 103, 106) sts F

Rnd 4 (WS): ch1, sc in first st and in each of next 75 (81, 88, 91) sts, sc in next ch2sp, bo in next sc, sc in next ch2sp, sc in each of next 8 (8, 9, 9) sts, join with sl st in first st, turn; 87 (93, 101, 104) sts G

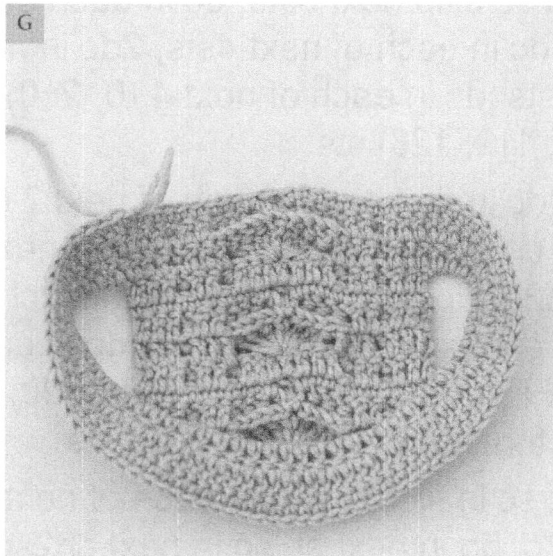

Rnd 5 (RS): ch1, dc in first and in each of next 2 (2, 3, 3) sts, FPtr around next FPdc one row below, dc in each of next 2sts, FPtr3tog working around next 3FPdc one row below, dc in each of next 7sts, FPtr3tog working around next 3FPdc one row below, dc in each of next 2sts, FPtr around next FPdc one row below, dc in each of next 69 (75, 82, 85) sts, join with sl st in first st; 87 (93, 101, 104) sts

Rnd 6 (RS): ch1, dc in first and in each of next 2 (2, 3, 3) sts, FPdc around next FPtr, dc in each of next 3sts, skip next 3sts, (3tr, ch1, dc, ch1, 3tr) in next st, skip next 3sts, dc in each of next 3sts, FPdc around next FPtr, dc in each of next 69 (75, 82, 85) sts, join with sl st in first st; 89 (95, 103, 106) sts

Rnd 7 (RS): ch1, dc in first and in each of next 2 (2, 3, 3) sts, FPdc around next FPdc, dc in each of next 2sts, skip next dc, FPdc around each of next 3tr, ch2, skip next ch, sc in next dc, ch2, skip next ch, FPdc around each of next 3tr, skip next dc, dc in each of next 2sts, FPdc around next FPdc, dc in each of next 69 (75, 82, 85) sts, turn; 89 (95, 103, 106) sts

Rnd 8: repeat Rnd 4

Rnd 9: repeat Rnd 5

Rnd 10 (RS): ch1, dc in first and in each of next 2 (2, 3, 3) sts, FPdc around next FPtr, dc in each of next 3sts, skip next 3sts, (3tr, ch1, dc, ch1, 3tr) in next st, skip next 3sts, dc in each of next 3sts, FPdc around next FPtr, *dc in each of next 4sts, 2dc in next st; repeat from * to last 4 (0, 2, 0) sts, dc in each of next 4 (0, 2, 0) sts, join with sl st in first st; 102 (110, 119, 123) sts

Rnd 11 (RS): ch1, dc in first and in each of next 2 (2, 3, 3) sts, FPdc around next FPdc, dc in each of next 2sts, skip next dc, FPdc around each of next 3tr, ch2, skip next ch, sc in next dc, ch2, skip next ch, FPdc around each of next 3tr, skip next dc, dc in each of next 2sts, FPdc around next FPdc, dc in each of next 82 (90, 98, 102) sts, join with sl st in first st, turn; 102 (110, 119, 123) sts

Rnd 12 (WS): ch1, sc in first st and in each of next 88 (96, 104, 108) sts, sc in next ch2sp, bo in next st, sc in next ch2sp, sc in each of next 8 (8, 9, 9) sts, join with sl st in first st, turn; 100 (108, 117, 121) sts

Rnd 13 (RS): ch1, dc in first and in each of next 2 (2, 3, 3) sts, FPtr around next FPdc one row below, dc in each of next 2sts, FPtr3tog working around next 3FPdc one row below, dc in each of next 7sts, FPtr3tog working around next 3FPdc one row below, dc in each of next 2sts, FPtr around next FPdc one row below, dc in each of next 82 (90, 98, 102) sts, join with sl st in first st; 100 (108, 117, 121) sts

Rnd 14 (RS): ch1, dc in first and in each of next 2 (2, 3, 3) sts, FPdc around next FPtr, dc in each of next 3sts, skip next 3sts, (3tr, ch1, dc, ch1, 3tr) in next st, skip next 3sts, dc in each of next 3sts, FPdc around next FPtr, dc in each of next 82 (90, 98, 102) sts, join with sl st in first st; 102 (110, 119, 123) sts

Repeat Rnds 11 through 14 once more.

Repeat Rnds 11 through 13 once more, fasten off and continue with Bottom Back and Crotch H

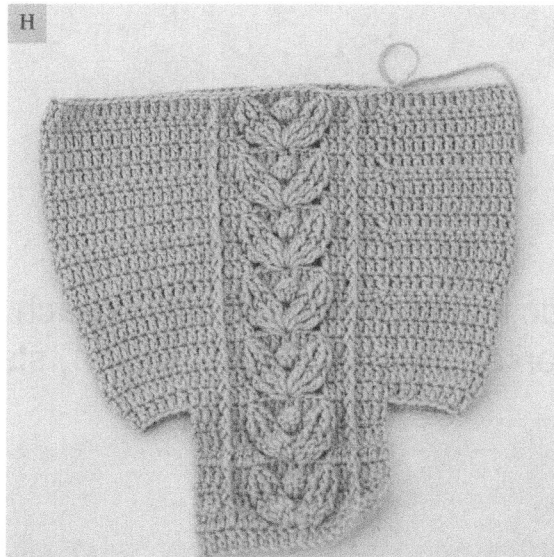

BOTTOM BACK AND CROTCH

Skip 16 (18, 20, 21) dc from the first FPtr of the front to the right and place a marker into the next st, skip 16 (18, 20, 21) dc from the second FPtr of the front to the left and place a marker in next st I

Row 1 (RS): ch1, dc in first marked st and in each st to the next marked st, dc in marked st, turn; 53 (57, 62, 64) sts

Row 2 (WS): ch1, dc in first st, dc2tog twice, dc in each next st to last 5sts, dc2tog twice, dc in last st, turn; 49 (53, 58, 60) sts

Repeat Row 2 – 9 (10, 11, 12) more times; 13 (13, 14, 12) sts K

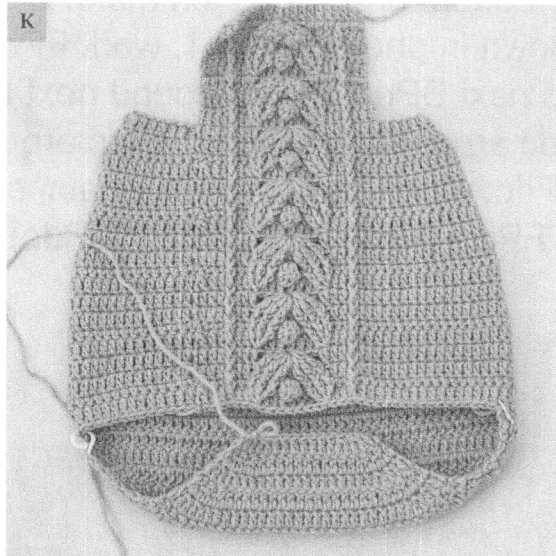

Do not fasten off but continue with Edging.

EDGING

Rnd 1 (RS): ch1, 3dc in first st, work evenly dc across the Bottom, work dc in each st across the Front and work evenly dc across the other side of Bottom, 4dc on the corner of the Crotch and in each st across the Crotch, dc in same st as first 3dc and join with sl st in first st; (number of sts is not important here, but it has to be an even number) L

Rnd 2 (RS): ch1, (FPdc around next dc, BPdc around next dc) to end, join with sl st in first st

Rnd 3 (RS): on the bottom area of crotch make 2 buttonholes, mark two BPdc sts as shown in photo M , ch1, work FPdc around first FPdc, BPdc around next BPdc, FPdc around next FPdc, *ch1, skip marked BPdc, (FPdc around next FPdc, BPdc around next BPdc) to the next marked BPdc; repeat from * once again, continue to work (FPdc around next FPdc, BPdc around next BPdc) to end, join with sl st in first st

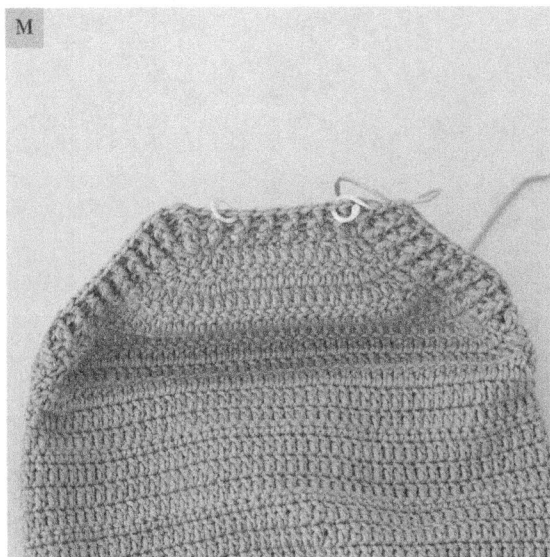

Rnd 4 (RS): ch1, work FPdc around each FPdc, BPdc around each BPdc to end, sc in each ch1 for buttonholes, join with sl st in first st, fasten off N

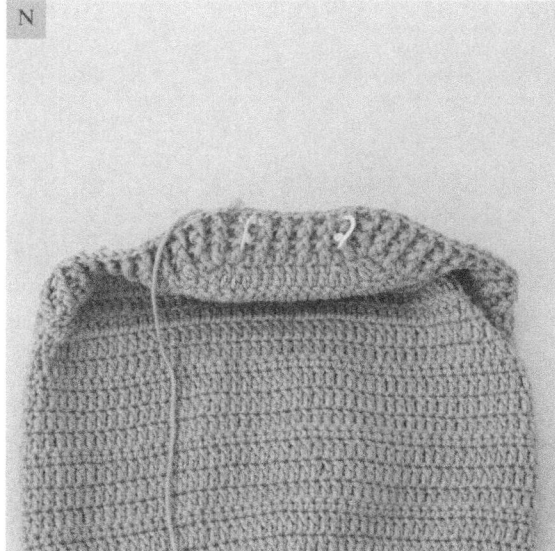

On the edging, work dc in row ends close together to slightly gather the fabric.

Front Edging

Join yarn into the first st of the Front Bib and work

Rnd 1 (RS): ch1, 3dc in first st, *FPdc around next st, BPdc around next st; repeat from * to last 2sts, FPdc around next st, 4dc in last st, evenly work 15 (15, 20, 20) dc across the side of the Bib; repeat from * across the Back, evenly work 15 (15, 20, 20) dc across other side of bib working last st in same st as first 3dc, join with sl st in first st; 98 (102, 118, 120) sts [O]

Rnd 2 (RS): ch1, BPdc around first dc, *FPdc around next dc, BPdc around next dc; repeat from * to end, join with sl st in first st, fasten off.

STRAPS

Skip 14 (16, 16, 16) sts from the Front Bib, join in next st and work P

Row 1: ch1, dc in first and in each of next 4 (4, 6, 6) sts, turn; 5 (5, 7, 7) sts Q

Repeat Row 1 – 13 (14, 17, 18) more times or until desired length.

Next Row: ch1, dc in first and in next 1 (1, 2, 2) sts, ch1, skip next st, dc in each of next 2 (2, 3, 3) sts, turn; 5 (5, 7, 7) sts

Last Row: ch1, sc in first and in each next st including ch1sp, fasten off R

Skip 7 (7, 7, 9) sts from the first strap, join in next st and work the second strap in exact same way as the first one, fasten

off S

RUFFLE

Join into the first FPdc of the Front Bib and work:

Row 1 (RS): dc in first st T , 3dc around same FPdc, work 4 dc around each next FPdc or FPtr to end, turn U

Row 2 (WS): ch1, dc in first st, *ch1, dc in next st; repeat from * to end, turn

Row 3 (RS): ch1, sc in first dc, *ch1, skip next ch1, sc in next dc; repeat from * to end, fasten off V

For second ruffle join into the first FPdc at the bottom of the romper, and repeat Rows 1 through 3 as for the first ruffle, fasten off W X

FINISHING

Weave in all ends (see Finishing Techniques).

Sew on the buttons (see Finishing Techniques) on the Front Bib, working through the bib and the end of the Ruffle as shown in photo Y , and do the same at the bottom as shown in photo Z

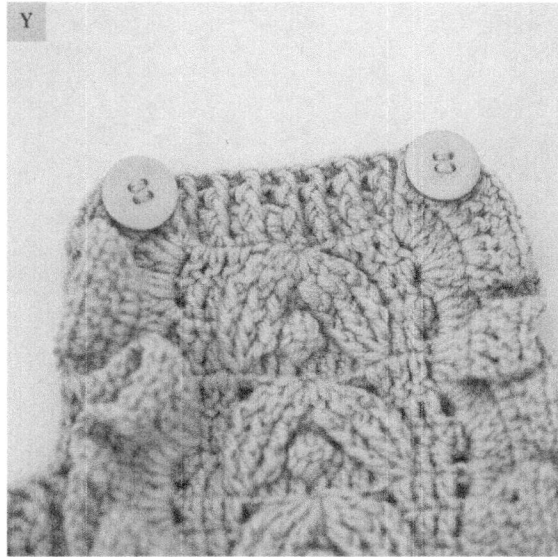

CLASSIC BONNET

~ ★★☆ ~

A bonnet is a very sweet accessory to add to your baby's wardrobe, but it can look cute on older children as well. I used a sock weight yarn to achieve this lightweight and fluffy fabric, but you could choose a sport weight yarn to achieve a thicker and warmer bonnet – just remember to always check the gauge!

SIZES AND MEASUREMENTS OF FINISHED GARMENT

Size	Head circumference	Bonnet depth measured front to back	Bonnet height measured top to bottom
0–6m	38cm/15in	14cm/5½in	15cm/6in
6–12m	43cm/17in	16cm/6¼in	17cm/6¾in
1–2y	45cm/17¾in	17cm/6¾in	18cm/7in
3–4y	48cm/19in	18cm/7in	20cm/7¾in

GAUGE (TENSION)

22 sts and 10 rows in dc to measure 10 x 10cm (4 x 4in) using 3mm (D/3) hook (or size required to obtain gauge)

SPECIAL STITCHES

FPdc, BPdc, bo (4-dc bobble), FPsc, FPdc3tog (see Special Stitches)

MATERIALS

3 LIGHT

- 120 (160, 200, 240) meters or 131 (174, 219, 261) yards of any fingering or sock weight yarn
  Suggested yarn: Katia United Socks, 75% wool, 25% polyamide, shade 14, 25g (¾oz), 100m (109yd)
- 3mm (D/3) crochet hook (or size required to obtain gauge)

Pattern is written for size 0–6m, changes for 6–12m, 1–2y and 3–4y are in (…).

Ch1 at the beginning of each round doesn't count as a stitch.

BACK OF THE HEAD AND FIRST SECTION

Row 1 (RS): ch11 (13, 15, 17), dc in 4th ch from hook (ch3 counts as first dc here and throughout), dc in each next ch to last ch, 7dc in last ch, rotate the work and work on opposite side into remaining loop of foundation chain, dc in each of next 8 (10, 12, 14) sts, turn; 23 (27, 31, 35) sts A

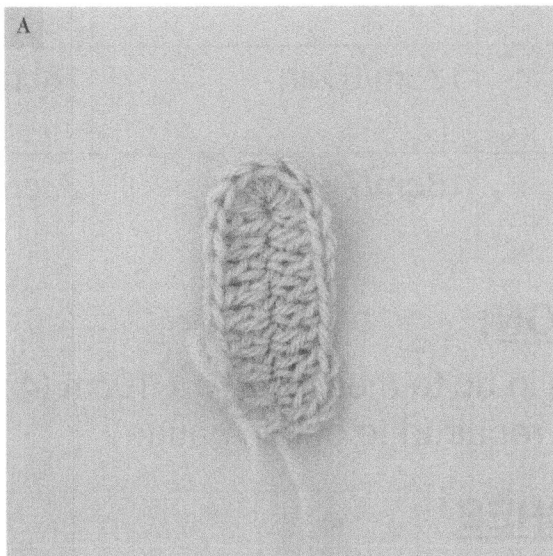

Row 2 (WS): ch1, sc in first st, FPsc around each of next st to last st, sc in last st, turn; 23 (27, 31, 35) sts B

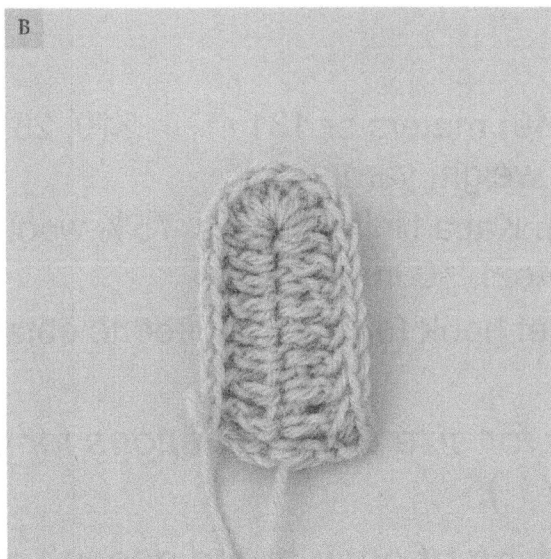

Row 3 (RS): ch1, but pull it to the height of dc (here and throughout where next st is dc), dc in first st and in each of next 7 (9, 11, 13) sts, 2dc in each of next 7sts, dc in each of next 8 (10, 12, 14) sts, turn; 30 (34, 38, 42) sts C

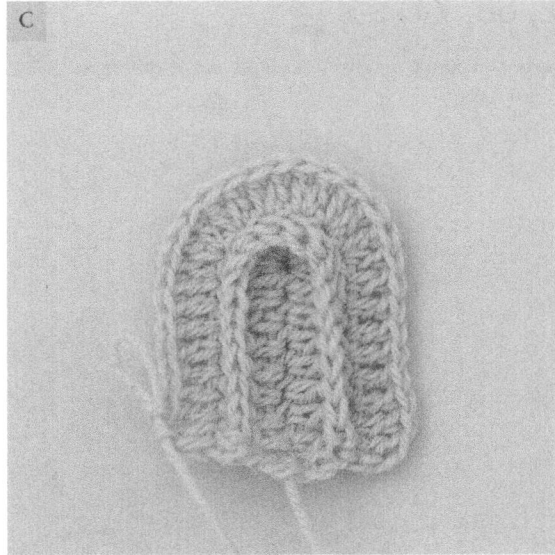

Row 4 (WS): ch1, sc in first st, FPsc around each next st to last st, sc in last st, turn; 30 (34, 38, 42) sts

Row 5 (RS): ch1, dc in first st and in each of next 7 (9, 11, 13) sts, 2dc in each of next 14sts, dc in each of next 8 (10, 12, 14) sts, turn; 44 (48, 52, 56) sts D

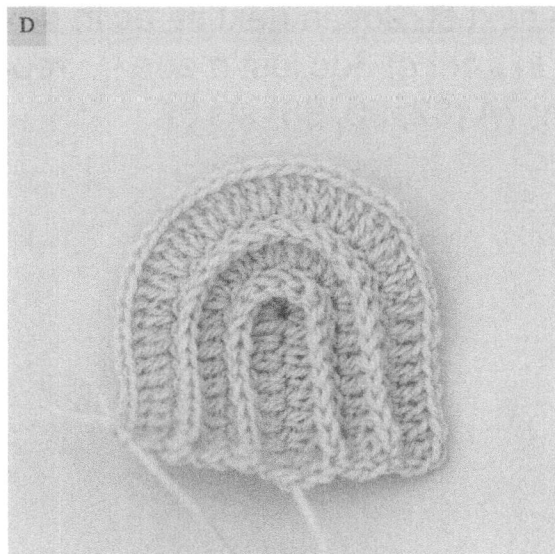

Row 6 (WS): ch1, sc in first st, FPsc around each next st to last st, sc in last st, turn; 44 (48, 52, 56) sts

Row 7 (RS): ch1, dc in first st and in each of next 15 (16, 17, 18) sts, 2dc in each of next 12 (14, 16, 18) sts, dc in each of next 16 (17, 18, 19) sts, turn; 56 (62, 68, 74) sts E

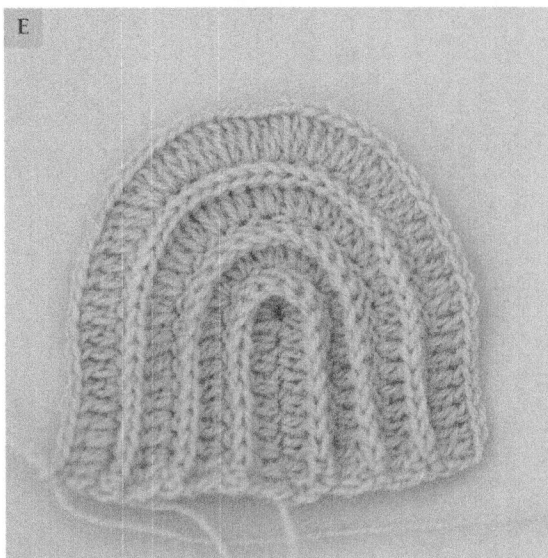

Row 8 (WS): ch1, sc in first st, FPsc around each next st to last st, sc in last st, turn; 56 (62, 68, 74) sts

Row 9 (RS): ch1, dc in first st, *skip next 2sts, tr in next st F , working behind tr just made work 2dc in first skipped st, dc in next skipped st G , skip next st, 2dc in next st, dc in next st H , tr in skipped st working in front of 3dc just made I ; repeat from * to last st, dc in last st, turn; 74 (82, 90, 98) sts J

F

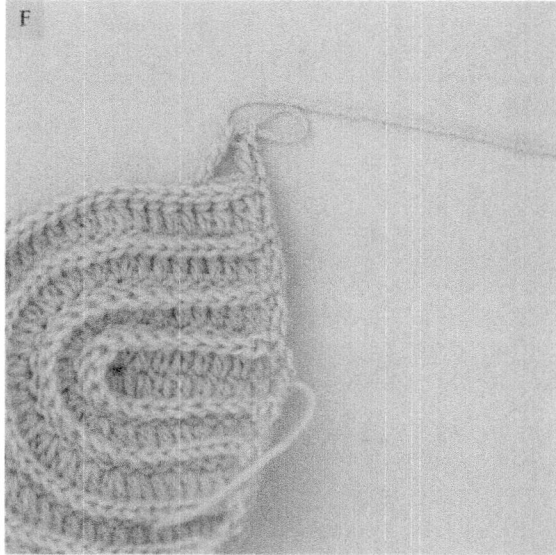

G

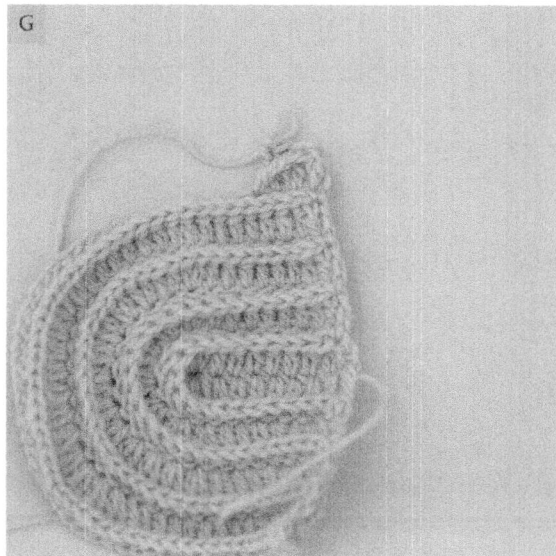

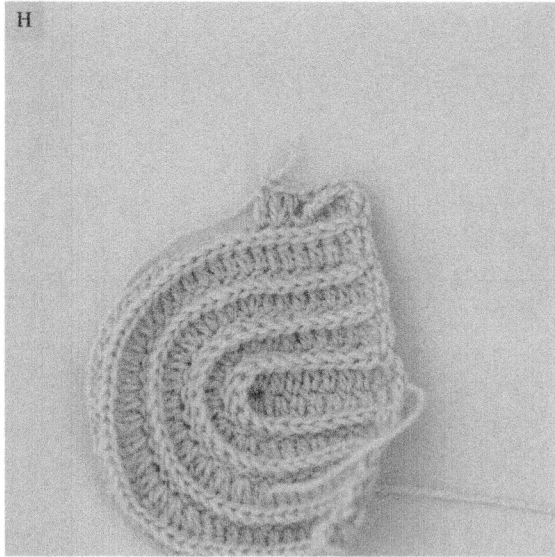

H

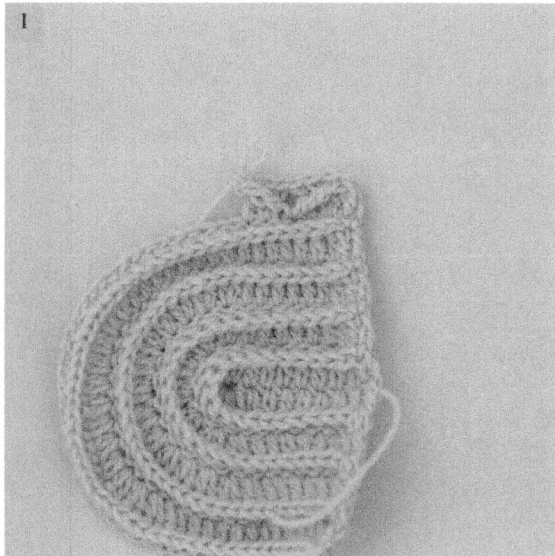

I

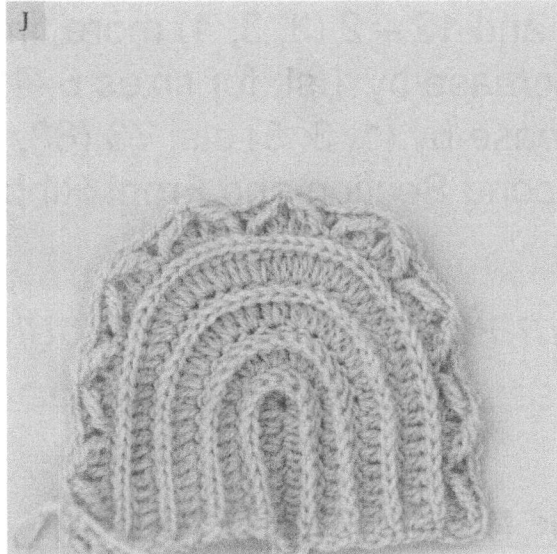

Row 10 (WS): ch1, sc in first st and in each next st to end, turn; 74 (82, 90, 98) sts

Row 11 (RS): ch1, dc in first st, *skip next 3sts, tr in next st, working behind tr just made work dc in each skipped st, skip next st, dc in each of next 3sts, tr in skipped st working in front of 3dc just made; repeat from * to last st, dc in last st, turn; 74 (82, 90, 98) sts K

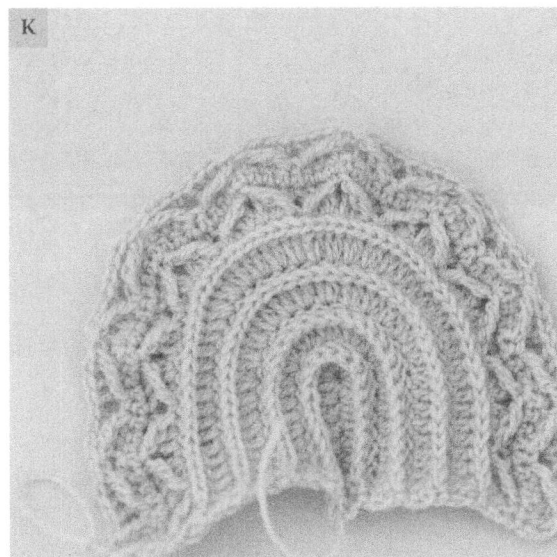

Row 12 (WS): ch1, sc in first st and in each next st to end, turn; 74 (82, 90, 98) sts

Repeat Rows 11 and 12 – 2 (3, 3, 4) more times, in last row for size 0–6m decrease by 1 st, for sizes 6–12m, 1–2y and 3–4y evenly increase by (1, 3, 5) sts; 73 (83, 93, 103) sts, continue with Second Section and Front Ribbing.

Quick to make, this bonnet would make a beautiful gift for a new baby.

SECOND SECTION AND FRONT RIBBING

Row 1 (RS): ch1, dc in first and in next st, *skip next 4sts, (3tr, ch1, dc, ch1, 3tr) in next st, skip next 4sts, dc in next st L ; repeat from * to last st, dc in last st, turn; 7 (8, 9, 10) shells made M

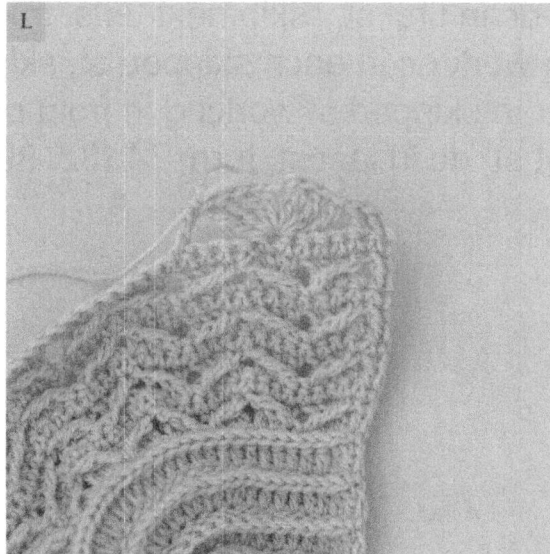

Row 2 (WS): ch1, sc in first and in each next st, sc in each ch1sp, turn; 73 (83, 93, 103) sts

Row 3 (RS): ch1, sc in first and in next st, *FPdc around each of next 3tr one row below, ch1, skip next st, sc in next st, ch1, skip next sc, FPdc around each of next 3tr one row below, sc in next st N ; repeat from * to last st, sc in last st, turn; 73 (83, 93, 103) sts including all ch

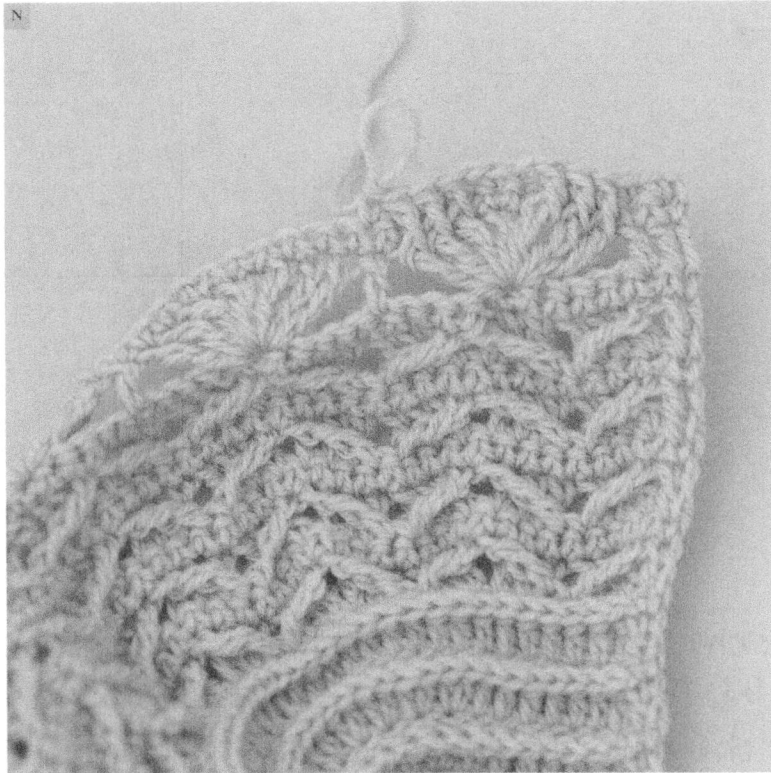

Row 4 (WS): ch1, sc in first and in each of next 4sts, *sc in next ch1sp, bo in next sc, sc in next ch1sp, sc in each of next 7sts; repeat from * to end, but in last repeat work sc in each of next 5sts, turn; 73 (83, 93, 103) sts O

Row 5 (RS): ch1, sc in first and in next st, *FPdc3tog working around next 3tr one row below, ch2, skip next 3sts, sc in next bo, ch2, skip next 3sts, FPdc3tog working around next 3tr one row below, sc in next st P ; repeat from * to last st, sc in last st, turn; 73 (83, 93, 103) sts including all ch

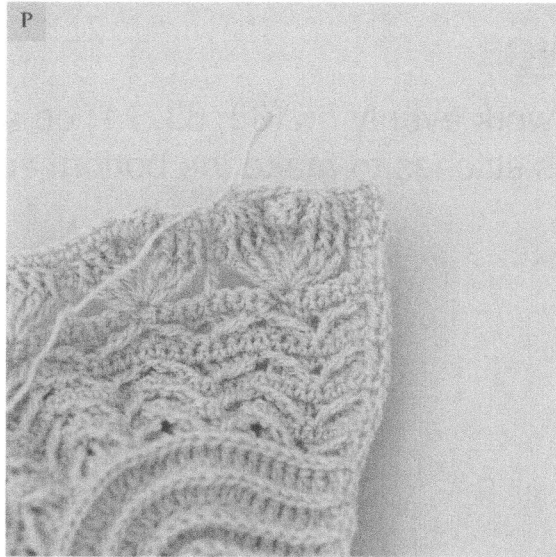

Row 6 (WS): ch1, dc in first and in each next st, 2dc in each ch2sp to end, turn; 59 (67, 75, 83) sts Q

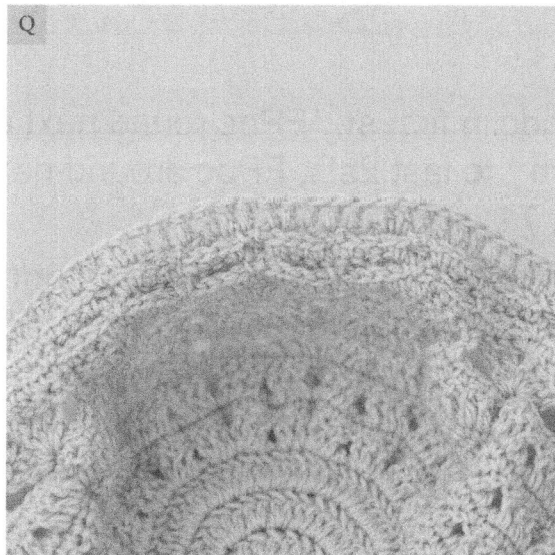

Row 7 (RS): ch1, hdc in first st, *FPdc around next dc, BPdc around next dc; repeat from * to last 2sts, FPdc around next st, hdc in last st,

turn; 59 (67, 75, 83) sts

Row 8 (WS): ch1, hdc in first st, work FPdc around each FPdc and BPdc around each BPdc to last st, hdc in last st; 59 (67, 75, 83) sts, rotate and work across the bottom edge and continue with the Bottom Edging.

BOTTOM EDGING

Row 1 (WS): ch1, work evenly 55 (63, 63, 71) dc across, turn: R , you might work less stitches to make the bottom edging tighter

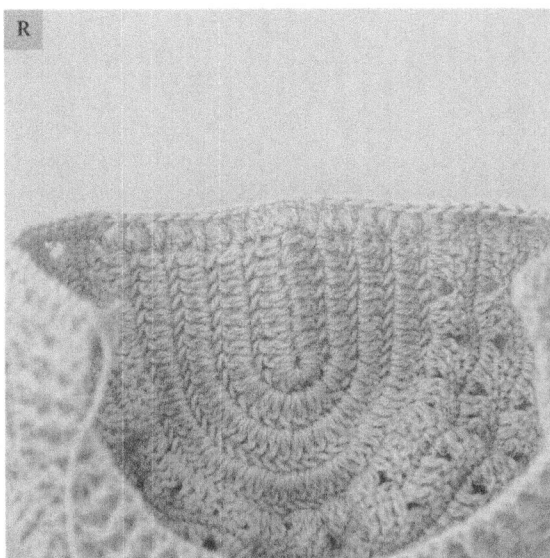

Row 2 (RS): ch1, hdc in first st, *FPdc round next dc, BPdc around next dc; repeat from * to last 2sts, FPdc around next dc, hdc in last st, turn; 55 (63, 63, 71) sts

Row 3 (WS): ch1, hdc in first st, work FPdc around each FPdc and BPdc around each BPdc to last st, hdc in last st; 55 (63, 63, 71) sts

Row 4 (RS): ch61, sc in 2nd ch from hook and in each next ch, sc in each next st across the bottom edging S , ch61, sc in 2nd ch from hook and in each next ch, sl st into the base of last sc of the bottom T , fasten off

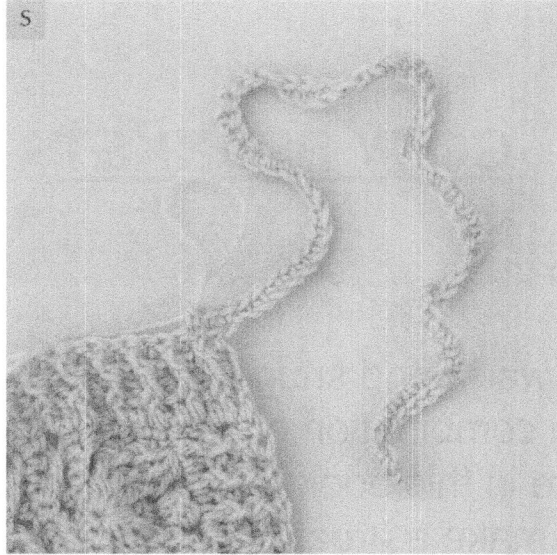

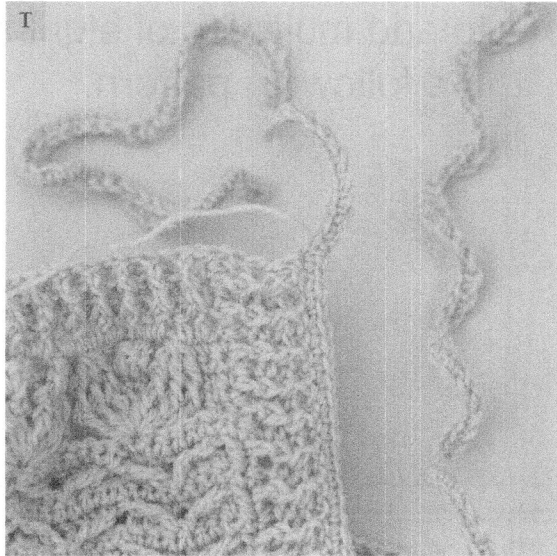

FINISHING

Weave in all ends (see Finishing Techniques).

COZY BLANKET

~ ★★☆ ~

For this warm and snuggly blanket I brought together a combination of stitches that I've used elsewhere in this book for other designs. It will therefore make a great matching accessory for many of them. If you'd like a larger blanket all you need to do is to add multiples of eight stitches to the following pattern.

SIZE AND MEASUREMENT OF FINISHED BLANKET

Size	Length x width
One size	80 x 80cm (31½ x 31½in)

GAUGE (TENSION)

19 sts and 9 rows in dc to measure 10 x 10cm (4 x 4in) using 3.5mm (E/4) hook (or size required to obtain gauge)

SPECIAL STITCHES

FPdc, BPdc, bo (4-dc bobble), v-st, crossed dc (see Special Stitches)

MATERIALS

3 LIGHT

- 1250 meters or 1368 yards of any DK weight or light worsted weight yarn
  Suggested yarns: Laines du Nord Holiday, 70% wool, 30% acrylic, shade 610, 50g (1¾oz), 125m (136yd)
- 3.5mm (E/4) crochet hook (or size required to obtain gauge)

Ch1 at the beginning of each round doesn't count as a stitch.

BLANKET

Row 1 (WS): ch148, dc in 4th ch from hook (ch3 counts as first dc) and in each next ch to end, turn; 146 sts

Row 2 (RS): ch1 (but pull it to the height of dc here and throughout where next st is dc), dc in first st, *skip next 3sts, tr in next st A , working behind tr just made work dc in each skipped st B , skip next st, dc in each of next 3sts, tr in skipped st working in front of 3dc just made C ; repeat from * to last st, dc in last st, turn; 146 sts

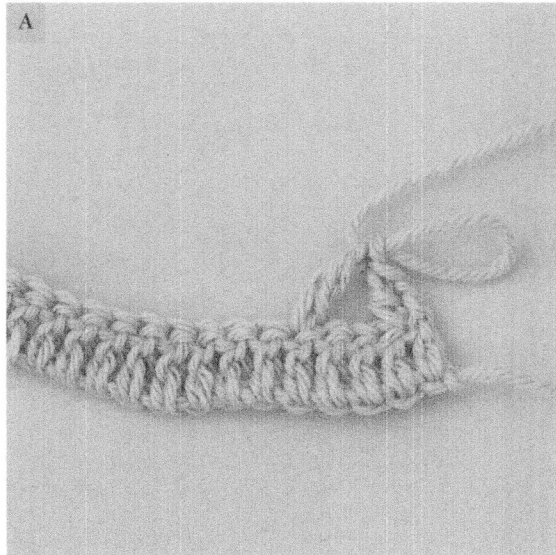

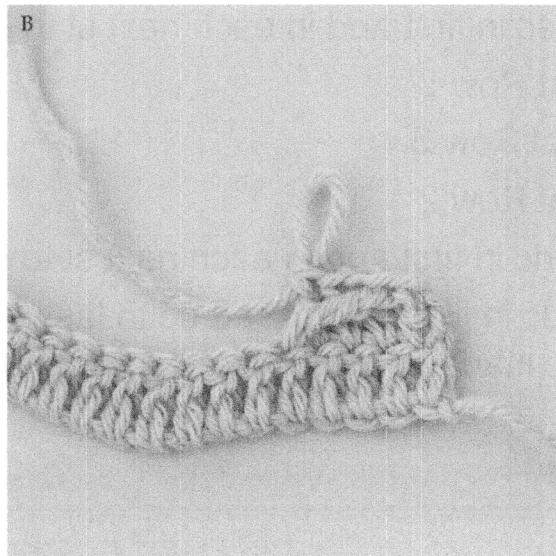

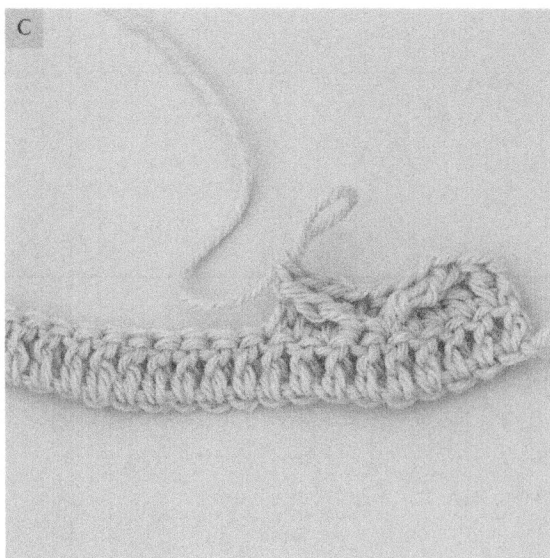

Row 3 (WS): ch1, sc in first and in each next st to end, turn; 146 sts

Row 4 (RS): repeat Row 2

Row 5 (WS): repeat Row 3

Row 6 (RS): repeat Row 2

Row 7 (WS): ch1, dc in first and in each next st to end, turn; 146 sts

Row 8 (RS): ch1, dc in first st, crossed dc to last st, dc in last st, turn; 48 crossed dc made, in total 146 sts including all chs D

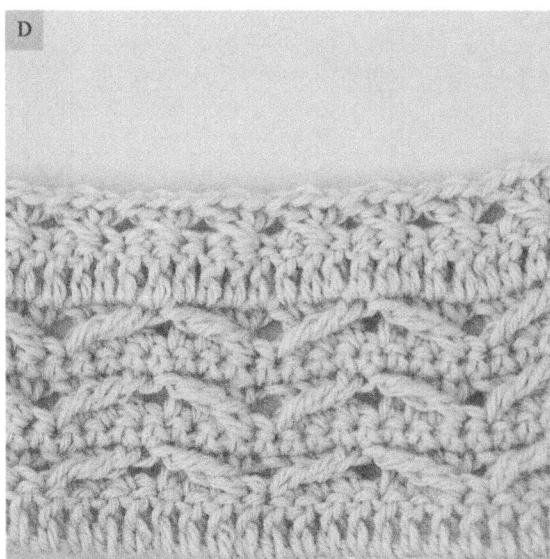

Row 9 (WS): ch1, sc in first st, sc in next st, *bo in next ch1sp, sc in each of next 2sts; repeat from * to end, turn; 146 sts

Row 10 (RS): repeat Row 8 E

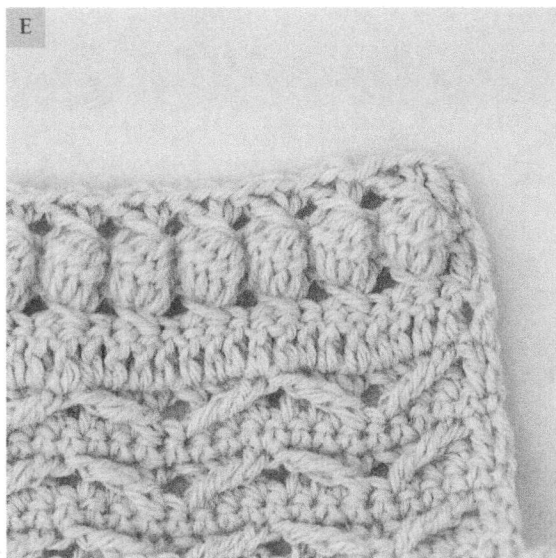

Row 11 (WS): ch1, dc in first and in each next st, dc in each ch1sp to end, turn; 146 sts

Row 12 (RS): ch1, sc in first st, *skip next st, v-st in next st, skip next st, sc in next st; repeat from * to last st, dc in last st, turn; 146 sts

Row 13 (WS): ch1, sc in first st, 2dc in next sc, *skip next dc, sc in next ch1sp, skip next dc, v-st in next sc; repeat from * to end, but instead of last v-st work 2dc in last sc, turn; 146 sts F

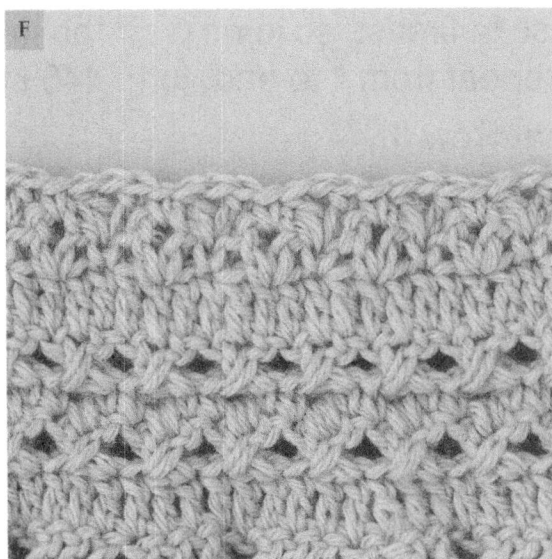

Row 14 (RS): ch1, sc in first st, *skip next dc, v-st in next sc, skip next dc, sc in next ch1sp; repeat from * to last 5sts, skip next dc, v-st in next sc, skip next dc, sc in next dc, dc in last st, turn; 146 sts

Row 15 (WS): repeat Row 13

Row 16 (RS): repeat Row 14

Row 17 (WS): repeat Row 13

Row 18 (RS): repeat Row 14

Row 19 (WS): ch1, dc in first and in each next st, dc in each ch1sp to end, turn; 146 sts

Row 20 (RS): ch1, dc in first st, crossed dc to last st, dc in last st, turn; 48 crossed dc made, in total 146 sts including all chs

Row 21 (WS): ch1, sc in first st, sc in next st, *bo in next ch1sp, sc in each of next 2sts; repeat from * to end, turn; 146 sts

Row 22 (RS): repeat Row 20

Row 23 (WS): ch1, dc in first and in each next st, dc in each ch1sp to end, turn; 146 sts

Repeat Rows 2 through 23 – 3 more times.

Repeat Rows 2 through 6 once more G

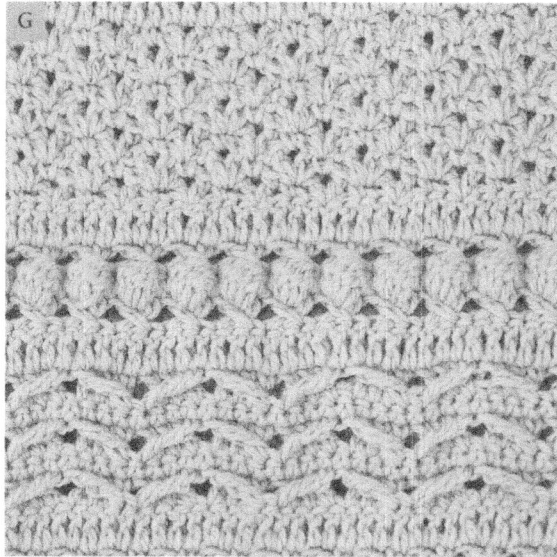

Last Row (WS): ch1, dc in first and in each next st to last st, 6dc in last st, and continue to work evenly dc across the side edge of the blanket to the last row (approximately 2dc per 1cm/⅜in), work 5dc into the base of next dc and join with sl st in next dc, fasten off H

Rotate the work, turn to RS and join into the first dc I , work 5dc into the base of same dc and continue to work evenly dc across the side edge of the blanket to the last row (approximately 2dc per 1cm/⅜in), work 5dc into the base of ch3 (first dc of first row) and join with sl st in top of ch3 J ; at this point you should have dc all the way around the blanket and 6 dc on each corner (st amount is not important but it has to be even number), don't fasten off but continue with Edging.

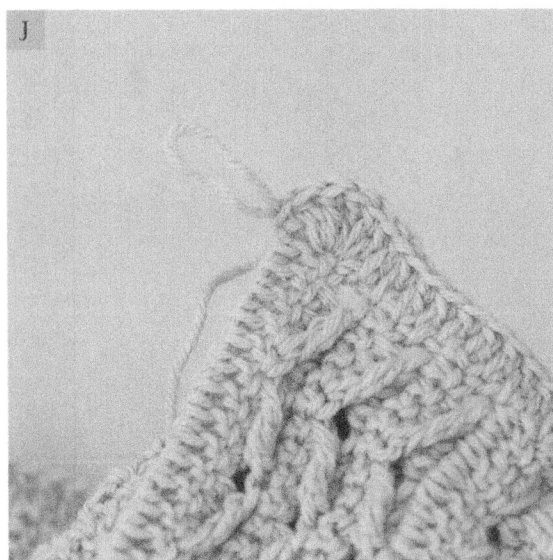

EDGING

Rnd 1 (RS): ch1, FPdc around first dc, *BPdc around next dc, FPdc around next dc; repeat from * to last st, BPdc around last st, join with sl st in first st K

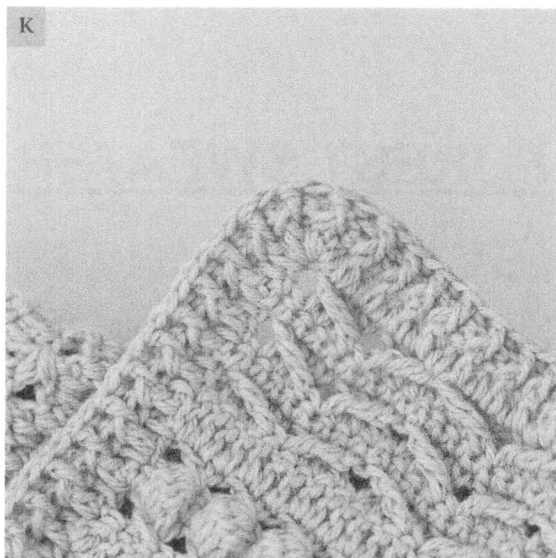

Rnd 2 (RS): ch1, FPdc around first FPdc, *BPdc around next BPdc, FPdc around next FPdc; repeat from * to last st, but on the corners work (2BPdc around next BPdc, FPdc around next FPdc, 2BPdc around next BPdc), BPdc around last BPdc, join with sl st in first st L

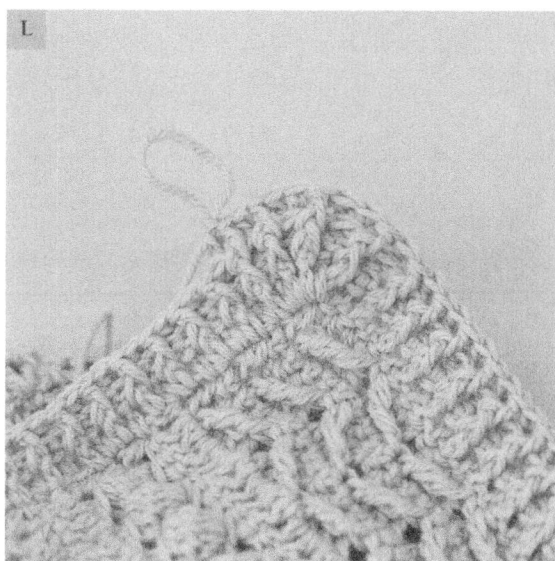

Rnd 3 (RS): ch1, FPdc around each FPdc, BPdc around each BPdc, join with sl st in first st, fasten off.

FINISHING

Weave in all ends (see Finishing Techniques).

FOREST SWEATER

~ ★☆☆ ~

The soft merino yarn that I chose, plus the simple design of this sweater make it a perfect everyday cozy top to slip on for outdoor adventures. The Forest Sweater is worked from the top down and is completely seamless. Make it in any color you like and it will be great for both boys and girls.

SIZES AND MEASUREMENTS OF FINISHED GARMENT

Size	Chest	Length	Sleeve length to underarm
0–6m	50cm/19¾in	27cm/10½in	14cm/5½in
6–12m	54cm/21¼in	30cm/11¾in	18cm/7in
1–2y	61cm/24in	33cm/13in	22cm/8½in
3–4y	66cm/26in	40cm/15¾in	26cm/10¼in

GAUGE (TENSION)

20 sts and 10 rows in dc to measure 10 x 10cm (4 x 4in) using 3.5mm (E/4) hook (or size required to obtain gauge)

SPECIAL STITCHES

v-st, FPdc, BPdc, dc2tog (see Special Stitches)

MATERIALS

3 LIGHT

- 400 (528, 600, 720) meters or 437 (576, 656, 786) yards of any DK weight or light worsted weight yarn
  Suggested yarns: Katia Prime Merino, 100% virgin wool, shade 12, 50g (1¾oz), 120m (131yd)
- 3.5mm (E/4) crochet hook (or size required to obtain gauge)

Pattern is written for size 0–6m, changes for 6–12m, 1–2y and 3–4y are in (…).

Ch1 at the beginning of each round doesn't count as a stitch.

Attention – some rounds are worked on WS, some on RS, follow instructions to turn.

YOKE

Foundation chain: work loosely, pull each chain longer (it has to pass over child's head), ch56 (60, 68, 72), join with sl st in first ch.

Rnd 1 (RS): ch1, but pull it to the height of dc here and throughout where next st is dc, dc in first and in each next ch to end, join with sl st in first st; 56 (60, 68, 72) sts A

Rnd 2 (RS): ch1, dc in first st, *dc in each of next 5 (5, 7, 7) sts, v-st in next st, dc in each of next 21 (23, 25, 27) sts**, v-st in next st, repeat from * to ** once more, dc in same st as first dc, ch1 and join with sl st in first dc to complete last v-st, turn; 64 (68, 76, 80) sts including all ch here and throughout

Rnd 3 (WS): ch1, skip first dc (you will have to work last st in it at the end of rnd here and throughout), 2dc in next ch1sp, *[sc in next st, hdc in next st] 11 (12, 13, 14) times, sc in next st, (2dc, ch1, 2dc) in next ch1sp, [sc in next st, hdc in next st] 3 (3, 4, 4) times, sc in next st**, (2dc, ch1, 2dc) in next ch1sp, repeat from * to ** once more, 2dc in same ch1sp as first 2dc, ch1 and join with sl st in first dc to complete last v-st, turn; 80 (84, 92, 96) sts B

Rnd 4 (RS): ch1, skip first dc, dc in next ch1sp, *dc in each of next 11 (11, 13, 13) sts, v-st in next ch1sp, dc in each of next 27 (29, 31, 33) sts**, v-st in next ch1sp, repeat from * to ** once more, dc in same ch1sp as first dc, ch1 and join with sl st in first dc to complete last v-st, turn; 88 (92, 100, 104) sts

Rnd 5 (WS): ch1, skip first dc, 2dc in next ch1sp, *[sc in next st, hdc in next st] 14 (15, 16, 17) times, sc in next st, (2dc, ch1, 2dc) in next ch1sp, [sc in next st, hdc in next st] 6 (6, 7, 7) times, sc in next st**, (2dc, ch1, 2dc) in next ch1sp, repeat from * to ** once more, 2dc in

same ch1sp as first 2dc, ch1 and join with sl st in first dc to complete last v-st, turn; 104 (108, 116, 120) sts

Rnd 6 (RS): ch1, skip first dc, dc in next ch1sp, *dc in each of next 17 (17, 19, 19) sts, v-st in next ch1sp, dc in each of next 33 (35, 37, 39) sts**, v-st in next ch1sp, repeat from * to ** once more, dc in same ch1sp as first dc, ch1 and join with sl st in first dc to complete last v-st, turn; 112 (116, 124, 128) sts

Rnd 7 (WS): ch1, skip first dc, 2dc in next ch1sp, *[sc in next st, hdc in next st] 17 (18, 19, 20) times, sc in next st, (2dc, ch1, 2dc) in next ch1sp, [sc in next st, hdc in next st] 9 (9, 10, 10) times, sc in next st**, (2dc, ch1, 2dc) in next ch1sp, repeat from * to ** once more, 2dc in same ch1sp as first 2dc, ch1 and join with sl st in first dc to complete last v-st, turn; 128 (132, 140, 144) sts

Rnd 8 (RS): ch1, skip first dc, dc in next ch1sp, *dc in each of next 23 (23, 25, 25) sts, v-st in next ch1sp, dc in each of next 39 (41, 43, 45) sts**, v-st in next ch1sp, repeat from * to ** once more, dc in same ch1sp as first dc, ch1 and join with sl st in first dc to complete last v-st, turn; 136 (140, 148, 152) sts

Rnd 9 (WS): ch1, skip first dc, 2dc in next ch1sp, *[sc in next st, hdc in next st] 20 (21, 22, 23) times, sc in next st, (2dc, ch1, 2dc) in next ch1sp, [sc in next st, hdc in next st] 12 (12, 13, 13) times, sc in next st**, (2dc, ch1, 2dc) in next ch1sp, repeat from * to ** once more, 2dc in same ch1sp as first 2dc, ch1 and join with sl st in first dc to complete last v-st, turn; 152 (156, 164, 168) sts

For size 0–6m

Continue with Divide for Sleeves and Body.

For sizes 6–12m, 1–2y and 3–4y

From now on for increases work only v-st in all rnds.

Rnd 10 (RS): ch1, skip first dc, dc in next ch1sp, *dc in each of next (29, 31, 31) sts, v-st in next ch1sp, dc in each of next (47, 49, 51) sts**, v-st in next ch1sp, repeat from * to ** once more, dc in same ch1sp as first dc, ch1 and join with sl st in first dc to complete last v-st, turn; (164, 172, 176) sts

Rnd 11 (WS): ch1, skip first dc, dc in next ch1sp, *[sc in next st, hdc in next st] (24, 25, 26) times, sc in next st, v-st in next ch1sp, [sc in next st, hdc in next st] (15, 16, 16) times, sc in next st**, v-st in next ch1sp, repeat from * to ** once more, dc in same ch1sp as first dc, ch1 and join with sl st in first dc to complete last v-st, turn; (172, 180, 184) sts

For size 6–12 m

Continue with Divide for Sleeves and Body.

For sizes 1–2y and 3–4y

Rnd 12 (RS): ch1, skip first dc, dc in next ch1sp, *dc in each of next (35, 35) sts, v-st in next ch1sp, dc in each of next (53, 55) sts**, v-st in next ch1sp, repeat from * to ** once more, dc in same ch1sp as first dc, ch1 and join with sl st in first dc to complete last v-st, turn; (188, 192) sts

Rnd 13 (WS): ch1, skip first dc, dc in next ch1sp, *[sc in next st, hdc in next st] (27, 28) times, sc in next st, v-st in next ch1sp, [sc in next st, hdc in next st] (18, 18) times, sc in next st**, v-st in next ch1sp, repeat from * to ** once more, dc in same ch1sp as first dc, ch1 and join with sl st in first dc to complete last v-st, turn; (196, 200) sts

For size 1–2y

Continue with Divide for Sleeves and Body.

For size 3–4y

Rnd 14 (RS): ch1, skip first dc, dc in next ch1sp, *dc in each of next 39sts, v-st in next ch1sp, dc in each of next 59sts**, v-st in next ch1sp, repeat from * to ** once more, dc in same ch1sp as first dc, ch1 and join with sl st in first dc to complete last v-st, turn; 208 sts

Rnd 15 (WS): ch1, skip first dc, dc in next ch1sp, *[sc in next st, hdc in next st] 30 times, sc in next st, v-st in next ch1sp, [sc in next st, hdc in next st] 20 times, sc in next st**, v-st in next ch1sp, repeat from * to ** once more, dc in same ch1sp as first dc, ch1 and join with sl st in first dc to complete last v-st, turn; continue with Divide for Sleeves and Body; 216 sts

DIVIDE FOR SLEEVES AND BODY

Rnd 1 (RS): ch1, dc in first st, dc in next ch1sp, ch5, skip next 29 (33, 39, 43) sts for an armhole, dc in next ch1sp, dc in each of next 45 (51, 57, 63) sts, dc in next ch1sp, ch5, skip next 29 (33, 39, 43) sts for an armhole, dc in next ch1sp, dc in each of next 44 (50, 56, 62) sts, join with sl st in first st, turn; 104 (116, 128, 140) sts D

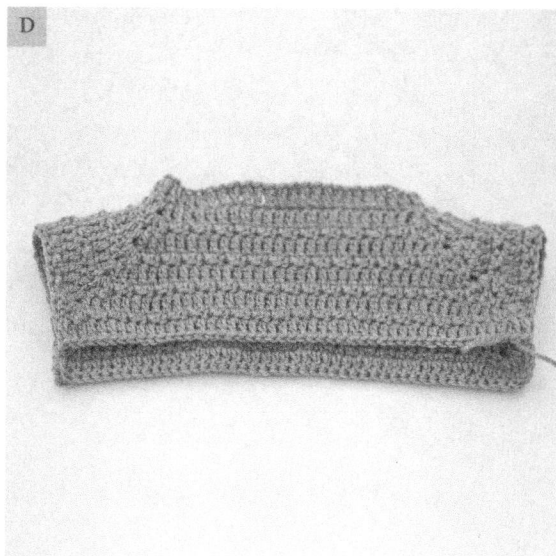

Rnd 2 (WS): ch1, sc in first st, *hdc in next st, sc in next st; repeat from * to last st, hdc in last st and join with sl st in first st, turn; 104 (116, 128, 140) sts

Rnd 3 (RS): ch1, dc in first and in each next st to end, join with sl st in first st, turn; 104 (116, 128, 140) sts

Repeat Rnds 2 and 3 – 8 (10, 12, 14) more times or until desired length, don't turn but continue with Ribbing E

RIBBING

Rnd 1 (RS): ch1, FPdc around first dc, *BPdc around next dc, FPdc around next dc; repeat from * to last st, BPdc around last dc, join with sl st in first st; 104 (116, 128, 140) sts

Rnd 2 (RS): ch1, FPdc around each FPdc, BPdc around each BPdc, join with sl st in first st; 104 (116, 128, 140) sts

Repeat Rnd 2 – 2 (2, 3, 3) more times or until desired length, fasten off F

SLEEVES

Join yarn in middle of underarm G , work in rnds and turn after each rnd.

Rnd 1 (RS): ch1, work evenly 38 (42, 48, 52) dc around the armhole, join with sl st in first st, turn; 38 (42, 48, 52) sts

Rnd 2 (WS): ch1, *sc in next st, hdc in next st; repeat from * to end, join with sl st in first st, turn; 38 (42, 48, 52) sts

Rnd 3 (RS): ch1, dc in first st, dc2tog, dc in each next st to last 2sts, dc2tog, join with sl st in first st, turn; 36 (40, 46, 50) sts H

Repeat Rnds 2 and 3 – 2 (3, 4, 5) more times; 32 (34, 38, 40) sts

Rnd 8 (10, 12, 14) (WS): ch1, *sc in next st, hdc in next st; repeat from * to end, join with sl st in first st, turn; 32 (34, 38, 40) sts

Rnd 9 (11, 13, 15) (RS): ch1, dc in first st, dc in each next st to end, join with sl st in first st, turn; 32 (34, 38, 40) sts

Repeat last two rnds – 4 (5, 6, 7) more times or until desired length, don't turn, but work the Cuff.

Second Sleeve

Work in exactly the same way as first sleeve.

CUFF

Rnd 1 (RS): ch1, FPdc around first dc, *BPdc around next dc, FPdc around next dc; repeat from * to last st, BPdc around last dc and join with sl st in first st; 32 (34, 38, 40) sts

Rnd 2 (RS): ch1, FPdc around each FPdc and BPdc around each BPdc to end, join with sl st in first st; 32 (34, 38, 40) sts

Repeat Rnd 2 – 2 (2, 3, 3) more times or until desired length, fasten off I J

Second Cuff

Work in exactly the same way on second sleeve.

COLLAR

Rnd 1 (RS): join yarn into the middle of the back collar and work ch1 K , FPdc around first dc, *BPdc around next dc, FPdc around next dc* repeat from * to last st, BPdc around next st, join with sl st in first st; 56 (60, 68, 72) sts L

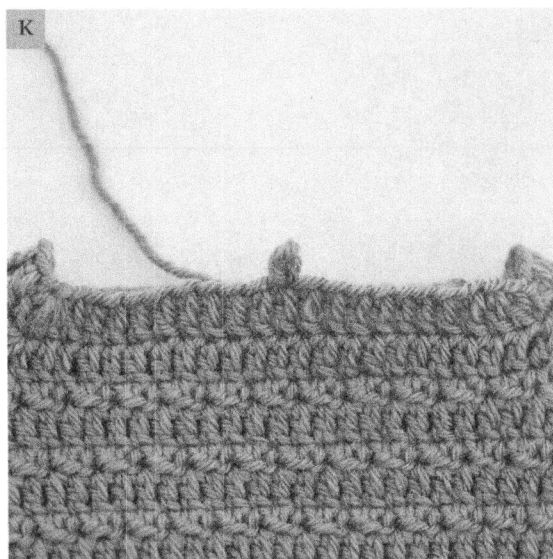

Rnd 2 (RS): ch1, FPdc around first FPdc, *BPdc around next BPdc, FPdc around next FPdc; repeat from * to last st, BPdc around last BPdc, join with sl st in first st; 56 (60, 68, 72) sts

Repeat Rnd 2 – 2 more times, fasten off.

FINISHING

Weave in all ends, wash and dry flat (see Finishing Techniques).

FAVORITE HOODIE

~ ★★☆ ~

This hoodie is worked top down, it's seamless, easy to make, and so comfortable to wear. It's bound to become a favorite! I used beautiful alpaca yarn, but bear in mind this can be a bit itchy. Look out for baby alpaca, which is much softer, and if your little one has very sensitive skin consider using merino wool, cashmere or another blended yarn.

SIZES AND MEASUREMENTS OF FINISHED GARMENT

Size	Chest	Length	Sleeve length to underarm
0–6m	50cm/19¾in	27cm/10½in	14cm/ 5½in
6–12m	54cm/21¼in	30cm/11¾in	18cm/7in
1–2y	60cm/23½in	33cm/13in	22cm/8½in
3–4y	64cm/25¼in	40cm/15¾in	26cm/10¼in

GAUGE (TENSION)

18 sts and 9 rows in dc to measure 10 x 10cm (4 x 4in) using 4mm (G/6) hook (or size required to obtain gauge)

SPECIAL STITCHES

FPdc, BPdc, FPtr, bo (4-dc bobble), v-st, dc2tog (see Special Stitches)

MATERIALS

3 LIGHT

- 400 (480, 560, 640) meters or 437 (525, 612, 700) yards of any worsted weight yarn
  Suggested yarns: Katia Concept Essential Alpaca, 70% superfine alpaca, 30% merino superwash, shade 74, 50g (1¾oz), 80m (87yd)
- 4mm (G/6) crochet hook (or size required to obtain gauge)
- 3 or more buttons, approximately 2cm (¾in) diameter

Pattern is written for size 0–6m, changes for 6–12m, 1–2y and 3–4y are in (…).

Ch1 at the beginning of each round doesn't count as a stitch.

YOKE

Row 1 (RS): ch48 (50, 50, 54), dc in 4th ch from the hook (ch3 counts as first dc), dc in each next ch, turn; 46 (48, 48, 52) dc

Row 2 (WS): ch1, sc in first st, sc in each of next 2sts, bo in next st, sc in next st, bo in next st, sc in each of next 2 (2, 2, 3) sts, v-st in next st, sc in each of next 5sts, v-st in next st, sc in each of next 16 (18, 18, 20) sts, v-st in next st, sc in each of next 5sts, v-st in next st, sc in each of next 2 (2, 2, 3) sts, bo in next st, sc in next st, bo in next st, sc in each of next 3sts, turn; 54 (56, 56, 60) sts A

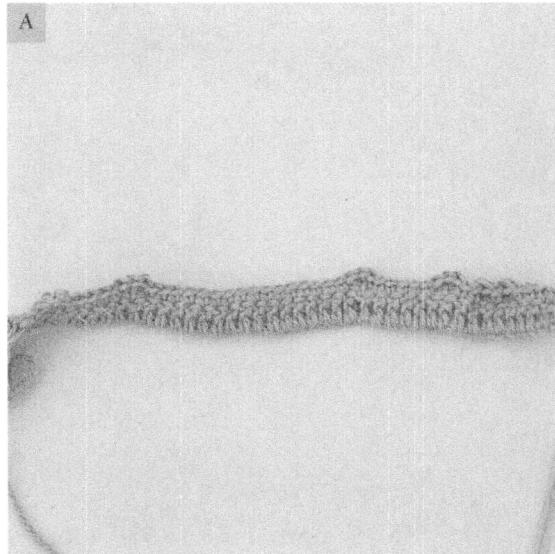

A

Row 3 (RS): ch1 (pull it to the height of dc here and throughout where next st is dc), dc in first st, FPtr around next dc two rows below, dc in each of next 5sts, FPtr around next dc two rows below, dc in next 1 (1, 1, 2) sts, (2dc, ch1, 2dc) in next ch1sp B , dc in each of next 7sts, (2dc, ch1, 2dc) in next ch1sp, dc in each of next 18 (20, 20, 22) sts, (2dc, ch1, 2dc) in next ch1sp, dc in each of next 7sts, (2dc, ch1, 2dc) in next ch1sp, dc in next 1 (1, 1, 2) sts, FPtr around next dc two rows below, dc in each of next 5sts, FPtr around next dc two rows below, dc in last st, turn; 70 (72, 72, 76) sts C

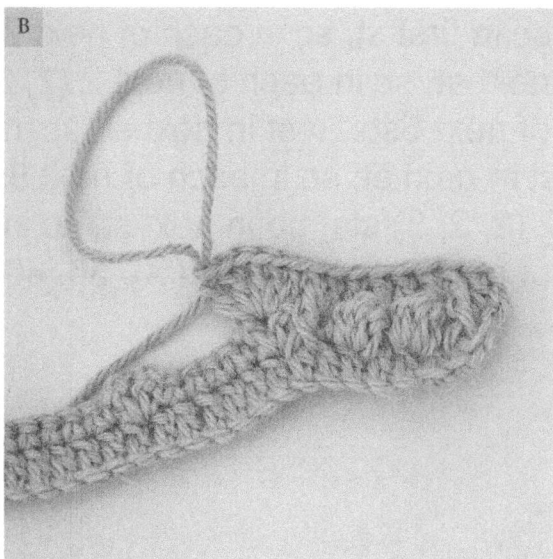

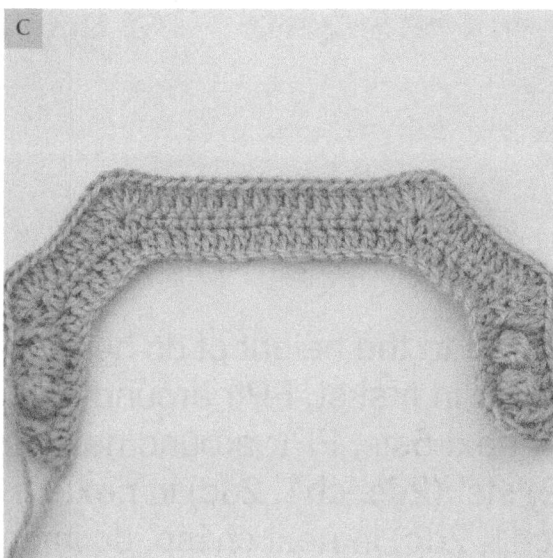

Row 4 (WS): ch1, sc in first st, sc in each of next 3sts, bo in next st, sc in each of next 6 (6, 6, 7) sts, v-st in next ch1sp, sc in each of next 11sts, v-st in next ch1sp, sc in each of next 22 (24, 24, 26) sts, v-st in next ch1sp, sc in each of next 11sts, v-st in next ch1sp, sc in each of next 6 (6, 6, 7) sts, bo in next st, sc in each of next 4sts, turn; 78 (80, 80, 84) sts

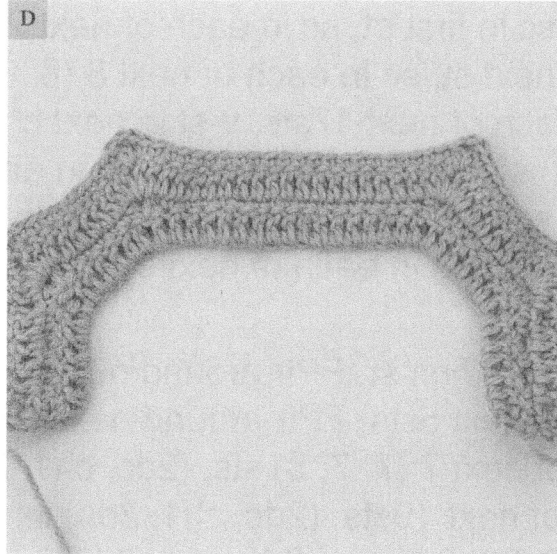

Row 5 (RS): ch1, dc in first st, FPtr around next FPtr two rows below, dc in each of next 5sts, FPtr around next FPtr two rows below, dc in each of next 4 (4, 4, 5) sts, (2dc, ch1, 2dc) in next ch1sp, dc in each of next 13sts, (2dc, ch1, 2dc) in next ch1sp, dc in each of next 24 (26, 26, 28) sts, (2dc, ch1, 2dc) in next ch1sp, dc in each of next 13sts, (2dc, ch1, 2dc) in next ch1sp, dc in each of next 4 (4, 4, 5) sts, FPtr around next FPtr two rows below, dc in each of next 5sts, FPtr around next FPtr two rows below, dc in last st, turn; 94 (96, 96, 100) sts

Row 6 (WS): ch1, sc in first st, sc in each of next 2sts, bo in next st, sc in next st, bo in next st, sc in each of next 8 (8, 8, 9) sts, v-st in next ch1sp, sc in each of next 17sts, v-st in next ch1sp, sc in each of next 28 (30, 30, 32) sts, v-st in next ch1sp, sc in each of next 17sts, v-st in next ch1sp, sc in each of next 8 (8, 8, 9) sts, bo in next st, sc in next st, bo in next st, sc in each of next 3sts, turn; 102 (104, 104, 108) sts

Row 7 (RS): ch1, dc in first st, FPtr around next FPtr two rows below, dc in each of next 5sts, FPtr around next FPtr two rows below, dc in each of next 7 (7, 7, 8) sts, (2dc, ch1, 2dc) in next ch1sp, dc in each of next 19sts, (2dc, ch1, 2dc) in next ch1sp, dc in each of next 30 (32, 32, 34) sts, (2dc, ch1, 2dc) in next ch1sp, dc in each of next 19sts, (2dc, ch1, 2dc) in next ch1sp, dc in each of next 7 (7, 7, 8) sts, FPtr around next FPtr two rows below, dc in each of next 5sts, FPtr around next FPtr two rows below, dc in last st, turn; 118 (120, 120, 124) sts

Row 8 (WS): ch1, sc in first st, sc in each of next 3sts, bo in next st, sc in each of next 12 (12, 12, 13) sts, v-st in next ch1sp, sc in each of next 23sts, v-st in next ch1sp, sc in each of next 34 (36, 36, 38) sts, v-st in next ch1sp, sc in each of next 23sts, v-st in next ch1sp, sc in each of next 12 (12, 12, 13) sts, bo in next st, sc in each of next 4sts, turn; 126 (128, 128, 132) sts

Row 9 (RS): ch1, dc in first st, FPtr around next FPtr two rows below, dc in each of next 5sts, FPtr around next FPtr two rows below, dc in each of next 10 (10, 10, 11) sts, (2dc, ch1, 2dc) in next ch1sp, dc in each of next 25sts, (2dc, ch1, 2dc) in next ch1sp, dc in each of next 36 (38, 38, 40) sts, (2dc, ch1, 2dc) in next ch1sp, dc in each of next 25sts, (2dc, ch1, 2dc) in next ch1sp, dc in each of next 10 (10, 10, 11) sts, FPtr around next FPtr two rows below, dc in each of next 5sts, FPtr around next FPtr two rows below, dc in last st, turn; 142 (144, 144, 148) sts

Row 10 (WS): ch1, sc in first st, sc in each of next 2sts, bo in next st, sc in next st, bo in next st, sc in each of next 14 (14, 14, 15) sts, v-st in next ch1sp, sc in each of next 29sts, v-st in next ch1sp, sc in each of next 40 (42, 42, 44) sts, v-st in next ch1sp, sc in each of next

29sts, v-st in next ch1sp, sc in each of next 14 (14, 14, 15) sts, bo in next st, sc in next st, bo in next st, sc in each of next 3sts, turn; 150 (152, 152, 156) sts F

For sizes 0–6m and 6–12m

Continue with Divide for Sleeves and Body.

For sizes 1–2y and 3–4y

Row 11 (RS): ch1, dc in first st, FPtr around next FPtr two rows below, dc in each of next 5sts, FPtr around next FPtr two rows below, dc in each of next (13, 14) sts, v-st in next ch1sp, dc in each of next 31sts, v-st in next ch1sp, dc in each of next (44, 46) sts, v-st in next ch1sp, dc in each of next 31sts, v-st in next ch1sp, dc in each of next (13, 14) sts, FPtr around next FPtr two rows below, dc in each of next 5sts, FPtr around next FPtr two rows below, dc in last st, turn; (160, 164) sts

Row 12 (WS): ch1, sc in first st, sc in each of next 3sts, bo in next st, sc in each of next (17, 18) sts, v-st in next ch1sp, sc in each of next 33sts, v-st in next ch1sp, sc in each of next (46, 48) sts, v-st in next ch1sp, sc in each of next 33sts, v-st in next ch1sp, sc in each of next (17, 18) sts, bo in next st, sc in each of next 4sts, turn; (168, 172) sts

Continue with Divide for Sleeves and Body.

DIVIDE FOR SLEEVES AND BODY

Row 1 (RS): ch1, dc in first st, FPtr around next FPtr two rows below, dc in each of next 5sts, FPtr around next FPtr two rows below, dc in each of next 13 (13, 15, 16) sts, dc in next ch1sp, ch4 (5, 5, 5), skip next 31 (31, 35, 35) sts for an armhole, dc in next ch1sp, dc in each of next 42 (44, 48, 50) sts, dc in next ch1sp, ch4 (5, 5, 5), skip next 31 (31, 35, 35) sts for an armhole, dc in next ch1sp, dc in each of next 13 (13, 15, 16) sts, FPtr around next FPtr two rows below, dc in each of next 5sts, FPtr around next FPtr two rows below, dc in last st, turn; 96 (100, 108, 112) sts including all chs
G

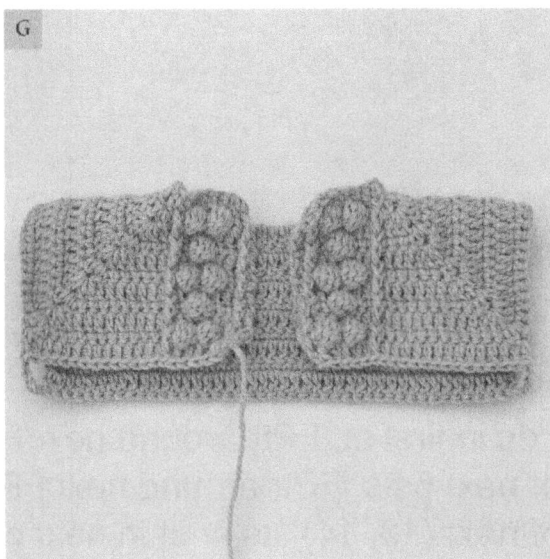

For sizes 0–6m and 6–12m

Row 2 (WS): ch1, sc in first st, sc in each of next 3sts, bo in next st, sc in each of next 86 (90) sts, bo in next st, sc in each of next 4sts, turn; 96 (100) sts

For sizes 1–2y and 3–4y

Row 2 (WS): ch1, sc in first st, sc in each of next 2sts, bo in next st, sc in next st, bo in next st, sc in each of next (96, 100) sts, bo in next st, sc in next st, bo in next st, sc in each of next 3sts, turn; (108, 112) sts

For all sizes

Row 3 (RS): ch1, dc in first st, FPtr around next FPtr two rows below, dc in each of next 5sts, FPtr around next FPtr two rows below, dc in each of next 80 (84, 92, 96) sts, FPtr around next FPtr two rows below, dc in each of next 5sts, FPtr around next FPtr two rows below, dc in last st, turn; 96 (100, 108, 112) sts

For sizes 0–6m and 6–12m

Row 4 (WS): ch1, sc in first st, sc in each of next 2sts, bo in next st, sc in next st, bo in next st, sc in each of next 84 (88) sts, bo in next st, sc in next st, bo in next st, sc in each of next 3sts, turn; 96 (100) sts

For sizes 1–2y and 3–4y

Row 4 (WS): ch1, sc in first st, sc in each of next 3sts, bo in next st, sc in each of next (98, 102) sts, bo in next st, sc in each of next 4sts, turn; (108, 112) sts

For all sizes

Row 5 (RS): ch1, dc in first st, FPtr around next FPtr two rows below, dc in each of next 5sts, FPtr around next FPtr two rows below, dc in each of next 80 (84, 92, 96) sts, FPtr around next FPtr two rows below, dc in each of next 5sts, FPtr around next FPtr two rows below, dc in last st, turn; 96 (100, 108, 112) sts

Repeat Rows 2 through 5 – 2 (3, 4, 5) more times.

For sizes 0–6m and 6–12m

Repeat Row 2 and 3 once more and work Bottom Edging H

For sizes 1–2y and 3–4y

Continue with Bottom Edging.

BOTTOM EDGING

Row 1 (WS): ch1, sc in first st, sc in each of next 2sts, bo in next st, sc in next st, bo in next st, sc in each of next 2sts, skip next st, sc in each of next 81 (85, 93, 97) sts, bo in next st, sc in next st, bo in next st, sc in each of next 3sts, turn; 95 (99, 107, 111) sts

Row 2 (RS): ch1, dc in first st, FPtr around next FPtr two rows below, dc in each of next 5sts, FPtr around next FPtr two rows below, *dc in next st, FPtr around next dc two rows below; repeat from * to last 9sts, dc in next st, FPtr around next FPtr two rows below, dc in each of next 5sts, FPtr around next FPtr two rows below, dc in last st, turn; 95 (99, 107, 111) sts ▮

Row 3 (WS): ch1, sc in first st, sc in each of next 3sts, bo in next st, sc in each of next 85 (89, 97, 101) sts, bo in next st, sc in each of next 4sts, turn; 95 (99, 107, 111) sts

Row 4 (RS): ch1, dc in first st, FPtr around next FPtr two rows below, dc in each of next 5sts, FPtr around next FPtr two rows below, *dc in next st, FPtr around next FPtr two rows below; repeat from * to last 9sts, dc in next st, FPtr around next FPtr two rows below, dc in each of next 5sts, FPtr around next FPtr two rows below, dc in last st; 95 (99, 107, 111) sts

Don't fasten off, but work Front Edging.

FRONT EDGING

Right Front

Row 1 (RS): ch1, work evenly 44 (50, 56, 62) dc across the right front, turn; it can be any other even number of sts too, but don't make them too close or too far from each other, remember to work the same amount of stitches for the Left Front

Row 2 (WS): ch1, hdc in first st, BPdc around next dc, FPdc around next dc, BPdc around next dc, *ch1, skip next st, BPdc around next dc, [FPdc around next dc, BPdc around next dc] 5 times; repeat from * as many times as buttonholes you'd like to make, where you don't need to make buttonholes work FPdc around next dc, BPdc around next dc to last st, hdc in last st, turn; 44 (50, 56, 62) sts J

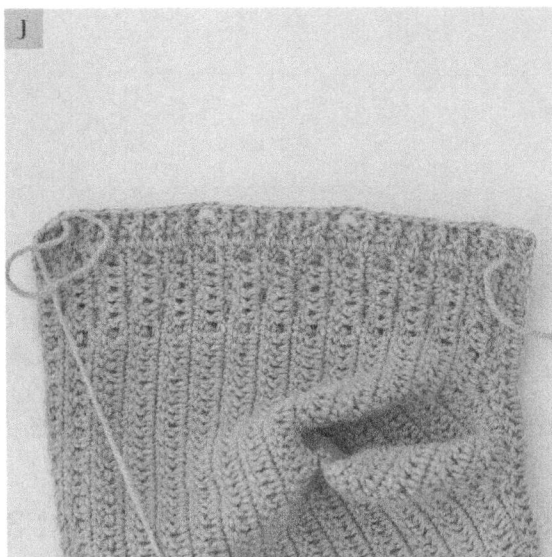

Row 3 (RS): ch1, hdc in first st, work BPdc around each BPdc, FPdc around each FPdc, sc in each ch1sp, to last st, hdc in last st; 44 (50, 56, 62) sts, fasten off

Left Front

On RS, join yarn into the first st of the collar and work across the left front.

Row 1 (RS): ch1, work evenly 44 (50, 56, 62) dc across the left front, turn

Row 2 (WS): ch1, hdc in first st, *FPdc around next dc, BPdc around next dc; repeat from * to last st, hdc in last st, turn; 44 (50, 56, 62) sts

Row 3 (RS): ch1, hdc in first st, *FPdc around next FPdc, BPdc around next BPdc; repeat from * to last st, hdc in last st; 44 (50, 56, 62) sts, fasten off

You can change this cardigan by working single crochet instead of bobbles.

HOOD

On RS, working into remaining loops of foundation chain, join yarn into the first FPtr on the collar and work K

Row 1 (RS): ch1, dc in first st, *2dc in next st, dc in next st; repeat from * 20 (21, 21, 23) more times, dc in next st, turn; 65 (68, 68, 74) sts L

Row 2 (WS): ch1, dc in first and in each next st, turn; 65 (68, 68, 74) sts

Row 3 (RS): ch1, dc in first and in each next st, turn; 65 (68, 68, 74) sts

Repeat Rows 2 and 3 – 7 (8, 9, 10) more times or until desired length M , fold the hood in half and working on WS join the top by working sl st in each st working through both layers N , fasten off.

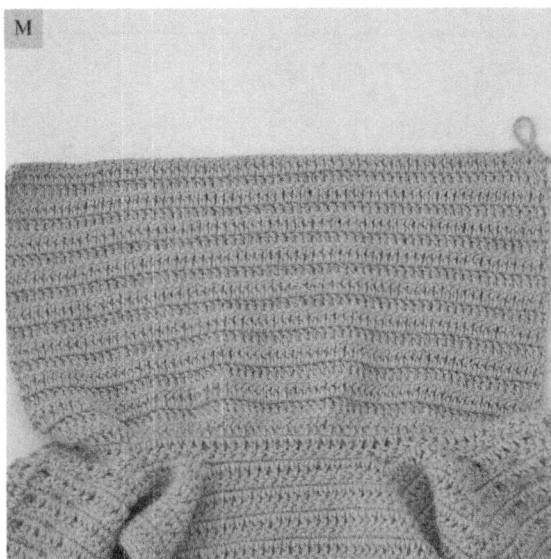

Join yarn at the base of Hood O and work sc evenly across to end, sl st in last st, fasten off P

SLEEVES

Join yarn in the middle of the underarm Q work in rnds and turn after each rnd.

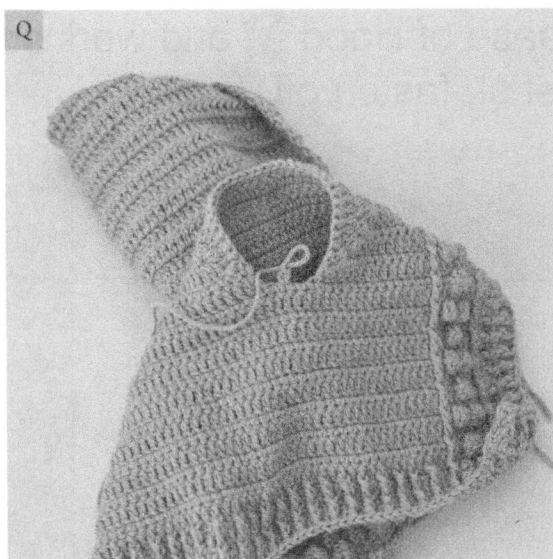

Rnd 1 (RS): ch1, work evenly 40 (42, 44, 44) dc around the armhole, join with sl st in first st, turn; 40 (42, 44, 44) sts

Rnd 2 (WS): ch1, sc in first and in each next st to end, join with sl st in first st, turn; 40 (42, 44, 44) sts

Rnd 3 (RS): ch1, dc in first st, [dc2tog] twice, dc in each next st to last 4sts, [dc2tog] twice, join with sl st in first st, turn; 36 (38, 40, 40) sts

Rnd 4 (WS): ch1, sc in first and in each next st to end, join with sl st in first st, turn; 36 (38, 40, 40) sts

Repeat Rnds 3 and 4 – 2 more times; 28 (30, 32, 32) sts

Rnd 9 (RS): ch1, dc in first and in each next st, join with sl st in first st, turn; 28 (30, 32, 32) sts

Rnd 10 (WS): ch1, sc in first and in each next st to end, join with sl st in first st, turn; 28 (30, 32, 32) sts

Repeat Rnds 9 and 10 – 2 (4, 6, 8) more times or until desired length, continue with Cuff.

Second Sleeve

Work in exactly the same way as first sleeve.

CUFF

Rnd 1 (RS): ch1, dc in first and in each next st, join with sl st in first st; 28 (30, 32, 32) sts

Rnd 2 (RS): ch1, FPdc around first dc, *BPdc around next dc, FPdc around next dc; repeat from * to last st, BPdc around last dc and join with sl st in first st; 28 (30, 32, 32) sts

Rnd 3 (RS): ch1, FPdc around each FPdc and BPdc around each BPdc to end, join with sl st in first st; 28 (30, 32, 32) sts

Repeat Rnd 3 – 0 (1, 2, 3) more times or until desired length, fasten off R

Second Cuff

Work in exactly the same way on second sleeve.

FINISHING

Weave in all ends (see Finishing Techniques).

Sew on buttons opposite the buttonholes (see Finishing Techniques).

JASMINE SWEATER

~ ★★☆ ~

The Jasmine Sweater uses an appealing mix of different stitches. It's worked from the top down with a circular yoke, then divided for the sleeves and body. This makes it completely seamless. The side slits add the perfect little detail to make it special – just what every sweater needs!

SIZES AND MEASUREMENTS OF FINISHED GARMENT

Size	Chest	Length	Sleeve length to underarm
0–6m	46cm/18¼in	27cm/10½in	16cm/6¼in
6–12m	53cm/21in	30cm/11¾in	18cm/7in
1–2y	57cm/22½in	38cm/15in	20cm/7¾in
3–4y	60cm/23½in	41cm/16¼in	23cm/9in

GAUGE (TENSION)

18 sts and 10 rows in dc to measure 10 x 10cm (4 x 4in) using 4mm (G/6) hook (or size required to obtain gauge)

SPECIAL STITCHES

bo (3-dc bobble), crossed dc, v-st, FPdc, BPdc (see Special Stitches)

MATERIALS

3 LIGHT

- 375 (450, 550, 625) meters or 411 (493, 602, 684) yards of any DK weight or light worsted weight yarn
  Suggested yarn: Rowan Alpaca Soft DK, 70% virgin wool, 30% alpaca, shade 202, 50g (1¾oz), 125m (136yd)
- 4mm (G/6) crochet hook (or size required to obtain gauge)

Pattern is written for size 0–6m, changes for 6–12m, 1–2y and 3–4y are in (…).

Ch1 at the beginning of round doesn't count as a stitch.

YOKE

The yoke is worked in rounds, mainly on RS, but for rows with bobbles you will have to turn and work on WS.

Foundation chain: work loosely, ch56 (58, 60, 66), join with sl st in first ch.

Rnd 1 (RS): ch1, but pull it to the height of dc here and throughout where next st is dc or bo, dc in first and in each next ch to end, join with sl st in first st; 56 (58, 60, 66) sts

Rnd 2 (RS): ch1, sc in first st, *ch2, skip next st, sc in next st; repeat from * to end, in last repeat instead of last sc join with sl st in first sc, turn; 28 (29, 30, 33) ch2sp made A

Rnd 3 (WS): ch1, bo in first sc, *sc in next ch2sp, bo in next sc; repeat from * to last ch2sp, sc in last ch2sp, join with sl st in first bo, turn; 28 (29, 30, 33) bo made B

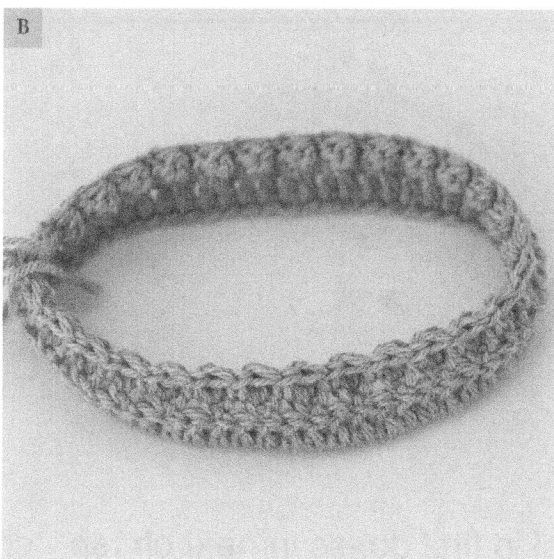

Rnd 4 (RS): ch1, 2dc in first st, 2dc in each next st to end, for size 0–6m in last st work only 1dc, for size 6–12m in last st work 3dc, join with sl st in first st; 111 (117, 120, 132) dc C

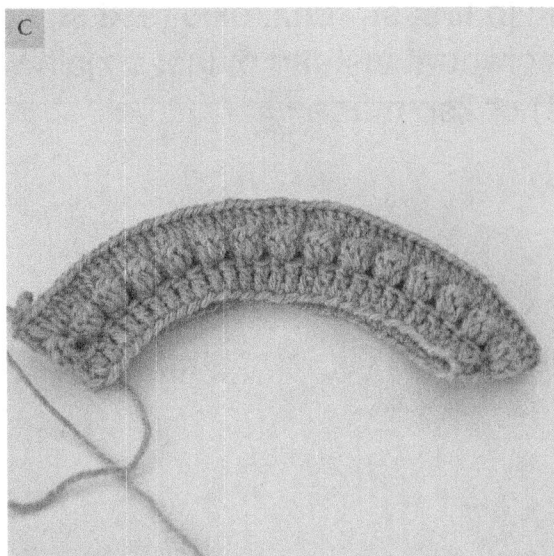

Rnd 5 (RS): ch1, skip first and next dc, dc in next st, ch1, dc in first skipped st working over dc just made, *crossed dc worked over next 3sts; repeat from * to end, join with sl st in first st; 37 (39, 40, 44) crossed dc made D

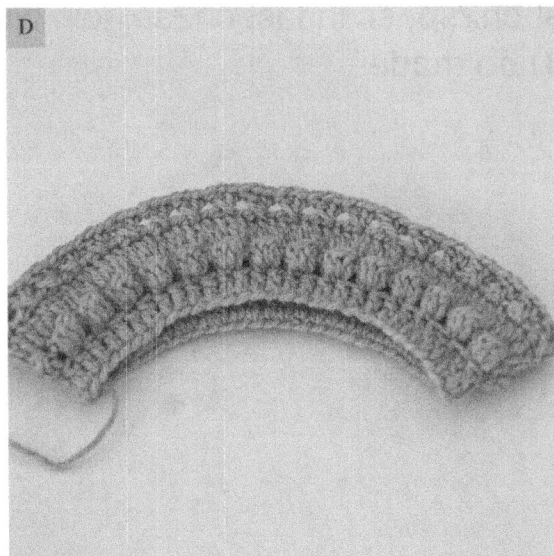

Rnd 6 (RS): ch1, skip first dc, sc in next ch1sp, *ch2, skip next 2dc, sc in next ch1sp; repeat from * to end, in last repeat instead of last

sc join with sl st in first st; 37 (39, 40, 44) ch2sp made █E

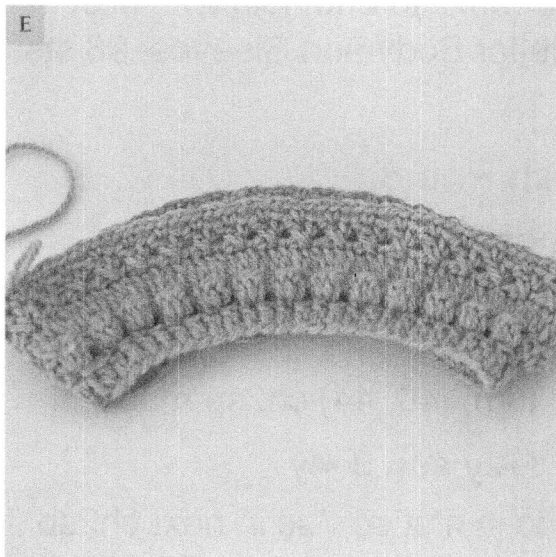

For size 0–6m

Rnd 7 (RS): ch1, sc in ch2sp to the right, *ch2, skip next sc, sc in next ch2sp; repeat from * to end, in last repeat instead of last sc join with sl st in first sc, turn; 37 ch2sp made █F

Rnd 8 (WS): ch1, bo in first sc, *sc in next ch2sp, bo in next sc; repeat from * to last ch2sp, sc in last ch2sp, join with sl st in first bo, turn; 37 bo made

Rnd 9 (RS): ch1, dc in first and in next st, *2dc in next st, dc in each of next 2sts; repeat from * to end, join with sl st in first st and continue with Divide for Body and Sleeves; 98 sts

For size 6–12m

Turn, continue with Rnd 8.

For sizes 1–2y and 3–4y

Rnd 7 (RS): ch1, sc in ch2sp to the right, *ch2, skip next sc, sc in next ch2sp; repeat from * to end, in last repeat instead of last sc join with sl st in first sc, turn; (40, 44) ch2sp made [F]

For sizes 6–12m, 1–2y and 3–4y

Rnd 8 (WS): ch1, bo in first sc, *sc in next ch2sp, bo in next sc; repeat from * to last ch2sp, sc in last ch2sp, join with sl st in first bo, turn; (39, 40, 44) bo made

Rnd 9 (RS): ch1, (2, 1, 3) dc in first st, 2dc in each next st to end, join with sl st in first st; (156, 159, 177) dc

Rnd 10 (RS): ch1, skip first and next dc, dc in next st, ch1, dc in first skipped st working over dc just made, *crossed dc worked over next 3sts; repeat from * to end, join with sl st in first st; (52, 53, 59) crossed dc made

Rnd 11 (RS): ch1, skip first dc, sc in next ch1sp, *ch2, skip next 2dc, sc in next ch1sp; repeat from * to end, in last repeat instead of last sc join with sl st in first st; (52, 53, 59) ch2sp made

For size 6–12m

Turn, continue with Rnd 13.

For sizes 1–2y and 3–4y

Rnd 12 (RS): ch1, sc in ch2sp to the right, *ch2, skip next sc, sc in next ch2sp; repeat from * to end, in last repeat instead of last sc join with sl st in first st, turn; (53, 59) ch2sp made

For sizes 6–12m, 1–2y and 3–4y

Rnd 13 (WS): ch1, bo in first sc, *sc in next ch2sp, bo in next sc; repeat from * to last ch2sp, sc in last ch2sp, join with sl st in first st,

turn; (52, 53, 59) bo made G

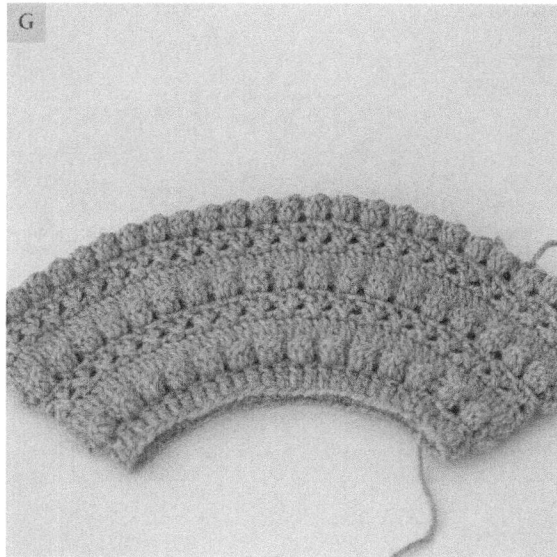

For sizes 6–12m and 1–2y

Continue with Divide for Body and Sleeves.

For size 3–4y

Rnd 14 (RS): ch1, dc in first and in each next st, join with sl st in first st and continue with Divide for Body and Sleeves; 118 dc

DIVIDE FOR BODY AND SLEEVES

For size 0–6m

Rnd 1 (RS): ch1, dc in first st, *2dc in next st, dc in each of next 2sts**; repeat from * 8 more times, ch3, skip next 21sts for an armhole, repeat from * to ** 9 more times, 2dc in next st, ch3, skip next 21sts for an armhole, join with sl st in first st; 81 sts H

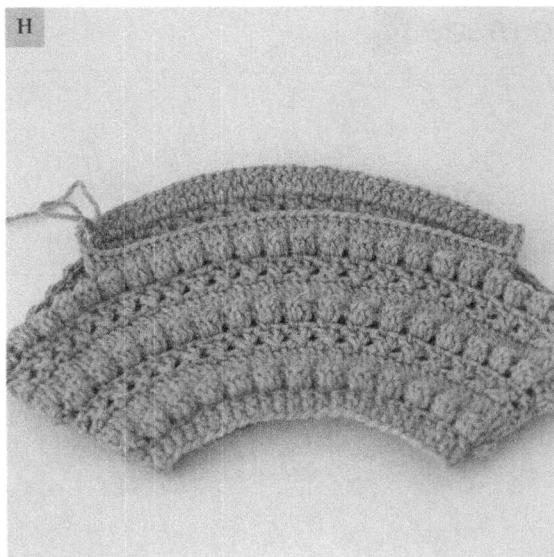

For size 6–12m

Rnd 1 (RS): ch1, 2dc in first st, *2dc in next st, dc in next st**; repeat from * 13 more times, ch4, skip next 23sts for an armhole, repeat from * to ** 14 more times, 2dc in next st, ch4, skip next 23sts for an armhole, join with sl st in first st; 96 sts

For size 1–2y

Rnd 1 (RS): ch1, dc in first st, *2dc in next st, dc in next st**; repeat from * 13 more times, 2dc in next st, ch6, skip next 23sts for an armhole, repeat from * to ** 15 more times, ch6, skip next 23sts for an armhole, join with sl st in first st; 102 sts

For size 3–4y

Rnd 1 (RS): ch1, 2dc in first st, *dc in each of next 2sts, 2dc in next st**; repeat from * 10 more times, ch8, skip next 25sts for an armhole, 2dc in next st, repeat from * to ** 11 more times, ch8, skip next 25sts for an armhole, join with sl st in first st; 108 sts

For all sizes

Rnd 2 (RS): ch1, sc in first st, v-st in next st, skip next st, *sc in next st, v-st in next st, skip next st; repeat from * to end, join with sl st in first st, turn; 27 (32, 34, 36) v-st made

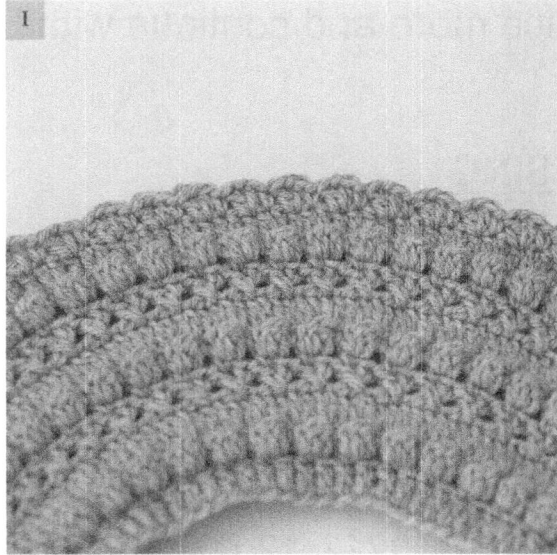

Rnd 3 (WS): ch1, dc in first sc, *skip next dc, sc in next ch1sp, skip next dc, v-st in next sc; repeat from * to end, in last repeat instead of last v-st work (dc, ch1) in same st as first dc and join with sl st in first st, turn; 27 (32, 34, 36) v-st made

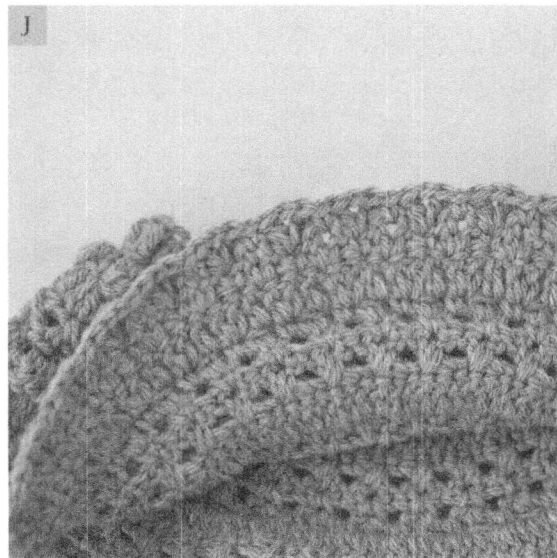

Rnd 4 (RS): ch1, sc in next ch1sp, *skip next dc, v-st in next sc, skip next dc, sc in next ch1sp; repeat from * to last sc, v-st in last sc, join with sl st in first st, turn; 27 (32, 34, 36) v-st made

Repeat Rnds 3 and 4 – 3 (4, 6, 8) more times.

Repeat Rnd 3 once more and continue with Back Decreasing.

BACK DECREASING

Work in rows.

Row 1 (RS): ch1, sc in next ch1sp, *skip next dc, v-st in next sc, skip next dc, sc in next ch1sp; repeat from * 11 (13, 13, 14) more times, turn; 12 (14, 14, 15) v-st made

Row 2 (WS): ch2 (doesn't count as st), skip first st and skip next dc, sc in next ch1sp, *skip next dc, v-st in next sc, skip next dc, sc in next ch1sp; repeat from * 10 (12, 12, 13) more times, skipping last 2sts turn; 11 (13, 13, 14) v-st made

Row 3: ch2 (doesn't count as st), skip first st and skip next dc, sc in next ch1sp, *skip next dc, v-st in next sc, skip next dc, sc in next ch1sp; repeat from * to end, skipping last 2sts turn; 10 (12, 12, 13) v-st made K

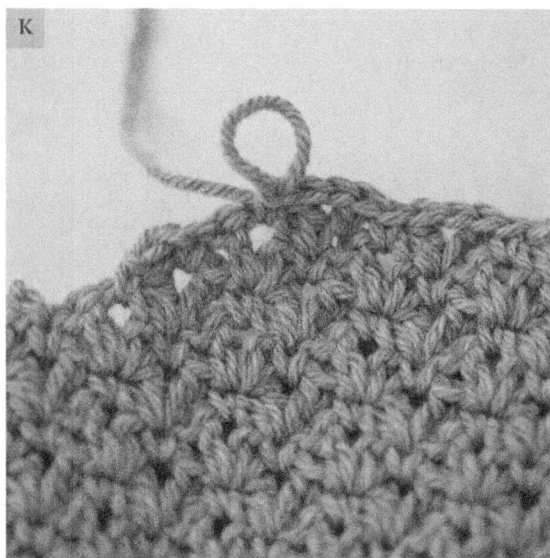

Repeat Row 3 – 3 (4, 4, 4) more times; 7 (8, 8, 9) v-sts made, fasten off L

FRONT DECREASING

On RS, skip 1 (1, 2, 2) v-sts from the Back and join yarn into the next ch1sp M ; work in rows.

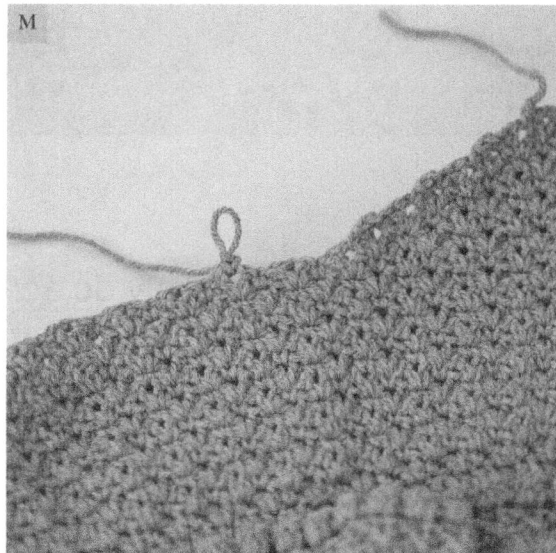

Row 1 (RS): ch1, sc in same ch1sp, *skip next dc, v-st in next sc, skip next dc, sc in next ch1sp; repeat from * 10 (13, 13, 14) more times, turn; 11 (14, 14, 15) v-st made

Row 2 (WS): ch2 (doesn't count as st), skip first st and skip next dc, sc in next ch1sp, *skip next dc, v-st in next sc, skip next dc, sc in next ch1sp; repeat from * 9 (12, 12, 13) more times, turn; 10 (13, 13, 14) v-st made

Row 3 (RS): ch2 (doesn't count as st), skip first st and skip next dc, sc in next ch1sp, *skip next dc, v-st in next sc, skip next dc, sc in next ch1sp; repeat from * to end, turn; 9 (12, 12, 13) v-st made

Repeat Row 3 – 3 (4, 4, 4) more times; 6 (8, 8, 9) v-sts made, don't fasten off, but continue with Edging N

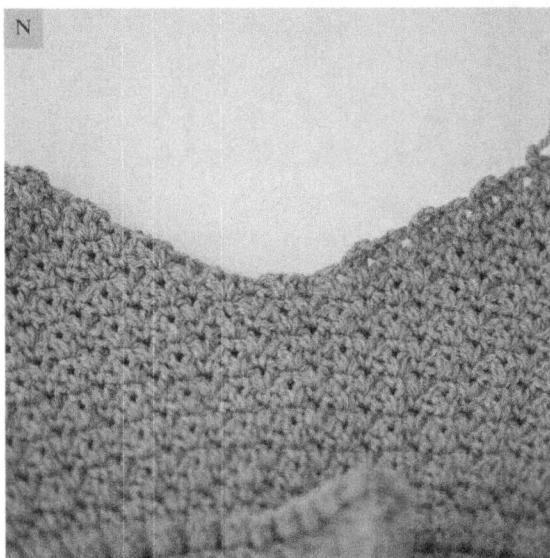

EDGING

Rnd 1 (RS): ch1, 3dc in first st, work evenly dc across the Front and the Back, on corners work twice 3dc in one st, at the end of rnd work 3dc in last st, join with sl st in first st (number of sts is not important here but it has to be even number) O

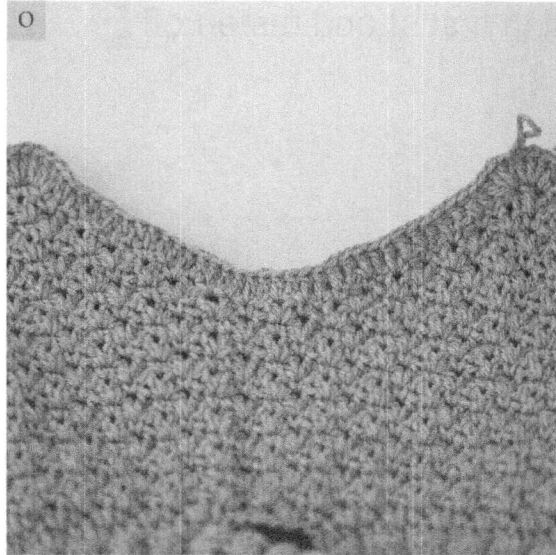

Rnd 2 (RS): ch1, FPdc around first dc, *BPdc around next dc, FPdc around next dc; repeat from * to last dc, BPdc around last dc, join with sl st in first st

Rnd 3 (RS): ch1, FPdc around first FPdc, *BPdc around next BPdc, FPdc around next FPdc; repeat from * to last st, but on the corners work (2BPdc around next BPdc, FPdc around next FPdc, 2BPdc around next BPdc) BPdc around last BPdc, join with sl st in first st P

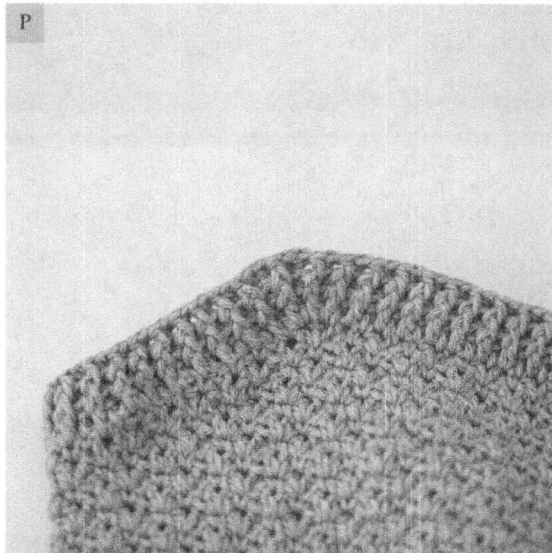

Rnd 4 (RS): ch1, FPdc around first FPdc, *BPdc around next BPdc, FPdc around next FPdc; repeat from * to last st, BPdc around last

BPdc, join with sl st in first st and fasten off

SLEEVES

On RS join yarn in middle of underarm turn after each round and work on both RS and WS.

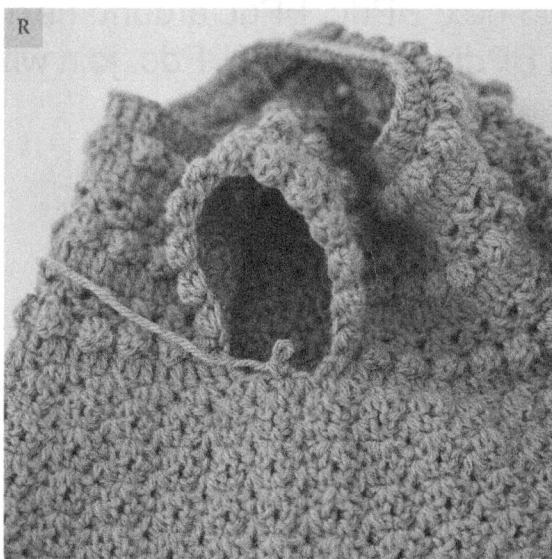

Rnd 1 (RS): ch1, sc in first st [skip 1st, v-st in next st, skip 1st, sc in next st], 8 (9, 10, 11)times evenly around the armhole, instead of last sc join with sl st in first st, turn; 8 (9, 10, 11) v-st made

Rnd 2 (WS): ch1, dc in first sc, *skip next dc, sc in next ch1sp, skip next dc, v-st in next sc; repeat from * to end, in last repeat instead of last v-st work (dc, ch1) in same st as first dc and join with sl st in first st, turn; 8 (9, 10, 11) v-st made

Rnd 3 (RS): ch1, sc in next ch1sp, *skip next dc, v-st in next sc, skip next dc, sc in next ch1sp; repeat from * to last sc, v-st in last sc, join with sl st in first st, turn; 8 (9, 10, 11) v-st made

Repeat Rnds 2 and 3 – 5 (8, 10, 12) more times or until the sleeve is 13 (15, 17, 20)cm/5 (6, 6¾, 8)in long, measured from underarm, or until desired length, (cuff will add approximately 3cm/1¼in).

Second Sleeve

Work in the same way as first sleeve.

CUFF

Rnd 1 (RS): ch1, dc in first sc, *skip next dc, 2dc in next ch1sp, skip next dc, dc in next sc; repeat from * to last v-st, 2 (1, 2, 1) dc in last ch1sp and join with sl st in first st; 24 (26, 30, 32) sts S

Rnd 2 (RS): ch1, FPdc around first dc, *BPdc around next dc, FPdc around next dc; repeat from * to last st, BPdc around last dc, join

with sl st in first st; 24 (26, 30, 32) sts

Rnd 3 (RS): ch1, FPdc around first FPdc, *BPdc around next BPdc, FPdc around next FPdc; repeat from * to last st, BPdc around last BPdc, join with sl st in first st; 24 (26, 30, 32) sts

Repeat Rnd 3 – one more time, fasten off T

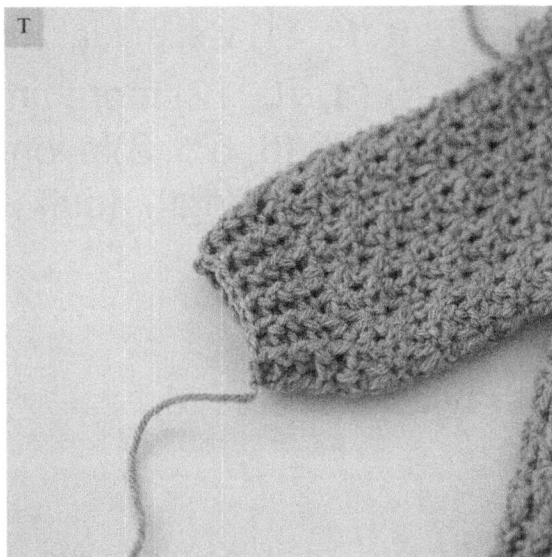

Second Cuff

Work in the same way on second sleeve.

COLLAR

Join yarn into the first st of collar, into the remaining loop and work:

Rnd 1 (RS): ch1, FPdc around first dc U , *BPdc around next dc, FPdc around next dc; repeat from * to last st, BPdc around next st, join with sl st in first st; 56 (58, 60, 66) sts

Rnd 2 (RS): ch1, FPdc around first FPdc, *BPdc around next BPdc, FPdc around next FPdc; repeat from * to last st, BPdc around last BPdc, join with sl st in first st; 56 (58, 60, 66) sts

Repeat Rnd 2 – one more time, fasten off

FINISHING

Weave in ends, wash and block (see Finishing Techniques).

CLOUD DRESS

~ ★★☆ ~

This dress is all about texture! As well as working picot and popcorn shells (amongst other stitches), you'll also learn a new, very stretchy, foundation chain. When I made the Cloud Dress I chose a cotton/wool blend yarn to make it soft and fluffy – like a cloud! – but you could use 100% cotton yarn if you prefer.

SIZES AND MEASUREMENTS OF FINISHED GARMENT

Size	Chest	Length
0–6m	51cm/20in	30cm/11¾in
6–12m	54cm/21¼in	35cm/13¾in
1–2y	60cm/23½in	40cm/15¾in
3–4y	64cm/25¼in	45cm/17¾in

GAUGE (TENSION)

20 sts and 9 rows in dc to measure 10 x 10cm (4 x 4in), using 3.5mm (E/4) hook (or size required to obtain gauge)

SPECIAL STITCHES

v-st, popcorn, popcorn shell, crossed dc, picot, picot shell (see Special Stitches)

MATERIALS

3 LIGHT

- 340 (450, 560, 700) meters or 370 (493, 613,767) yards of any DK weight or light worsted weight yarn
  Suggested yarn: Laines du Nord Spring Wool, 50% wool, 50% cotton, shade 04, 50g (1¾oz), 140m (153yd)
- 4.5mm (7) crochet hook (only for foundation chain), and 3.5mm (E/4) crochet hook (or size required to obtain gauge)

Pattern is written for size 0–6m, changes for 6–12m, 1–2y and 3–4y are in (…).

Ch1 at the beginning of each round doesn't count as a stitch.

YOKE

Foundation chain: with 4.5mm (7) hook, *ch1, hdc in bottom loop of ch1; repeat from * 25 (26, 28, 30) more times A B C D , join with sl st in first ch; foundation ch has to be loose and elastic; 52 (54, 58, 62) sts including all chs E

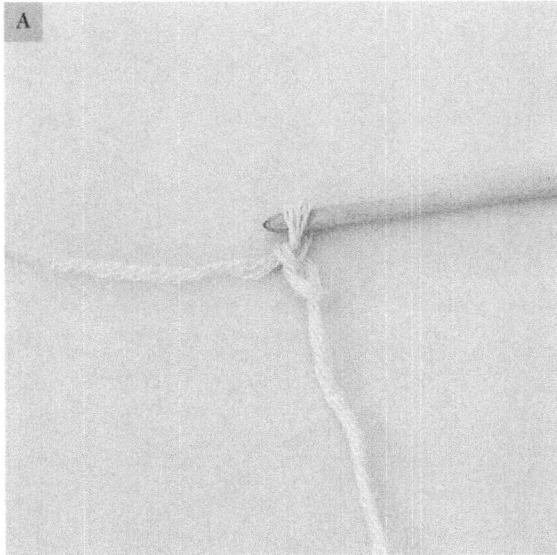

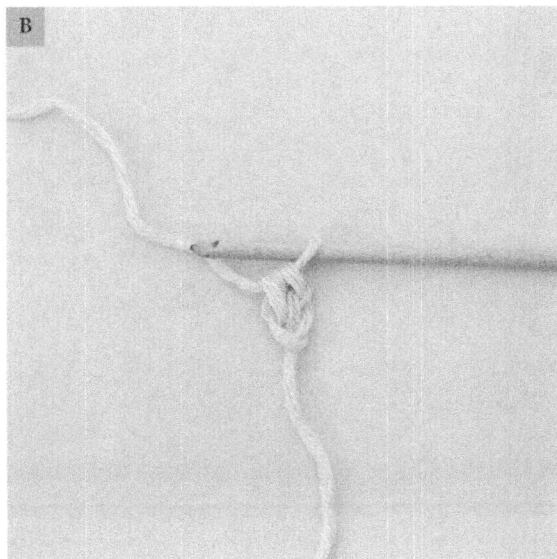

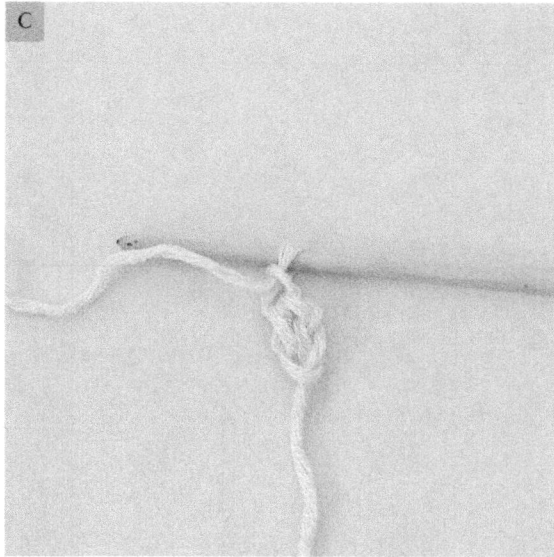

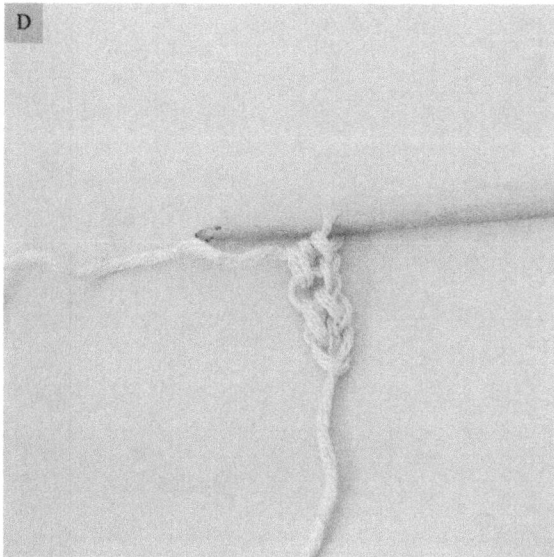

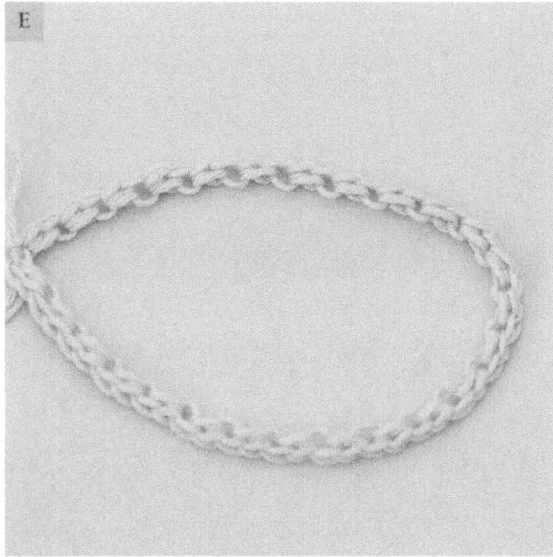

Simpler option is to work ch52 (54, 58, 62) (it has to be loose and elastic) and join with sl st in first ch.

Rnd 1 (RS): with 3.5mm (E/4) hook, ch1, but pull it to the height of dc here and throughout where next st is dc or popcorn, v-st in first st, *skip next st, v-st in next st; repeat from * to end, join with sl st in first st; 26 (27, 29, 31) v-sts made F

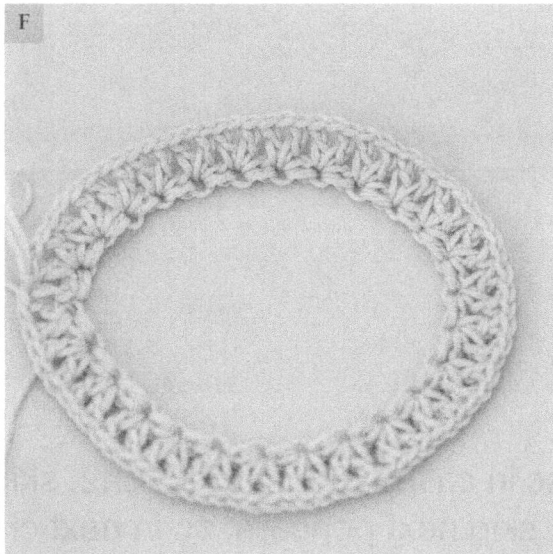

Rnd 2 (RS): ch1, skip first dc, *sc in next ch1sp, ch2, skip next 2dc; repeat from * to end, join with sl st in first st; 26 (27, 29, 31) ch2sp made G

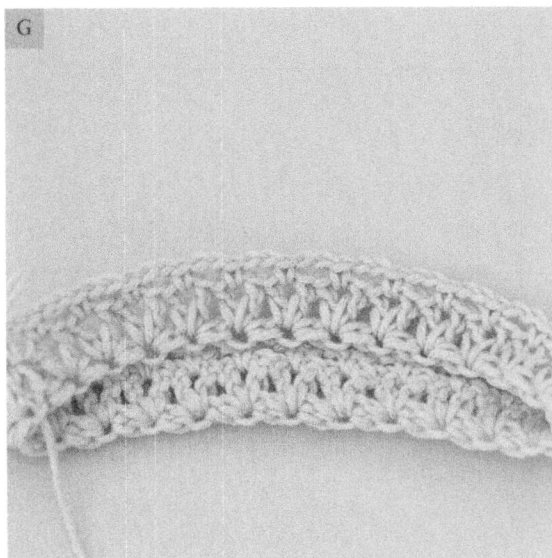

Rnd 3 (RS): ch1, *popcorn shell in next ch2sp, ch1, skip next sc; repeat from * to end, join with sl st in first popcorn; 26 (27, 29, 31) popcorn shells made H

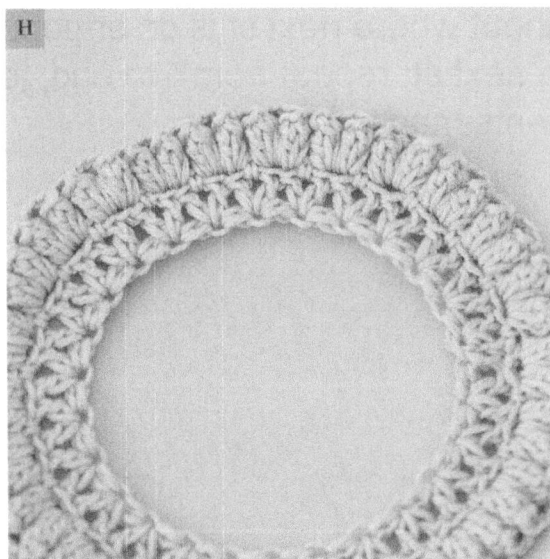

Rnd 4 (RS): ch1, sc in ch1sp to the right, *ch2, skip next popcorn, sc in next ch2sp, ch2, skip next popcorn, sc in next ch1sp; repeat from * to end, but instead of last sc join with sl st in first st; 52 (54, 58, 62) ch2sp made I

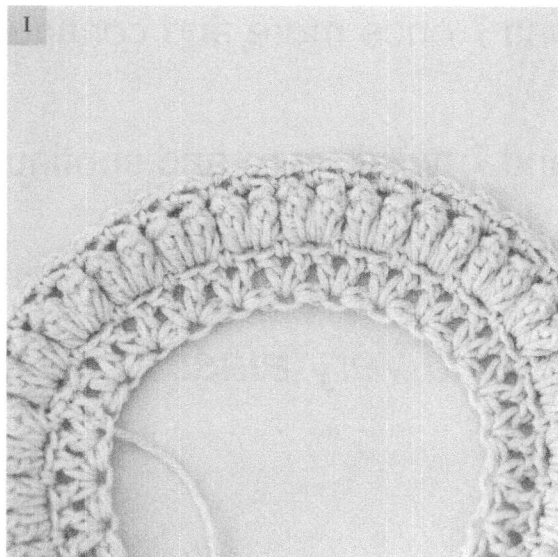

Rnd 5 (RS): ch1, *2dc in next ch2sp, ch1, skip next sc; repeat from * to end, join with sl st in first st; 52 (54, 58, 62) pairs of 2dc made

Rnd 6 (RS): ch1, sc in ch1sp to the right, *ch2, skip next 2dc, sc in next ch1sp; repeat from * to end, but instead of last sc join with sl st in first st; 52 (54, 58, 62) ch2sp made J

Rnd 7 (RS): ch1, *2dc in next ch2sp, ch1, skip next sc; repeat from * to end, join with sl st in first st; 52 (54, 58, 62) pairs of 2dc made

For size 0–6m

Continue with Back.

For sizes 6–12m and 1–2y

Repeat Rnds 6 and 7 once more and continue with Back.

For size 3–4y

Repeat Rnds 6 and 7 twice more and continue with Back.

> *Use this foundation chain every time you need a very elastic chain.*

BACK

Turn and work on WS.

Row 1 (WS): ch1, sc in next ch1sp, *ch2, skip next 2dc, sc in next ch1sp; repeat from * 13 (14, 15, 16) more times, turn; 14 (15, 16, 17) ch2sp made

Row 2 (RS): ch1, *popcorn shell in next ch2sp, ch1, skip next sc; repeat from * 13 (14, 15, 16) more times, ch4 (3, 5, 4), fasten off, but leave a tail K ; 14 (15, 16, 17) popcorn shells made

FRONT

On WS, skip next 12 (12, 13, 14) pairs of 2dc from Back for an armhole, and join yarn into next ch1sp.

Row 1 (WS): ch1, sc in ch1sp at base of ch1, *ch2, skip next 2dc, sc in next ch1sp; repeat from * 13 (14, 15, 16) more times, turn; 14 (15, 16, 17) ch2sp made

Row 2 (RS): ch1, *popcorn shell in next ch2sp, ch1, skip next sc; repeat from * 13 (14, 15, 16) more times, ch4 (3, 5, 4) L , join into the first popcorn of Back, leave the loop opened; 14 (15, 16, 17) popcorn shells made; pick up the ch4 (3, 5, 4) you left on Back and join it to the first popcorn of Front, fasten off M

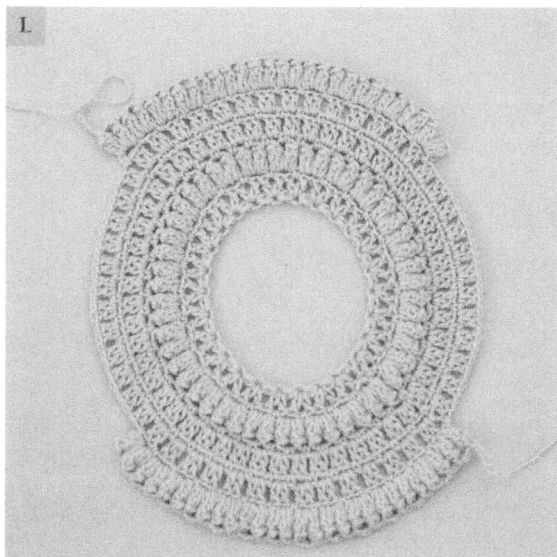

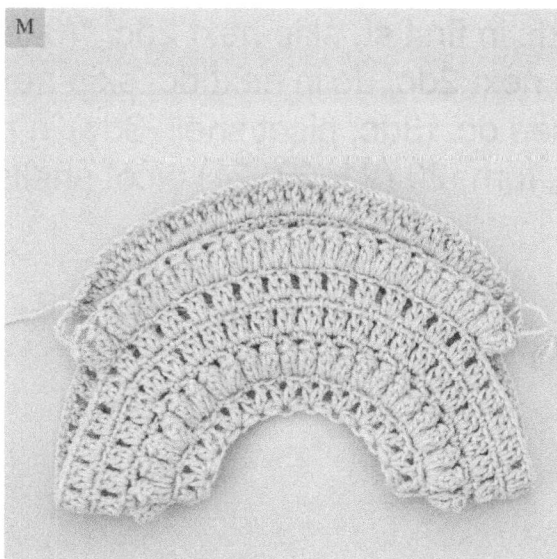

SKIRT PART

Rnd 1 (RS): ch1, dc in first st, 2dc in each ch2sp, 2dc in each ch1sp, 2dc in first ch of underarm and 1dc in each next ch (same for second underarm), skip all popcorns, join with sl st in first st; 119 (125, 137, 143) sts

Rnd 2 (RS): ch1, 2dc in first st, *skip next st, crossed dc worked over next 3sts, skip next st, 3dc in next st; repeat from * to last 4sts, skip next st, crossed dc, dc in same st as first 2dc of rnd, join with sl st in first st, turn; 20 (21, 23, 24) crossed dc made N

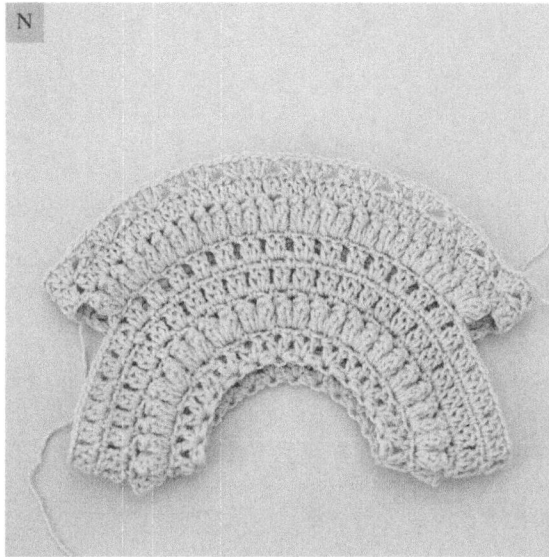

Rnd 3 (WS): ch1, dc in first st, skip next 2dc, *(3dc, picot shell, 3dc) in next ch1sp, skip next 2dc, dc in next dc, skip next 2dc; O repeat from * to last crossed dc, (3dc, picot shell, 3dc) in next ch1sp, join with sl st in first dc, turn; 20 (21, 23, 24) picot shells made P

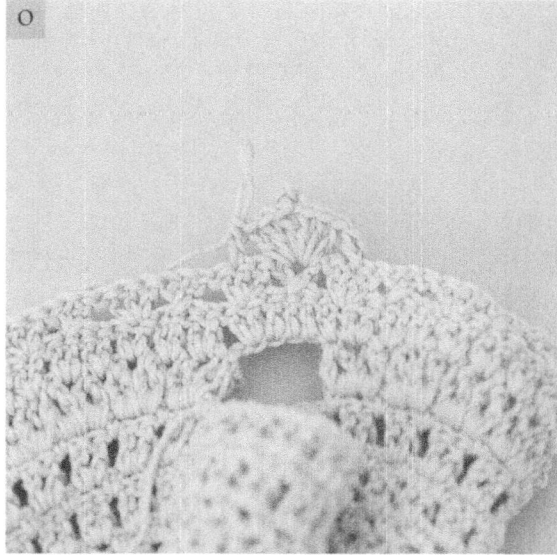

O

P

Rnd 4 (RS): ch1, 2dc in first st, *skip next 3dc and picot, dc in next dc, ch1, dc in last skipped dc leaving picot in front of work and working over previous dc Q , skip next 2dc, 3dc in next dc; repeat from * to end, but in last repeat instead of 3dc work dc in same st as first 2dc of rnd and join with sl st in first st, turn; 20 (21, 23, 24) crossed dc made

Rnd 5 (WS): ch1, dc in st at the base of ch1, skip next 2dc, *(3dc, picot shell, 3dc) in next ch1sp, skip next 2dc, dc in next dc, skip next 2dc; repeat from * to last crossed dc, (3dc, picot shell, 3dc) in next ch1sp, join with sl st in first st, turn; 20 (21, 23, 24) picot shells made

Repeat Rnds 4 and 5 – 5 (7, 9, 11) more times or until desired length, fasten off

SLEEVES

On WS, join yarn into the first ch1sp of armhole

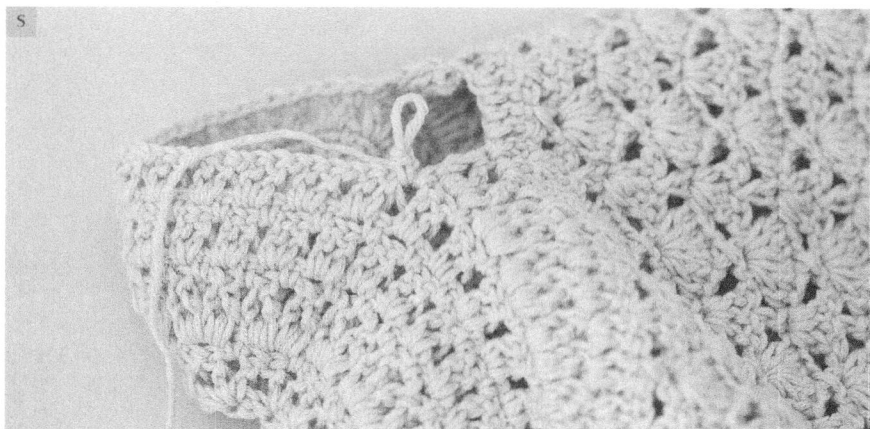

Row 1 (WS): ch1, sc in same sp, *skip next 2dc, (3dc, picot shell, 3dc) in next ch1sp; repeat from * to last ch1sp, sc in last ch1sp, fasten off T

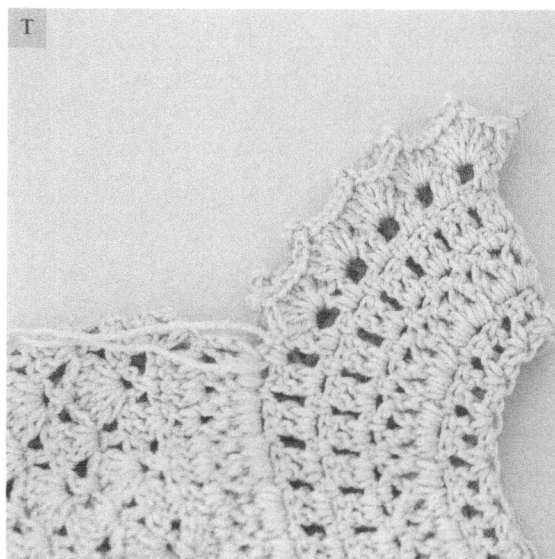

Second Sleeve

Work in exactly the same way as first sleeve.

FINISHING

Weave in all ends (see Finishing Techniques).

SWEET DRESS

~ ★½☆ ~

Everything is sweet about this dress, from its pretty collar to its frilly cuffs! To make it with short sleeves, just work an even number of ch3sp around the armhole (as mentioned in Cuff Edging – the amount of ch3sp will be different), then complete the cuff. The dress is worked top down – just be careful not to make the collar too tight.

SIZES AND MEASUREMENTS OF FINISHED GARMENT

Size	Chest	Length	Sleeve length to underarm
0–6m	50cm/19¾in	30cm/11¾in	12cm/4¾in
6–12m	55cm/21½in	36cm/14in	14cm/5½in
1–2y	60cm/23½in	42cm/16½in	18cm/7in
3–4y	63cm/24¾in	48cm/19in	22cm/8½in

GAUGE (TENSION)

20 sts and 10 rows in dc to measure 10 x 10cm (4 x 4in) using 4mm (G/6) hook (or size required to obtain gauge)

SPECIAL STITCHES

Shell (Sweet Dress shell), BPdc, bo, BPsc, dc2tog (see Special Stitches)

MATERIALS

3 **LIGHT**

- 400 (505, 605, 705) meters or 437 (550, 660, 770) yards of any DK weight or light worsted weight yarn
  Suggested yarns: Drops Cotton Merino, 50% cotton, 50% merino, shade 28, 50g (1¾oz), 110m (120yd)
- 4mm (G/6) crochet hook (or size required to obtain gauge)

Pattern is written for size 0–6m, changes for 6–12m, 1–2y and 3–4y are in (…).

Ch1 at the beginning of each round doesn't count as a stitch.

YOKE

Foundation chain: ch56 (60, 64, 68), join with sl st in first ch (it has to be loose and elastic to pass over child's head).

If the neckline turns out too large, at the very end you can work round of sc to make tighter.

Rnd 1 (RS): ch1, sc in first ch, *ch3, skip next ch, sc in next ch; repeat from * to end, instead of last sc join with sl st in first st; 28 (30, 32, 34) ch3sp made A

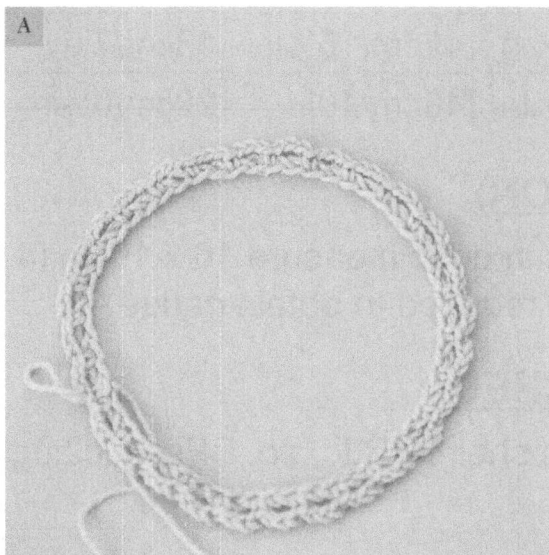

Rnd 2 (RS): ch1, skip first sc, *shell in next ch3sp, skip next sc, sc in next ch3sp, skip next sc; repeat from * to end and join with sl st in first st; 14 (15, 16, 17) shells made B

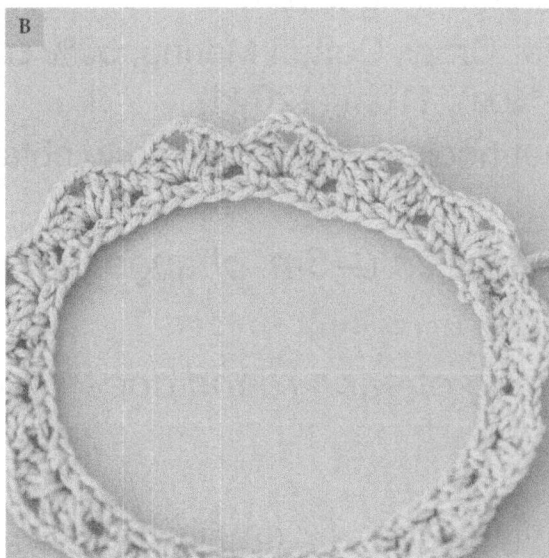

Rnd 3 (RS): ch1, BPdc around each of next 2dc, *ch2, sc in next ch3sp, ch2, BPdc around each of next 2dc, skip next sc, BPdc

around each of next 2dc C ; repeat from * to end, after skipping last sc join with sl st in first st; 126 (135, 144, 153) sts including all ch D

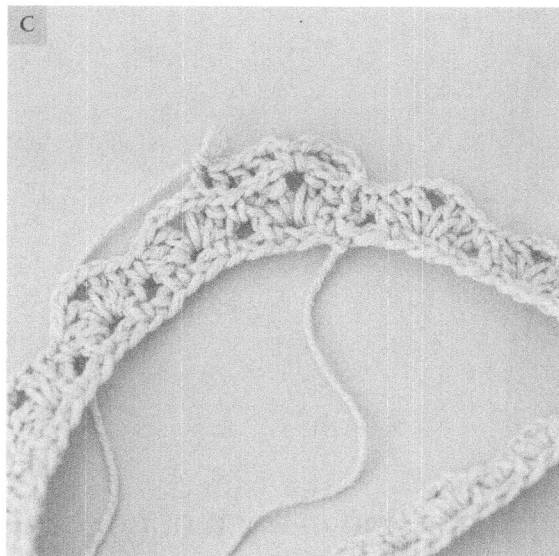

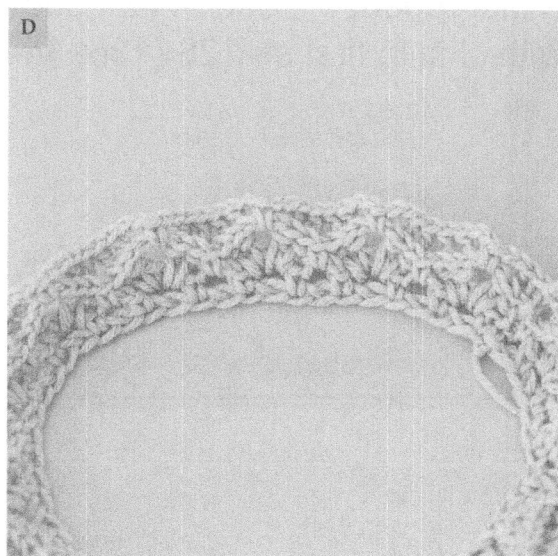

Rnd 4 (RS): ch1, dc in first and in each next st and 2dc in each ch2sp to end, for size 0–6m work 3dc in one ch2sp twice to increase by 2sts; for size 6–12m work 3dc in one ch2sp once to increase by 1st; for size 3–4y work 1dc in one ch2sp once to decrease by 1st, join with sl st in first st; 128 (136, 144, 152) sts E

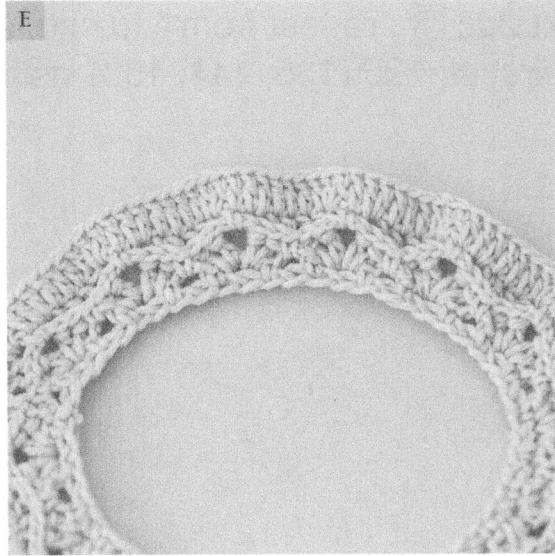

Rnd 5 (RS): ch1, dc in first and in each of next 2sts, *ch1, skip next st, bo in next st, ch1, skip next st, dc in each of next 5sts F ; repeat from * to end, but in last repeat instead of last 5dc work dc in each of next 2sts and join with sl st in first st; 128 (136, 144, 152) sts G

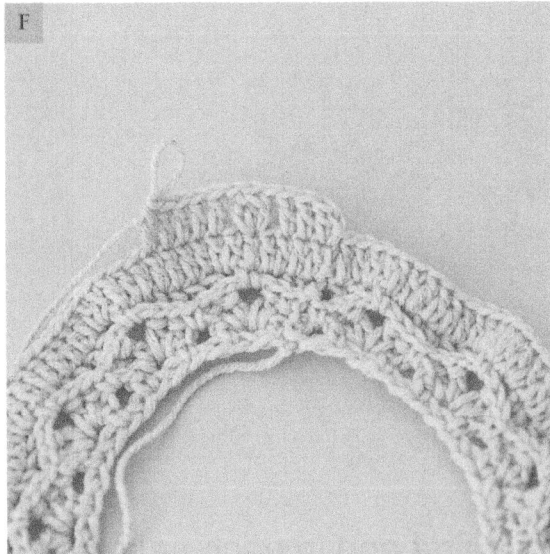

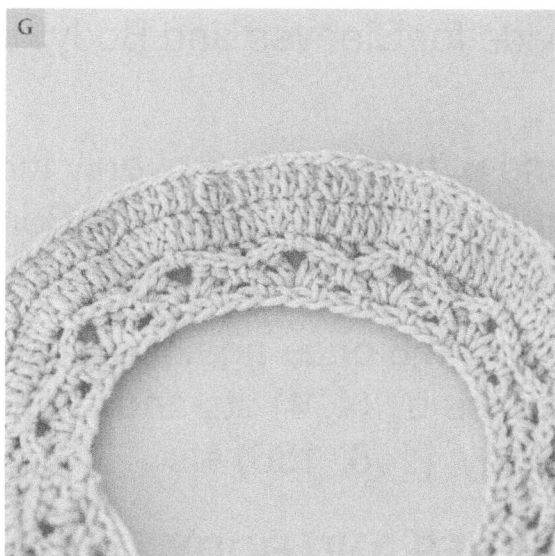

Rnd 6 (RS): ch1, dc in first and in each next st, dc in each ch1sp to end, join with sl st in first st; 128 (136, 144, 152) sts [H]

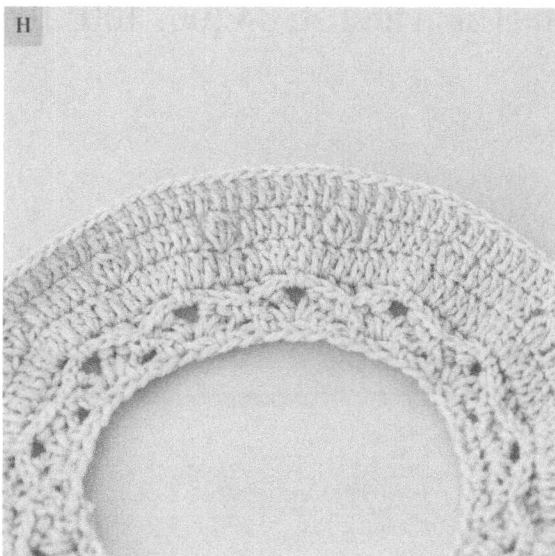

Rnd 7 (RS): ch1, bo in first st, *ch1, skip next st, dc in each of next 5sts, ch1, skip next st, bo in next st; repeat from * to last 7sts, ch1, skip next st, dc in each of next 5sts, ch1, skip last st, join with sl st in first st; 128 (136, 144, 152) sts including all chs

Rnd 8 (RS): ch1, dc in first and in each next st, dc in each ch1sp to end, join with sl st in first st; 128 (136, 144, 152) sts

For size 0–6m

Continue with Divide for Sleeves and Body.

For size 6–12m

Repeat Rnds 5 and 6, but in Rnd 6 evenly increase by 4sts and continue with Divide for Sleeves and Body; (140) sts

For sizes 1–2y and 3–4y

Repeat Rnds 5 through 8 once again, but in last repeat in Rnd 8 evenly increase by (4, 4) sts and continue with Divide for Sleeves and Body; (148, 156) sts

DIVIDE FOR SLEEVES AND BODY

Rnd 1 (RS): ch1, dc in first and in each of next 36 (41, 43, 45) sts, ch5 (6, 6, 7), skip next 27 (28, 30, 32) sts for sleeve, dc in each of next 37 (42, 44, 46) sts, ch5 (6, 6, 7), skip next 27 (28, 30, 32) sts for sleeve and join with sl st in first st; 84 (96, 100, 106) sts I

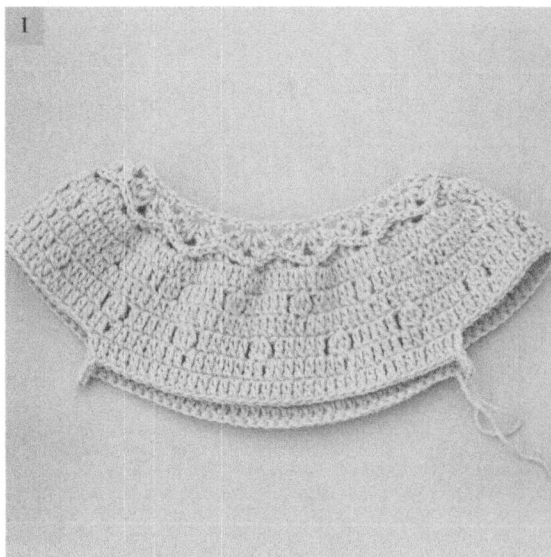

Rnd 2 (RS): ch1, sc in first st, *ch3, skip next st, sc in next st, ch3, skip next 2sts, sc in next st; repeat from * to end, in last repeat for size 0–6m you will have to skip 1st both times; for size 6–12m and 3–4y in last repeat you will have to skip 2sts both times; instead of last sc join with sl st in first st; 34 (38, 40, 42) ch3sp made J

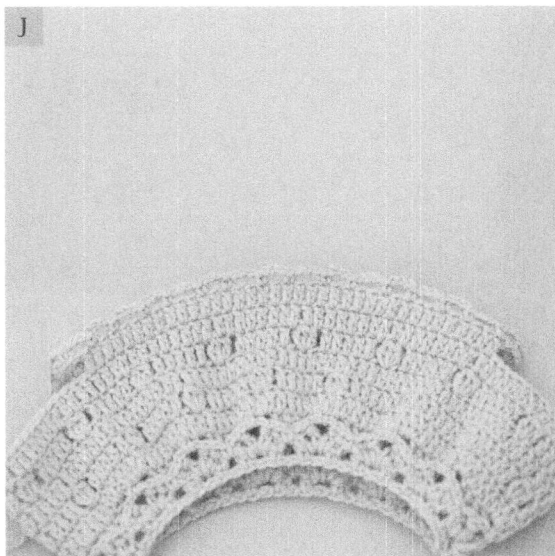

Rnd 3 (RS): ch1, skip first sc, *shell in next ch3sp, skip next sc, sc in next ch3sp, skip next sc; repeat from * to end and join with sl st in first st; 17 (19, 20, 21) shells made K

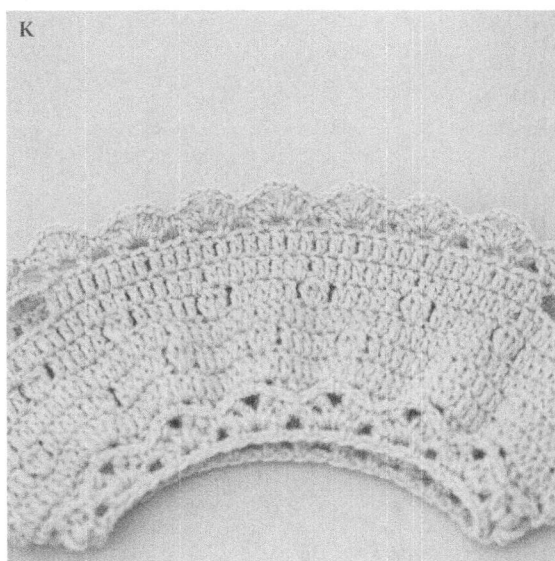

Rnd 4 (RS): ch1, BPdc around each of next 2dc, *ch2, sc in next ch3sp, ch2, BPdc around each of next 2dc, skip next sc, BPdc around each of next 2dc; repeat from * to end, after skipping last sc join with sl st in first st; 153 (171, 180, 189) sts including all ch L

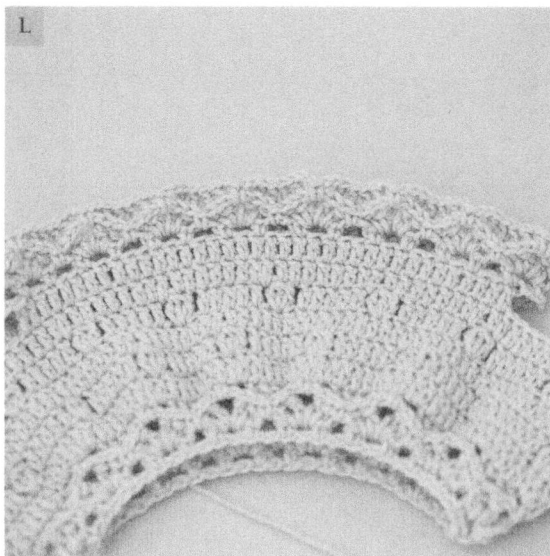

Rnd 5 (RS): ch1, dc in first and in next st, *dc in next ch2sp, dc in next sc, 2dc in next ch2sp, dc in each of next 4sts; repeat from * to end, join with sl st in first st; 136 (152, 160, 168) sts M

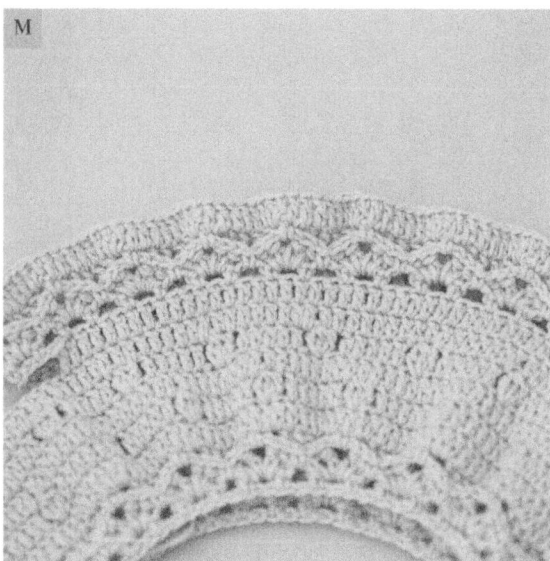

Rnd 6 (RS): ch1, dc in first and in each of next 2sts, *ch1, skip next st, bo in next st, ch1, skip next st, dc in each of next 5sts; repeat from * to end, but in last repeat instead of last 5dc work dc in each of next 2sts and join with sl st in first st; 136 (152, 160, 168) sts N

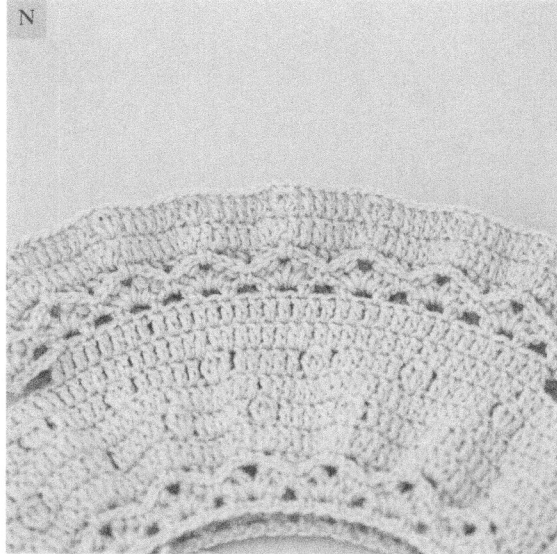

Rnd 7 (RS): ch1, dc in first and in each next st, dc in each ch1sp to end, join with sl st in first st; 136 (152, 160, 168) sts

Rnd 8 (RS): ch1, bo in first st, *ch1, skip next st, dc in each of next 5sts, ch1, skip next st, bo in next st; repeat from * to last 7sts, ch1, skip next st, dc in each of next 5sts, ch1, skip last st, join with sl st in first st; 136 (152, 160, 168) sts

Rnd 9 (RS): ch1, dc in first and in each next st, dc in each ch1sp to end, join with sl st in first st; 136 (152, 160, 168) sts

Repeat Rnds 6 through 9 – 2 (3, 5, 7) more times or until just short of desired length.

Repeat Rnds 6 and 7 once more and work Bottom Edging.

BOTTOM EDGING

Rnd 1 (RS): ch1, sc in first st, *ch3, skip next 2sts, sc in next st; repeat from * to last 3 (7, 3, 0) sts, for size 3–4y join with sl st in first st, for other sizes work ch3, skip next 1 (3, 1) sts, sc in next st, ch3, skip next 1 (3, 1) sts and join with sl st in first st; 46 (50, 54, 56) ch3sp made O

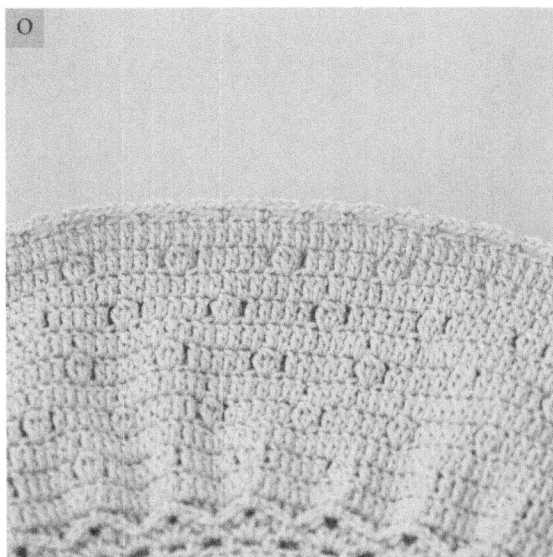

Rnd 2 (RS): ch1, skip first sc, *shell in next ch3sp, skip next sc, sc in next ch3sp, skip next sc; repeat from * to end and join with sl st in first st; 23 (25, 27, 28) shells made

Rnd 3 (RS): ch1, BPsc around each of next 2dc, *ch1, sc in next ch3sp, ch1, BPsc around each of next 2dc, skip next sc, BPsc around each of next 2dc; repeat from * to end, after skipping last sc join with sl st in first st; 161 (175, 189, 196) sts including all ch, fasten off P

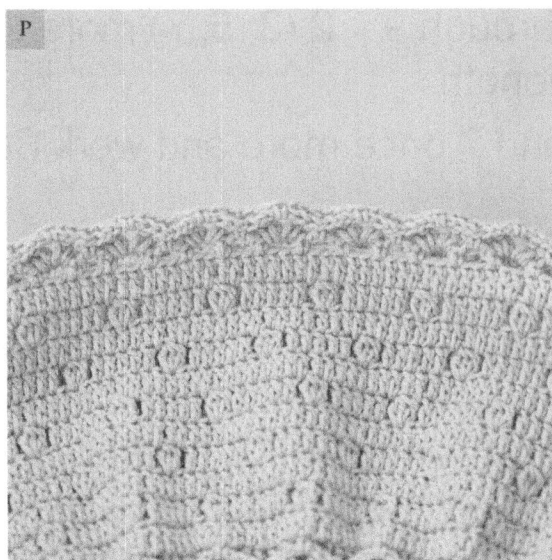

SLEEVES

On RS, join yarn into ch in the middle of the armhole

Rnd 1 (RS): ch1, dc in first st, [dc2tog] 3 times, work evenly 25 (27, 29, 31) dc around the armhole and [dc2tog] 3 times, join with sl st in first st; 32 (34, 36, 38) sts

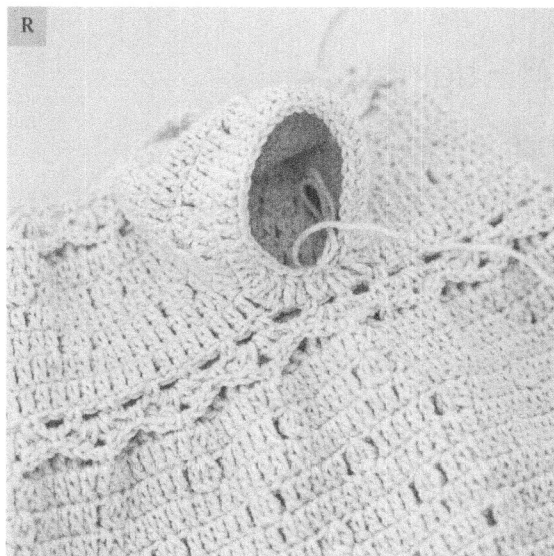

Rnd 2 (RS): ch1, BPdc around each next st to end, join with sl st in first st; 32 (34, 36, 38) sts

Rnd 3 (RS): ch1, dc in first and in each next st, join with sl st in first st; 32 (34, 36, 38) dc

Repeat Rnd 3 – 8 (10, 14, 16) more times, or until desired length, the Cuff Edging will add approximately 2cm/¾in.

For size 1–2y

Continue with Cuff Edging.

For sizes 0–6m and 3–4y

Last Rnd (RS): ch1, dc2tog, dc in each next st to last 2sts, dc2tog, join with sl st in first st; 30 (36) sts

Continue with Cuff Edging.

For size 6–12m

Last Rnd (RS): ch1, [dc2tog] twice, dc in each next st to last 4sts, [dc2tog] twice, join with sl st in first st; (30) sts

Continue with Cuff Edging.

Second Sleeve

Work in exactly the same way as first sleeve.

CUFF EDGING

Rnd 1 (RS): ch1, sc in first st, *ch3, skip next 2sts, sc in next st; repeat from * to end, but instead of last sc join with sl st in first st; 10 (10, 12, 12) ch3sp made

Rnd 2 (RS): ch1, skip first sc, *shell in next ch3sp, skip next sc, sc in next ch3sp, skip next sc; repeat from * to end and join with sl st in first st; 5 (5, 6, 6) shells made

Rnd 3 (RS): ch1, BPsc around each of next 2dc, *ch1, sc in next ch3sp, ch1, BPsc around each of next 2dc, skip next sc, BPsc around each of next 2dc; repeat from * to end, after skipping last sc join with sl st in first st; 35 (35, 42, 42) sts including all ch, fasten off
T

Second Cuff Edging

Work in exactly the same way on second sleeve.

FINISHING

Weave in all ends (see Finishing Techniques).

Try making a short sleeve version of the Sweet Dress for summer wear.

NORDIC SOCKS

~ ★★☆ ~

You work these socks starting at the toe. It's just a case of crocheting the toe and foot in a spiral, before switching to rows for the heel. The cuff is really easy to adjust so you can make it any length, for cozy baby toes or a toddler ankle sock. However you choose to style them, these socks will be perfect for both boys and girls.

SIZES AND MEASUREMENTS OF FINISHED GARMENT

Size	Foot length
0–6m	9cm/3½in
6–12m	10cm/4in
1–2y	12cm/4¾in
3–4y	14cm/5½in

GAUGE (TENSION)

24 sts and 26 rows in sc to measure 10 x 10cm (4 x 4in) using 2.5mm (C/2)hook (or size required to obtain gauge)

SPECIAL STITCHES

FPdc, BPdc, FPsc, puff, v-st (see Special Stitches)

MATERIALS

3 **LIGHT**

- 100 (140, 180, 200) meters or 109 (153, 196, 219) yards of any sock yarn

  Suggested yarn: Katia United Socks, 75% wool, 25% polyamide, shade 14, 25g (¾oz), 100m (109yd)
- 2.5mm (C/2) crochet hook (or size required to obtain gauge)
- 2 stitch markers

Pattern is written for size 0–6m, changes for 6–12m, 1–2y and 3–4y are in (…).

As these socks are worked in a spiral they might lean to one side, but after a wash and light blocking it will all even out.

Unless otherwise instructed, do not join your rounds.

TOE

Rnd 1 (RS): ch6, sc in 2nd ch from hook, sc in each of next 3ch, 3sc in last ch, rotating to work back along opposite side of the ch, sc in each of next 3ch, 2sc in remaining loop of first ch (12 sts) A

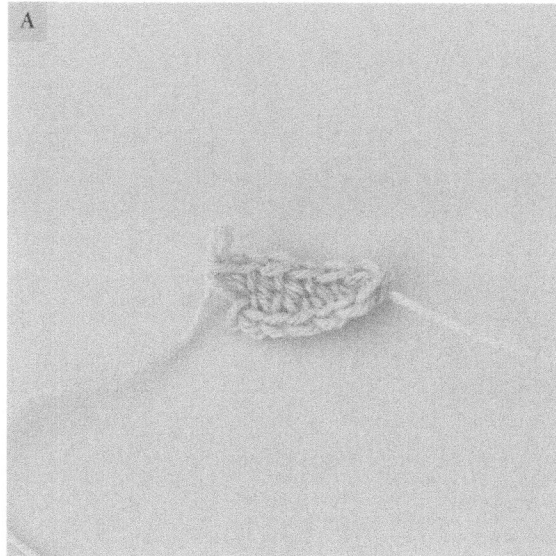

Rnd 2 (RS): 2sc in first st, sc in each of next 3sts, 2sc in next st, sc in next st and place a marker, 2sc in next st, sc in each of next 3sts, 2sc in next st, sc in next st and place a marker (16 sts) B

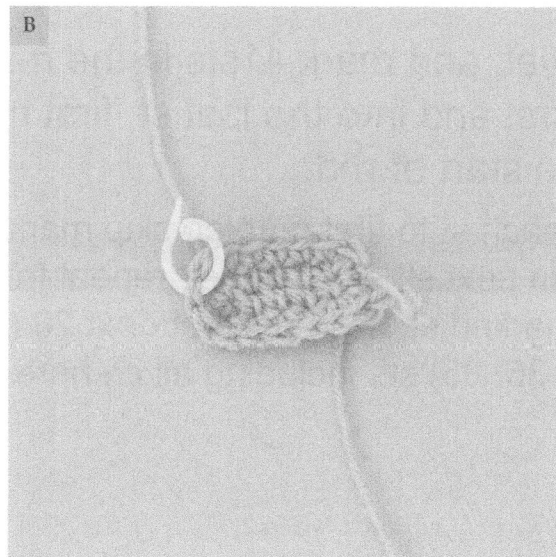

Rnd 3 (RS): 2sc in next st, *sc in each st to last st before marker, 2sc in next st, sc in marked st, move marker up**, 2sc in next st, repeat from * to ** once more (20 sts) C

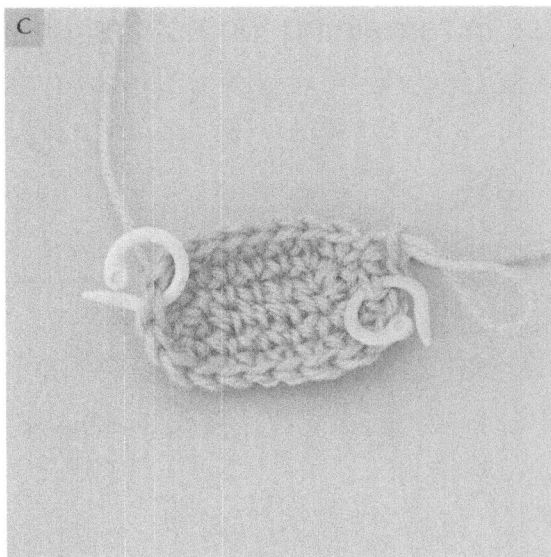

Repeat Rnd 3 working in spiral, and work 2sc in one st before and after each marker, until you have 31 (31, 35, 35) sts, remove markers.

FOOT

Lay the toe part flat, and mark 11sts in the middle, place marker into the first and into the last st, first marker (white one) will mark the start of rnd.

Rnd 1 (RS): sc in each st to first marker, skip marked st, *v-st in next st, skip next st, sc in next st, skip next st; repeat from * once more, v-st in next st, skip marked st, sc in each of next 20 (20, 24, 24) sc to end of rnd; 31 (31, 35, 35) sts including all ch here and throughout D

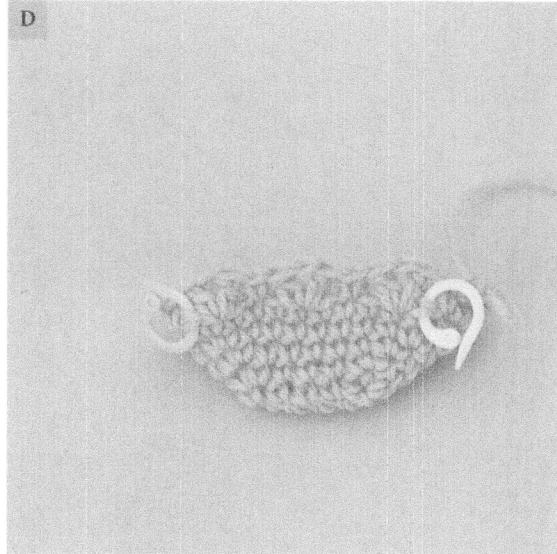

Rnd 2 (RS): ch1, skip next dc, *sc in next ch1sp, skip next dc, v-st in next sc, skip next dc; repeat from * once more, sc in next ch1sp, ch1, skip next dc, sc in each of next 20 (20, 24, 24) sc to end of rnd; 31 (31, 35, 35) sts

Rnd 3 (RS): skip ch1, *v-st in next sc, skip next dc, sc in next ch1sp, skip next dc; repeat from * once more, v-st in next sc, skip next ch1, sc in each of next 20 (20, 24, 24) sc to end of rnd; 31 (31, 35, 35) sts

Repeat Rnds 2 and 3 – 3 (4, 5, 6) more times or until desired length (to make them fit well I would suggest to try them on to see if it's time to make a heel or an extra repeat is necessary) E , continue with Heel.

HEEL

Turn and work on WS.

Row 1 (WS): ch1, FPsc around each of next 19 (19, 23, 23) sc, sc in last sc leaving the rest of the sts unworked, turn; 20 (20, 24, 24) sts

Row 2 (RS): ch1, sc in first and in each next st to end, turn; 20 (20, 24, 24) sts

Row 3 (WS): ch1, FPsc around first and each next st to end, sc in last st, turn 20 (20, 24, 24) sts

Repeat Rows 2 and 3 – 2 (3, 4, 5) more times F

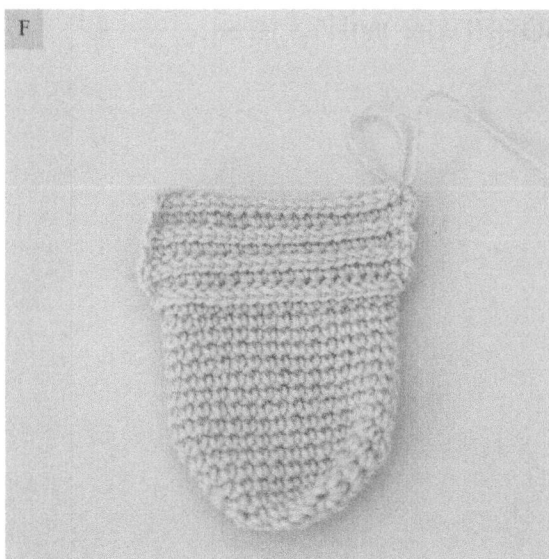

Fold the heel in half, RS together and work sl st across though both layers G , fasten off.

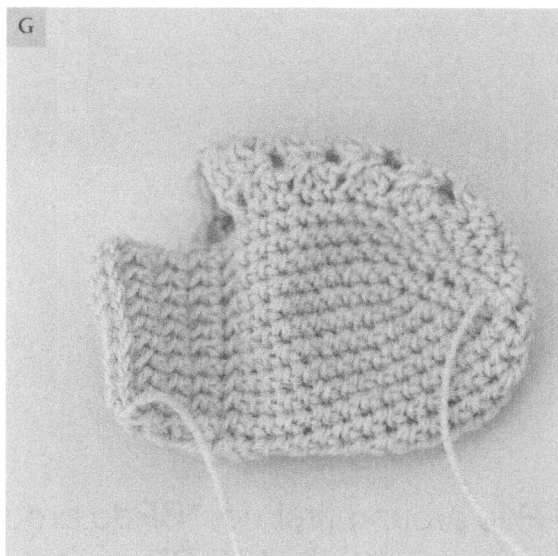

Turn the sock right side out and work Cuff.

CUFF

For some rnds you have to turn and work on WS.

Join yarn in the middle of the heel and work

Rnd 1 (RS): ch1, but pull it to the height of dc here and throughout, dc in first st and work evenly 29 (31, 33, 35) dc around the cuff, across the front work in each st and in each ch1sp, join with sl st in first st; 30 (32, 34, 36) sts H

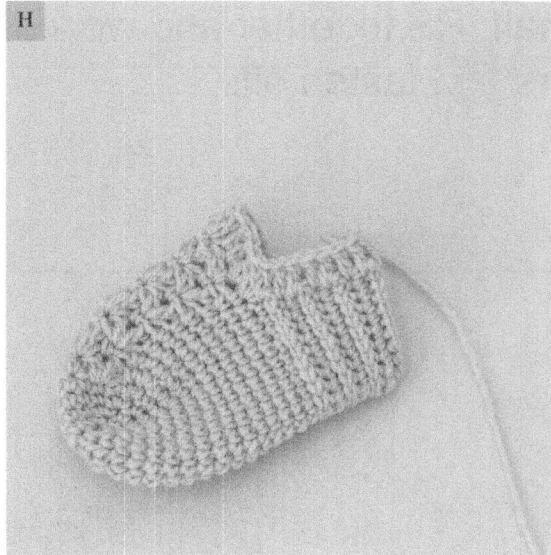

Rnd 2 (RS): ch1, FPdc around first dc, *BPdc around next dc, FPdc around next dc; repeat from * to last st, BPdc around next dc, join with sl st in first st, turn; 30 (32, 34, 36) sts I

Rnd 3 (WS): ch1, sc in first st, *puff in next st, sc in next st; repeat from * to last st, puff in next st and join with sl st in first st, turn; 30 (32, 34, 36) sts J

Rnd 4 (RS): ch1, dc in first st and in each next st to end, join with sl st in first st; 30 (32, 34, 36) sts K

Rnd 5 (RS): ch1, FPdc around first dc, *BPdc around next dc, FPdc around next dc; repeat from * to last st, BPdc around next dc, join with sl st in first st; 30 (32, 34, 36) sts

Repeat Rnds 3 through 5 once more or until desired length.

Last Rnd (RS): ch1, FPdc around first FPdc, *BPdc around next BPdc, FPdc around next FPdc; repeat from * to last st, BPdc around next BPdc, join with sl st in first st; 30 (32, 34, 36) sts L

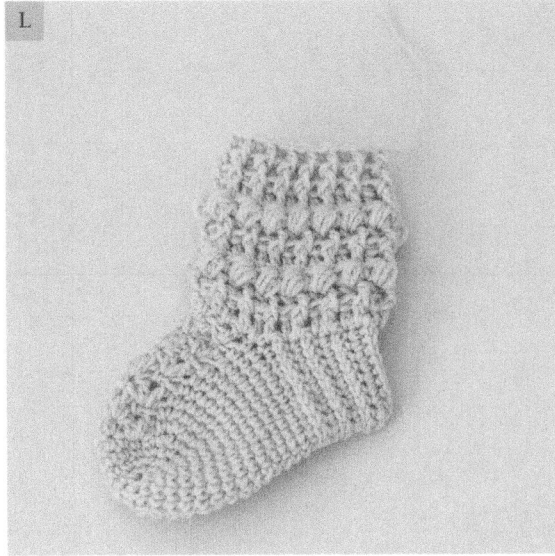

Make second sock in exactly the same way.

FINISHING

Weave in all ends (see Finishing Techniques).

SAGE TROUSERS

~ ★★☆ ~

Crochet trousers can be very comfortable – honestly! It's just important to work them quite loosely, so that the fabric turns out with plenty of stretch. The Sage Trousers are worked from the waist down and then divided for the legs, with the waist ribbing worked at the end. The texture is extremely soft and stretchy.

SIZES AND MEASUREMENTS OF FINISHED GARMENT

Size	Waist *	Length
0–6m	40cm/15¾in	30cm/11¾in
6–12m	42cm/16½in	35cm/13¾in
1–2y	45cm/17¾in	40cm/15¾in
3–4y	48cm/19in	45cm/17¾in

* suggested negative ease approximately 3–4cm (1⅛–1½in)

GAUGE (TENSION)

18 sts and 9 rows in dc to measure 10 x 10cm (4 x 4in), using 3.5mm (E/4)hook (or size required to obtain gauge)

SPECIAL STITCHES

FPdc, BPdc, BPdc2tog (see Special Stitches)

MATERIALS

3 LIGHT

- 242 (330, 385, 440) meters or 264 (360, 420, 480) yards of any DK weight or light worsted weight yarn
  Suggested yarn: Lana Gatto Harmony Free DK, 100% fine merino wool, shade 14012, 50g (1¾oz), 110m (120yd)
- 3.5mm (E/4) crochet hook (or size required to obtain gauge)

Pattern is written for size 0–6m, changes for 6–12m, 1–2y and 3–4y are in (…).

Ch1 at the beginning of each round doesn't count as a stitch.

BODY

Foundation chain: ch70 (75, 80, 85) and join with sl st in first ch

Rnd 1 (RS): ch1 pull it to the height of dc here and throughout where next st is dc, dc in first ch and in each next ch, join with sl st in first st; 70 (75, 80, 85) sts

Rnd 2 (RS): ch1, sc in first st, *ch3, skip next st, sc in next st, ch3, skip next 2sts, sc in next st; repeat from * to end, but in last repeat instead of last sc join with sl st in first st; 28 (30, 32, 34) sc and 28 (30, 32, 34) ch3sp made

Rnd 3 (RS): ch1, 2dc in first sc, *skip next ch3, 3dc in next sc; repeat from * to end, but in last repeat instead of last 3dc work dc in same st as first 2dc and join with sl st in first st; 84 (90, 96, 102) sts

Rnd 4 (RS): ch1, sc in first st, *ch3, skip next 2sts, sc in next st; repeat from * to end, but in last repeat instead of last sc join with sl st in first st; 28 (30, 32, 34) sc and 28 (30, 32, 34) ch3sp made

Repeat Rnds 3 and 4 – 6 (7, 7, 8) more times.

Repeat Rnd 3 once more, continue with Divide for Legs A

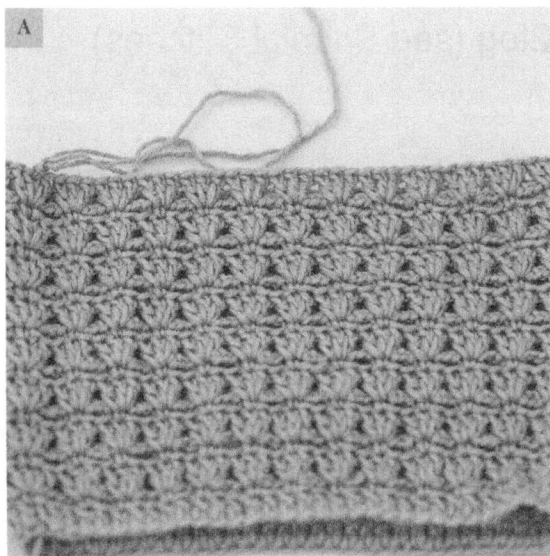

DIVIDE FOR LEGS

First Leg

Rnd 1 (RS): ch1, sc in first st, *ch3, skip next 2sts, sc in next st; repeat from * 13 (14, 15, 16) more times, ch3, join with sl st in first st; 15 (16, 17, 18) sc and 15 (16, 17, 18) ch3sp made B

Rnd 2 (RS): ch1, 2dc in first sc, *skip next ch3, 3dc in next sc; repeat from * 13 (14, 15, 16) more times, dc in each of next 3ch of crotch, dc in same st as first 2dc and join with sl st in first st; 48 (51, 54, 57) sts C

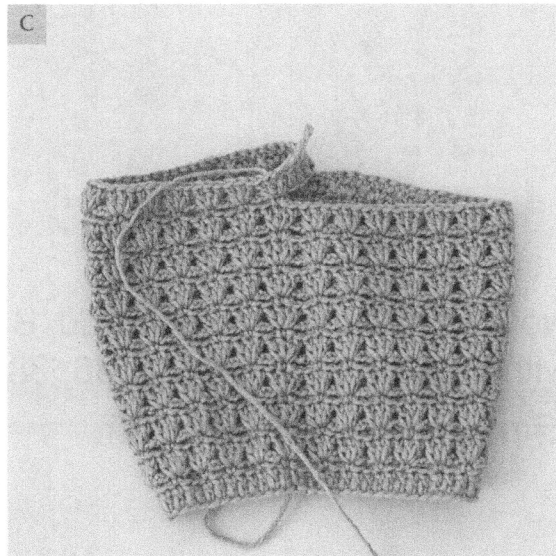

Rnd 3 (RS): ch1, sc in first st, *ch3, skip next 2sts, sc in next st; repeat from * to end, but in last repeat instead of last sc join with sl st in first st; 16 (17, 18, 19) sc and 16 (17, 18, 19) ch3sp made

Rnd 4 (RS): ch1, 2dc in first sc, *skip next ch3, 3dc in next sc; repeat from * to end, but in last repeat instead of last 3dc work dc in same st as first 2dc and join with sl st in first st; 48 (51, 54, 57) sts

Repeat Rnds 3 and 4 – 6 (10, 15, 18) more times or until desired length and continue with Cuff.

CUFF

Rnd 1 (RS): ch1, FPdc around first dc, *BPdc2tog, FPdc around next dc; repeat from * to end, but in last repeat instead of last FPdc join with sl st in first st; 32 (34, 36, 38) sts D

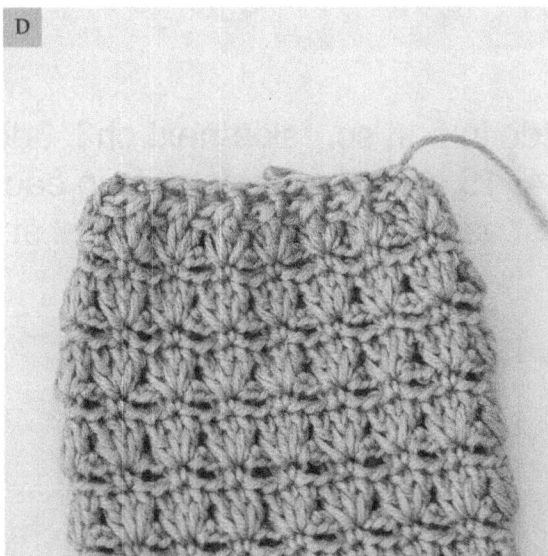

Rnd 2 (RS): ch1, work FPdc around each FPdc, BPdc around each BPdc to end, join with sl st in first st; 32 (34, 36, 38) sts

Repeat Rnd 2 – 3 more times, fasten off.

Second Leg

Join yarn into the base of first 3dc of the First Leg before the crotch and work:

Rnd 1 (RS): ch1, sc in first st, sc in remaining loop of each of next 3ch worked for crotch E , sc in next dc (the one in the middle of next 3dc), *ch3, skip next 2sts, sc in next st; repeat from * 13 (14, 15, 16) more times, join with sl st in first st; 19 (20, 21, 22) sc and 14 (15, 16, 17) ch3sp made F

Rnd 2 (RS): ch1, 2dc in first sc, dc in each of next 3sc, 3dc in next sc, *skip next ch3, 3dc in next sc; repeat from * 12 (13, 14, 15) more times, dc in next sc, join with sl st in first st; 48 (51, 54, 57) sts G

Rnd 3 (RS): ch1, sc in first st, *ch3, skip next 2sts, sc in next st; repeat from * to end, but in last repeat instead of last sc join with sl st in first st; 16 (17, 18, 19) sc and 16 (17, 18, 19) ch3sp made

Rnd 4 (RS): ch1, 2dc in first sc, *skip next ch3, 3dc in next sc; repeat from * to end, but in last repeat instead of last 3dc work dc in same st as first 2dc and join with sl st in first st; 48 (51, 54, 57) sts

Repeat Rnds 3 and 4 – 6 (10, 15, 18) more times or until desired length and continue with Cuff as for First Leg.

WAIST

Join yarn into the first dc of the waist and work:

Rnd 1 (RS): ch1, FPdc around first dc, *BPdc around next dc, FPdc around next dc* H ; repeat from * to last 1 (2, 1, 2) sts, for sizes 0–6m and 1–2y work BPdc around last st, for sizes 6–12m and 3–4y work BPdc2tog around 2 last sts, join with sl st in first FPdc; 70 (74, 80, 84) sts

Rnd 2 (RS): ch1, work FPdc around each FPdc, BPdc around each BPdc to end, join with sl st in first st; 70 (74, 80, 84) sts

Repeat Rnd 2 – 3 more times, fasten off

FINISHING

Weave in all ends (see Finishing Techniques).

SPRING ROMPER

~ ★★☆ ~

Rompers are so practical and versatile that you may find you want to make several – in different yarn weights – for all the seasons. Pop one on over a cozy onesie in winter, or with nothing but a diaper (nappy) underneath for hot summer days. Choose a cotton/wool blend yarn to ensure you achieve a stretchy and comfortable garment.

SIZES AND MEASUREMENTS OF FINISHED GARMENT

Size	Chest	Length from shoulders to bottom
0–6m	41cm/16¼in	35cm/13¾in
6–12m	44cm/17¼in	41cm/16in
12–18m	49cm/19¼in	43cm/17in
18–24m	51cm/20in	45cm/17¾in

GAUGE (TENSION)

19 sts and 10 rows in dc to measure 10 x 10cm (4 x 4in), using 3.5mm (E/4)hook (or size required to obtain gauge)

SPECIAL STITCHES

FPdc, BPdc, v-st (see Special Stitches)

MATERIALS

3 LIGHT

- 280 (350, 420, 500) meters or 306 (383, 460, 547) yards of any DK weight or light worsted weight yarn
  Suggested yarn: Laines du Nord Spring Wool, 50% wool, 50% cotton, shade 6, 50g (1¾oz), 140m (153yd)
- 3.5mm (E/4) crochet hook (or size required to obtain gauge)
- 2 stitch markers
- 2 buttons, approximately 2cm (¾in) diameter

Pattern is written for size 0–6m, changes for 6–12m, 12–18m and 18–24m are in (…).

Ch1 at the beginning of each round doesn't count as a stitch.

FRONT

Row 1 (RS): ch30 (32, 36, 38), sc in 2nd ch from hook and in each next ch, turn; 29 (31, 35, 37) sc

Row 2 (WS): ch1, (sc, dc) in first st, *skip next st, (sc, dc) in next st A ; repeat from * to last 2sts, skip next st, sc in last st, turn; 29 (31, 35, 37) sts

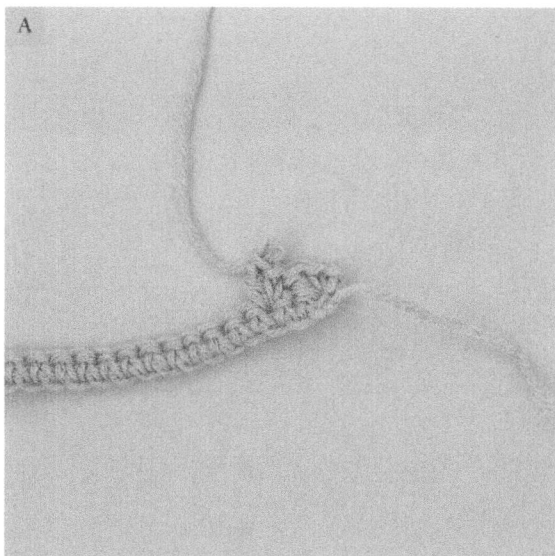

Row 3 (RS): ch1, (sc, dc) in back loop of first st B , *skip next st, (sc, dc) in back loop of next st C ; repeat from * to last 2sts, skip next st, sc in last st, turn; 29 (31, 35, 37) sts D

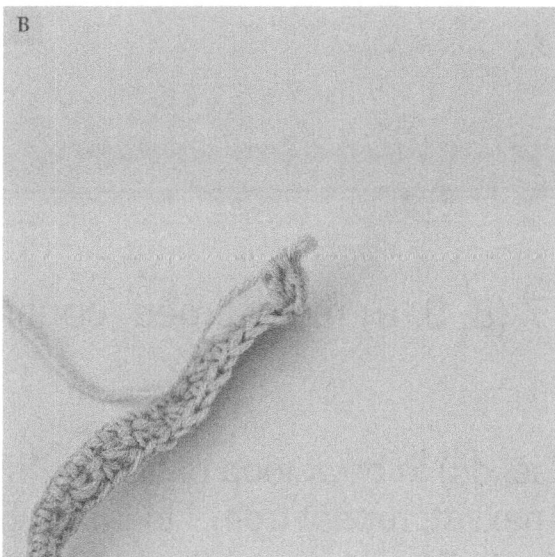

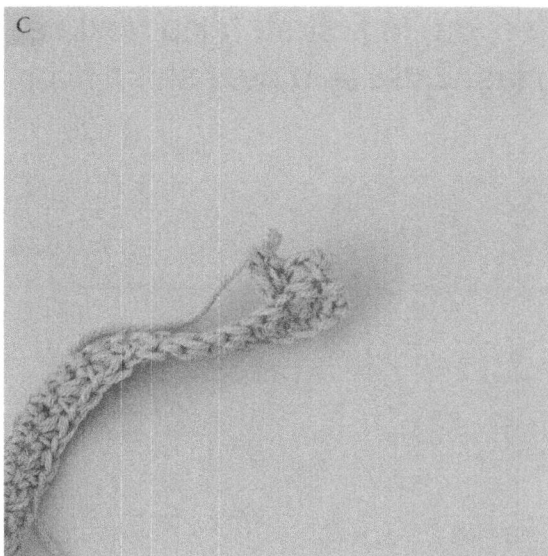

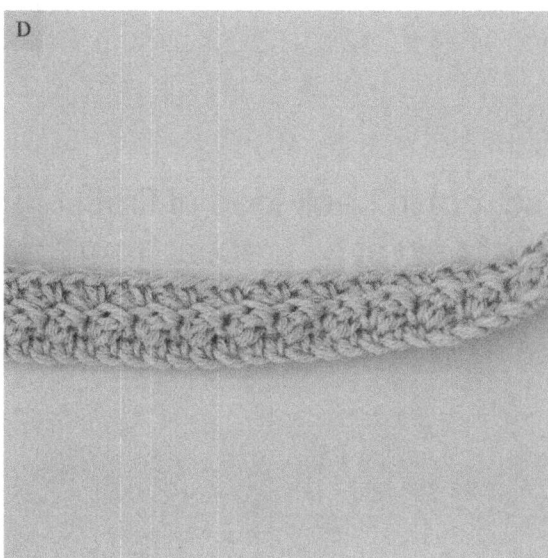

Repeat Row 3 – 7 (8, 9, 9) more times, continue with Body.

BODY

Rnd 1 (RS): ch1, (sc, dc) in back loop of first st, *skip next st, (sc, dc) in back loop of next st; repeat from * to last 2sts, skip next st, sc in last st, ch 39 (45, 49, 51) and join with sl st in first st; 68 (76, 84, 88) sts E

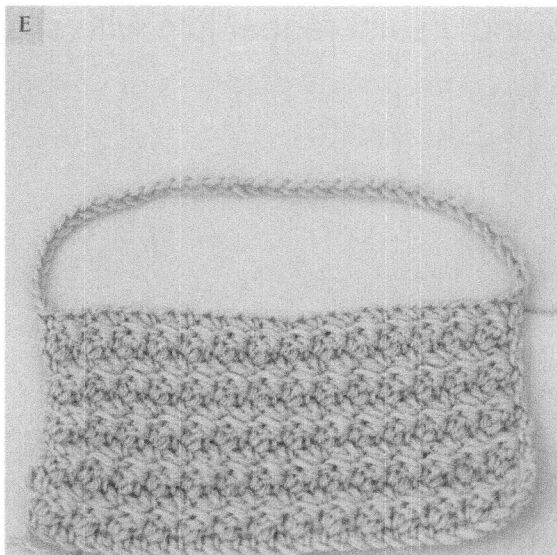

Rnd 2 (RS): working in both loops, ch1, dc in first st, dc in each of next 13 (14, 16, 17) sts, v-st in next st, dc in each of next 33 (37, 41, 43) sts, v-st in next st, dc in each of next 19 (22, 24, 25) sts and join with sl st in first st; 72 (80, 88, 92) sts including all chs **F**

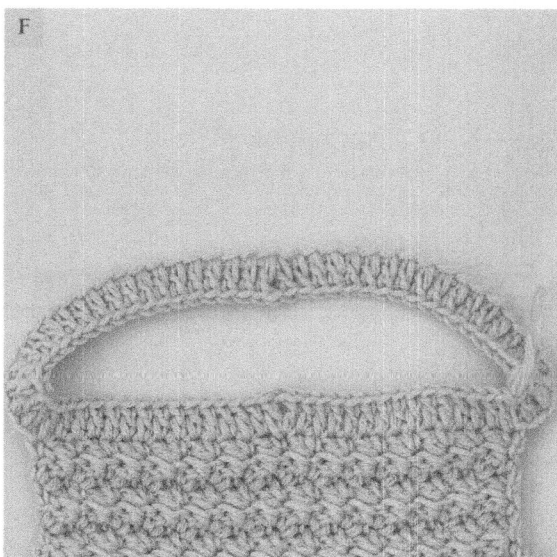

For sizes 0–6m and 18–24m

Rnd 3 (RS): ch1, FPdc around first dc, *BPdc around next dc, FPdc around next dc; repeat from * to ch1sp, v-st in ch1sp, FPdc around next dc **G** , repeat from * to ch1sp, v-st in ch1sp, FPdc around next dc, repeat from * to end, in last repeat join with sl st in first st; 76 (96) sts H

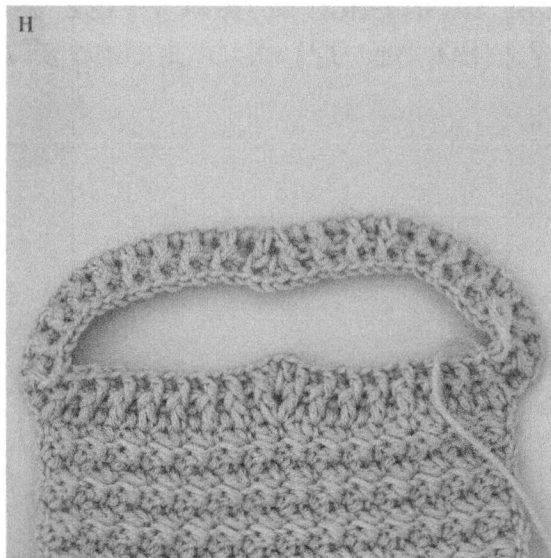

For sizes 6–12m and 12–18m

Rnd 3 (RS): ch1, BPdc around first st, *FPdc around next st, BPdc around next st; repeat from * to last st before ch1sp, FPdc around next st, v-st in ch1sp G , repeat from * to last st before ch1sp, FPdc around next st, v-st in ch1sp, repeat from * to end, in last repeat join with sl st in first st; (84, 92) sts H

For all sizes

Rnd 4 (RS): ch1, dc in first and in each next st to ch1sp, v-st in ch1sp, dc in each next st to ch1sp, v-st in ch1sp, dc in each st to end, join with sl st in first st; 80 (88, 96, 100) sts **I**

Rnd 5 (RS): repeat Rnd 4; 84 (92, 100, 104) sts
Rnd 6 (RS): repeat Rnd 4; 88 (96, 104, 108) sts **J**

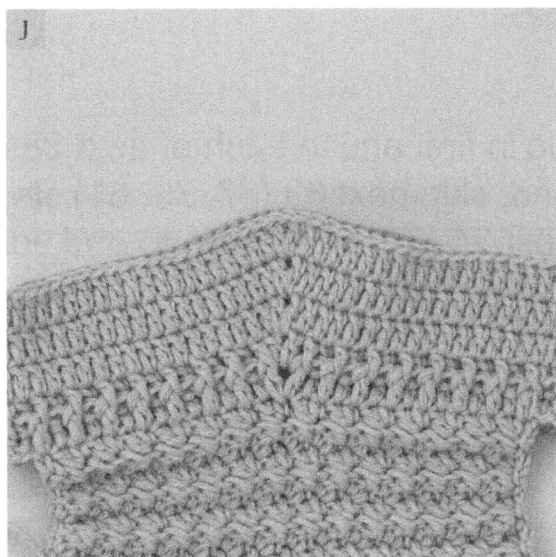

For sizes 0–6m and 18–24m

Rnd 7 (RS): ch1, FPdc around first dc, *BPdc around next dc, FPdc around next dc; repeat from * to ch1sp, v-st in ch1sp, FPdc around next dc, repeat from * to ch1sp, v-st in ch1sp, FPdc around next dc, repeat from * to end, in last repeat join with sl st in first st; 92 (112) sts

For sizes 6–12m and 12–18m

Rnd 7 (RS): ch1, BPdc around first dc, *FPdc around next dc, BPdc around next dc; repeat from * to last st before ch1sp, FPdc around next dc, v-st in ch1sp, repeat from * to last st before ch1sp, FPdc around next dc, v-st in ch1sp, repeat from * to end, in last repeat join with sl st in first st; (100, 108) sts

For all sizes

Repeat Rnds 4 through 7 – 2 (2, 3, 3) more times, in each rnd you will be increasing by 4sts; 124 (132, 156, 160) sts

Last Rnd (RS): ch1, dc in first and in each next st to ch1sp, v-st in ch1sp, dc in each next st to next ch1sp, v-st in ch1sp, dc in each st to end, join with sl st in first st; 128 (136, 160, 164) sts. Continue with Divide for Legs.

DIVIDE FOR LEGS

First Leg

Rnd 1 (RS): ch1, dc in first and in each of next 28 (29, 34, 36) sts, dc in next ch1sp, ch5, skip next 63 (67, 79, 81) sts, dc in next ch1sp K , dc in each of next 34 (37, 44, 44) sts to end, join with sl st in first st; 70 (74, 86, 88) sts including all chs L

Rnd 2 (RS): ch1, dc in first and in each next st including ch5 of crotch, join with sl st in first st; 70 (74, 86, 88) sts

Rnd 3 (RS): ch1, FPdc around first dc, *BPdc2tog around next 2dc, FPdc around next dc; repeat from * to last 3 (1, 1, 3) sts, BPdc around next st, for sizes 6–12m and 12–18m join with sl st in first st, for sizes 0–6m and 18–24m work FPdc around next st, BPdc around next st and join with sl st in first st; 48 (50, 58, 60) sts

Rnds 4–5 (RS): ch1, FPdc around each next FPdc and BPdc around each next BPdc to end, join with sl st in first st, fasten off; 48 (50, 58,

60) sts M

Crotch

Join yarn into ch1sp at the crotch N , dc in each remaining loop of ch5 worked for crotch O P , sl st in next ch1sp Q , continue with Second Leg.

333

Second Leg

Rnd 1 (RS): ch1, dc in same ch1sp as sl st, dc in each of next 63 (67, 79, 81) sts, dc in next ch1sp, dc in each dc of crotch and join with sl st in first st; 70 (74, 86, 88) sts R

Repeat Rnds 2 through 5 as for First Leg, fasten off S

STRAPS

First Strap

On RS, with back of romper facing you, skip 10 (11, 13, 14) sts from the left side of Front and join yarn into next st (it has to be BPdc).

Row 1 (RS): ch1, hdc in same st where joined, (FPdc around next FPdc, BPdc around next BPdc) twice, FPdc around next FPdc, hdc in next st, turn; 7 sts T

Row 2 (WS): ch1, hdc in first st, (BPdc around next BPdc, FPdc around next FPdc) twice, BPdc around next BPdc, hdc in next st, turn; 7 sts

Row 3 (RS): ch1, hdc in first st, (FPdc around next FPdc, BPdc around next BPdc) twice, FPdc around next FPdc, hdc in next st, turn; 7 sts

Repeat Rows 2 and 3 – 7 (8, 8, 9) more times or until desired length.

Repeat Row 2 once more and work Next Row.

Next Row (RS): ch1, hdc in first st, FPdc around next FPdc, ch1, skip next 3sts, FPdc around next FPdc, hdc in next st, turn; 5 sts

Last Row (WS): ch1, sc in first and in each next st including ch1sp, fasten off; 5 sts U

Second Strap

On RS, skip 5 (7, 9, 9) sts from the First Strap and join yarn into next st (it has to be BPdc) and work in exact same way as First Strap V W

FINISHING

Weave in all ends (see Finishing Techniques).

Sew on buttons opposite the buttonholes (sse Finishing Techniques).

A cotton/wool blend yarn is a lovely choice for this romper.

TRUFFLE DRESS

~ ★⯪☆ ~

Fun and easy to make, the Truffle Dress is likely to become your 'go to' dress pattern. It's so versatile! It can be dressed up or down, worn as an everyday dress or as a special occasion outfit. The length is easy to adjust too, so you can make it really short as a top, or long as a gown. And it would look wonderful in any number of light and bright colors!

SIZES AND MEASUREMENTS OF FINISHED GARMENT

Size	Chest	Length from shoulders to bottom
0–6m	46cm/18¼in	37cm/14½in
6–12m	50cm/19¾in	40cm/15¾in
1–2y	60cm/23½in	43cm/17in
3–4y	66cm/26in	46cm/18¼in

GAUGE (TENSION)

21 sts and 10 rows in dc to measure 10 x 10cm (4 x 4in) using 3.5mm (E/4)hook (or size required to obtain gauge)

SPECIAL STITCHES

FPdc, BPdc, working in third loop of hdc, v-st, dc2tog, picot, shell (Truffle Dress shell) (see Special Stitches)

MATERIALS

3 LIGHT

- 320 (480, 640, 800) meters or 350 (525, 700, 885) yards of any sport weight yarn
  Suggested yarn: Drops Safran, 100% cotton, shade 64, 50g (1¾oz), 160m (174yd)
- 3.5mm (E/4) crochet hook (or size required to obtain gauge)
- 2 stitch markers

Pattern is written for size 0–6m, changes for 6–12m, 1–2y and 3–4y are in (…).

Ch1 at the beginning of each round or row doesn't count as a stitch.

COLLAR

Foundation chain: work loosely, ch 72 (76, 80, 88), join with sl st in first ch.

Rnd 1: ch1, but pull it to the height of dc here and throughout where next st is dc, 2dc in first ch, dc in each of next 17 (18, 19, 21) ch, * (2dc, ch2, 2dc) in next ch, dc in each of next 17 (18, 19, 21) ch; repeat from * 2 more times, 2dc in same ch as first 2dc, ch2, join with sl st in first st; 92 (96, 100, 108) sts including all ch2 A

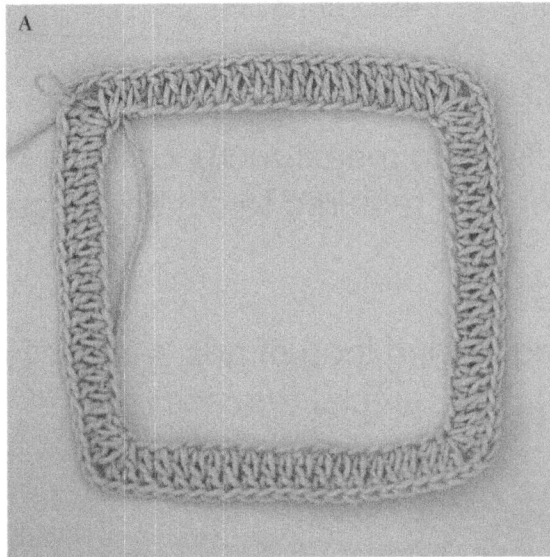

Rnd 2: ch1, but pull it to the height of hdc, 2hdc in ch2sp to the right B , *hdc in each dc to next ch2sp, 3hdc in next ch2sp; repeat from * 3 more times, but in last repeat work hdc in same ch2sp as first 2hdc and join with sl st in first st; 96 (100, 104, 112) sts C

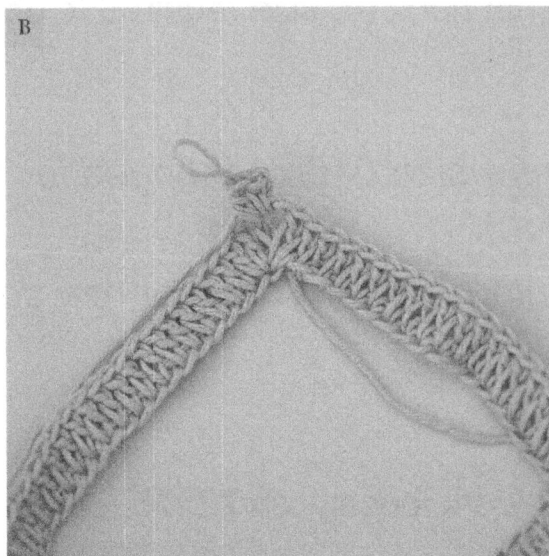

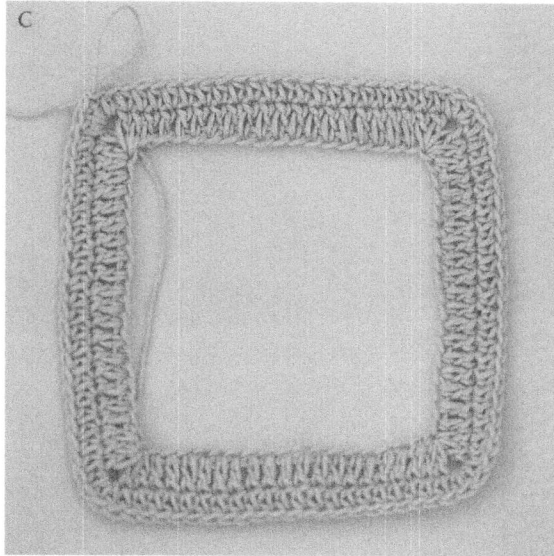

Rnd 3: working in third loop of each hdc, ch1, 2dc in first st D , *dc in each of next 23 (24, 25, 27) sts, (2dc, ch2, 2dc) in next st; repeat from * 3 more times, but in last repeat work (2dc, ch2) in same st as first 2dc and join with sl st in first st; 116 (120, 124, 132) sts including all ch2 E

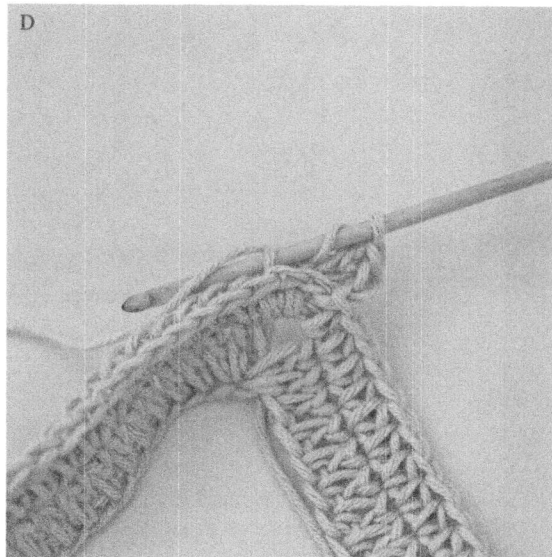

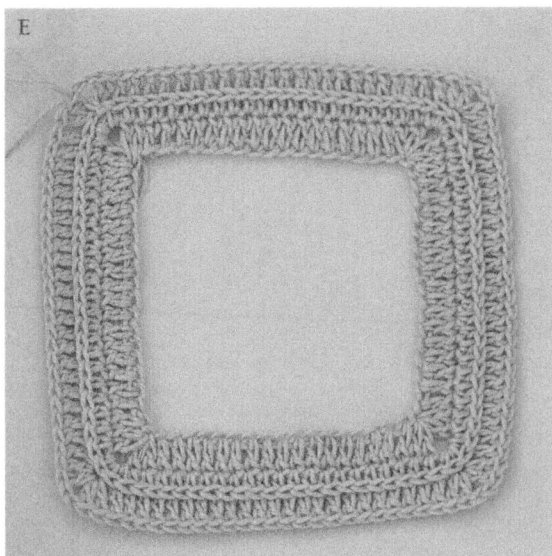

Rnd 4: ch1, 3dc in ch2sp to the right, *dc in each st to next ch2sp, 5dc in next ch2sp; repeat from * 3 more times, but in last repeat work 2dc in same ch2sp as first 3dc and join with sl st in first st; 128 (132, 136, 144) sts, fasten off F

FRONT

Fold the collar in half to shape V, joining line on the shoulder, RS facing, mark central 33 (35, 37, 41) sts of the collar as shown in G and join yarn into the first marked st.

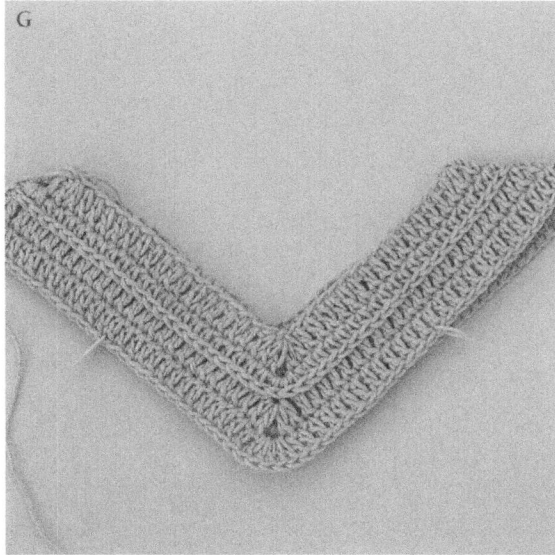

Row 1 (RS): ch4 (counts as first tr), tr in each of next 6 (7, 8, 10) sts, dc in each of next 6sts, sc in each of next 7sts, dc in each of next 6sts, tr in each of next 7 (8, 9, 11) sts, turn; 33 (35, 37, 41) sts H

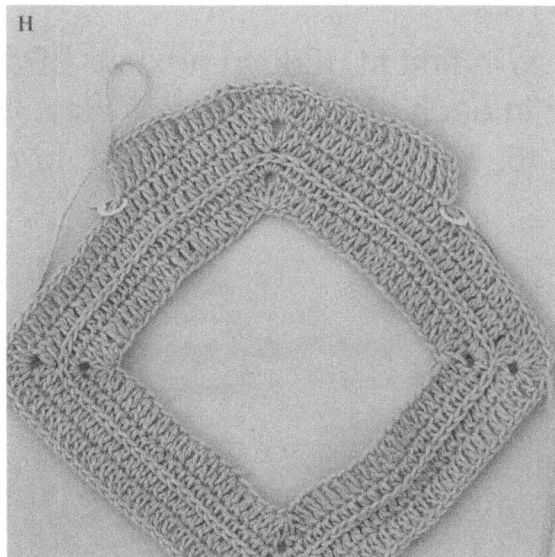

Row 2 (WS): ch1, dc in first st, [FPdc around next st, BPdc around next st] 6 (6, 7, 8) times, sc in each of next 7 (9, 7, 7) sts, [BPdc around next st, FPdc around next st] 6 (6, 7, 8) times, dc in last st, turn; 33 (35, 37, 41) sts I

Row 3 (RS): ch1, dc in first st, [BPdc around next st, FPdc around next st] 6 (6, 7, 8) times, sc in each of next 7 (9, 7, 7) sts, [FPdc around next st, BPdc around next st] 6 (6, 7, 8) times, dc in last st, turn; 33 (35, 37, 41) sts

Row 4 (WS): ch1, dc in first st, [2dc in next st, BPdc around next st] 6 (6, 7, 8) times, sc in each of next 7 (9, 7, 7) sts, [BPdc around next st, 2dc in next st] 6 (6, 7, 8) times, dc in last st, turn; 45 (47, 51, 57) sts J

For sizes 0–6m and 6–12m

Fasten off and continue with Back.

For sizes 1–2y and 3–4y

Row 5 (RS): ch1, dc in first st, [dc in each of next 2sts, FPdc around next st] (7, 8) times, dc in each of next 7sts, [FPdc around next st, dc in each of next 2sts] (7, 8) times, dc in last st, turn; (51, 57) sts

Row 6 (WS): ch1, dc in first st, [2dc in next st, dc in next st, BPdc around next st] (7, 8) times, dc in each of next 7sts, [BPdc around next st, dc in next st, 2dc in next st] (7, 8) times, dc in last st, turn; (65, 73) sts, fasten off.

BACK

Work in exact same way as Front K , but don't fasten off, turn and work Skirt Part.

The Truffle Dress is easy and versatile. Why not make more than one?

SKIRT PART

Rnd 1 (RS): ch1, dc in first st, *[dc in each of next 2 (2, 3, 3) sts, FPdc around next FPdc] 6 (6, 7, 8) times, dc in each of next 7 (9, 7,

7) sts, [FPdc around next FPdc, dc in each of next 2 (2, 3, 3) sts] 6 (6, 7, 8) times, dc in last st, ch3 (4, 5, 4) (for underarm)**, dc in first st of Front L ; repeat from * to ** once more, join with sl st in first st of Back; 96 (102, 140, 154) sts M

Rnd 2 (RS): ch1, 3dc in first st, *ch1, skip next 2 (2, 3, 3) sts, v-st in next st, ch1, skip next 2sts, 5dc in next st; repeat from * to end, in last repeat work 2dc in same st as first 3dc and join with sl st in first st; 16 (17, 20, 22) 5dc shells and 16 (17, 20, 22) v-sts made N

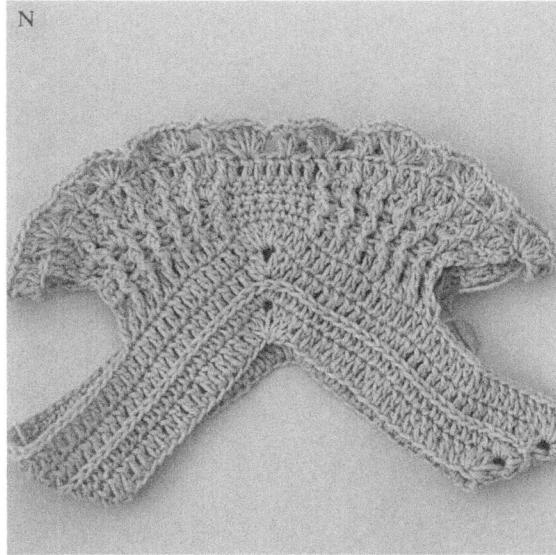

Rnd 3: ch1, dc in first st, dc in each of next 2sts, *ch1, v-st in next ch2sp, ch1, skip next dc, skip next ch1, dc in each of next 5dc; repeat from * to end, in last repeat work dc in each of next 2dc and join with sl st in first st; 176 (187, 220, 242) sts including all ch O

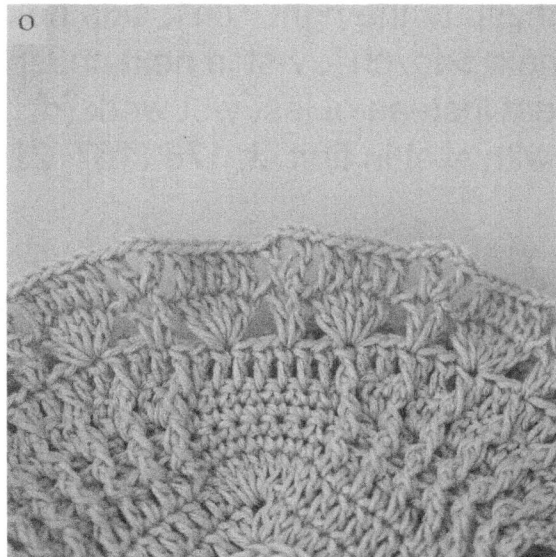

Rnd 4: repeat Rnd 3.

Rnd 5: ch1, dc in first st, dc2tog, *ch1, v-st in next ch2sp, ch1, skip next dc and next ch1, dc2tog, dc in next st, dc2tog; repeat from * to end, in last repeat work only one dc2tog and join with sl st in first st; 144 (153, 180, 198) sts including all ch P

349

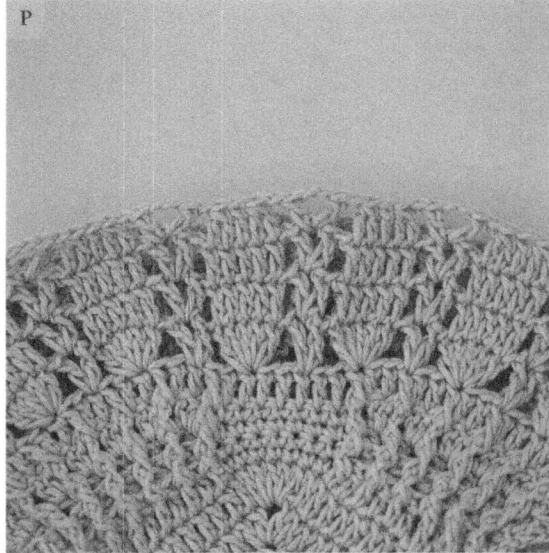

Rnd 6: ch1, dc in first st, *ch1, 5dc in next ch2sp, ch1, skip next ch1, skip next dc, v-st in next dc; repeat from * to end, but in last repeat instead of last v-st work (dc, ch2) in same st as first dc and join with sl st in first st; 176 (187, 220, 242) sts including all ch

Rnd 7: ch1, dc in ch2sp to the right, *ch1, skip next dc, skip next ch1, dc in each of next 5dc, ch1, v-st in next ch2sp; repeat from * to end, but in last repeat instead of last v-st work (dc, ch2) in same sp as first dc and join with sl st in first st; 176 (187, 220, 242) sts including all ch

Rnd 8: repeat Rnd 7

Rnd 9: ch1, dc in ch2sp to the right, *ch1, skip next ch1, dc2tog, dc in next st, dc2tog, ch1, v-st in next ch2sp; repeat from * to end, but in last repeat instead of last v-st work (dc, ch2) in same sp as first dc of round and join with sl st in first st; 144 (153, 180, 198) sts including all ch

Rnd 10: ch1, 3dc in ch2sp to the right, *ch1, skip next ch1, skip next dc, v-st in next dc, ch1, 5dc in next ch2sp; repeat from * to end, in last repeat work 2dc in same sp as first 3dc of the round and join with sl st in first st; 176 (187, 220, 242) sts including all ch

For size 0–6m

Repeat Rnds 3 through 8 once more and continue with Last Rnd Q

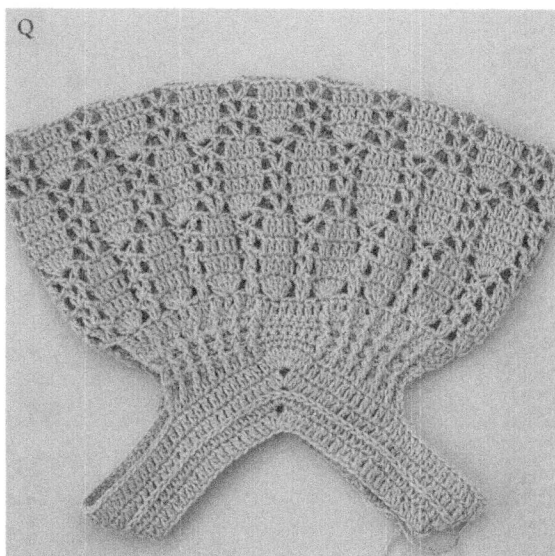

For size 6–12m

Repeat Rnds 3 through 10 once more and continue with Last Rnd.

For size 1–2y

Repeat Rnds 3 through 10.

Repeat Rnds 3 and 4 once more and continue with Last Rnd.

For size 3–4y

Repeat Rnds 3 through 10.

Repeat Rnds 3 through 8 once more and continue with Last Rnd.

For sizes 0–6m and 3–4y

Last Rnd: ch1, dc in ch2sp to the right, *ch1, skip next ch1, sc in next dc, skip next dc, picot shell in next dc, skip next dc, sc in next dc, ch1, v-st in next ch2sp; repeat from * to end, in last repeat work (dc, ch2) in same sp as first dc of the round and join with sl st in first st, fasten off R S

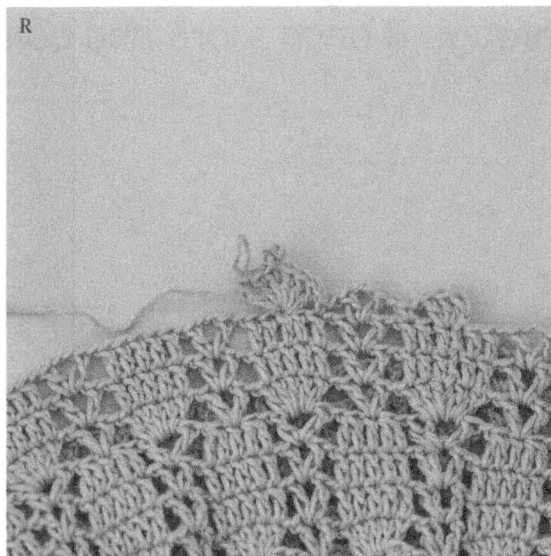

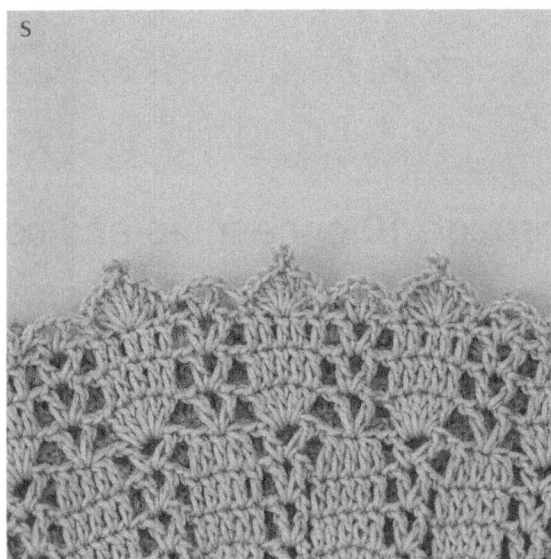

For sizes 6–12m and 1–2y

Last Rnd: ch1, 3dc in first st, *ch1, skip next dc, sc in next dc, skip next ch1, skip next dc, ch1, v-st in next ch2sp, ch1, skip next dc, skip next ch1, sc in next dc, skip next dc, picot shell in next dc; repeat from * to end, in last repeat work (3dc, picot) in same st as first 3dc of the round and join with sl st in first st, fasten off R S

RUFFLE

Join yarn into the remaining two loops of first hdc of the collar on the shoulder **T** and work:

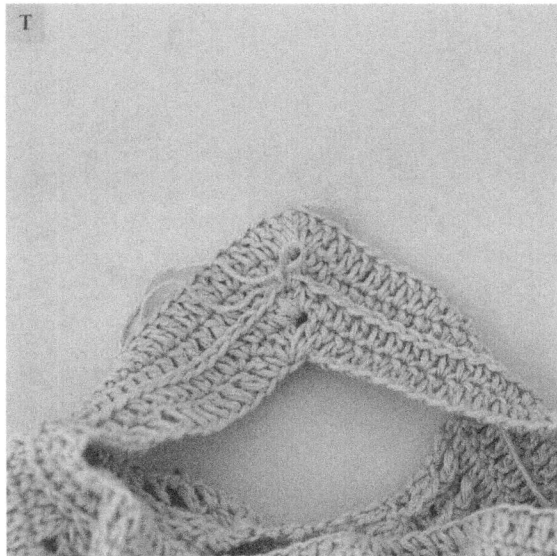

Rnd 1: ch1, dc in first st, *2dc in next st, 3dc in next st **U** ; repeat from * to end working always in both loops of hdc, join with sl st in first st

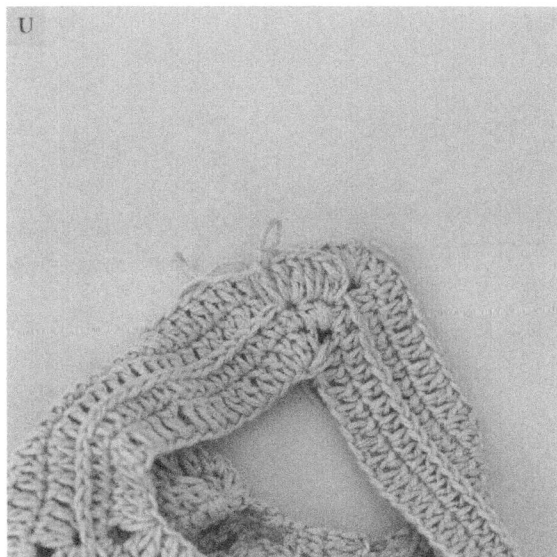

Rnds 2–3: ch1, dc in base of ch1, dc in each st to end, join with sl st in first st

Rnd 4: ch1, sc in each st to end, join with sl st in first st, fasten off **V**

FINISHING

After you have finished the dress, I suggest to work sc around the collar working into the remaining loop of foundation ch W , to prevent the straps from stretching out. This way you can also adjust the collar for a better fit.

You can work one round of sc around the armholes as well to make them more fitted if needed.

Weave in all ends (see Finishing Techniques).

Basic Stitches

Here are the main stitches that form the basis of most of the patterns in this book. They are also the building blocks for making most of the Special Stitches that follow in the next section.

CHAIN (CH)

Make a slip knot, place your hook into the loop, *yarn over and pull it through the loop; repeat from * as many times as needed A

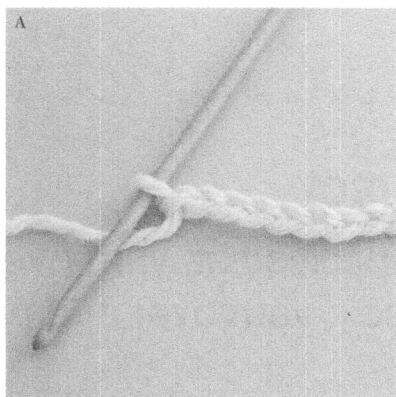

SLIP STITCH (SL ST)

Insert hook into specified st A , yarn over and pull it directly through both loops on the hook B

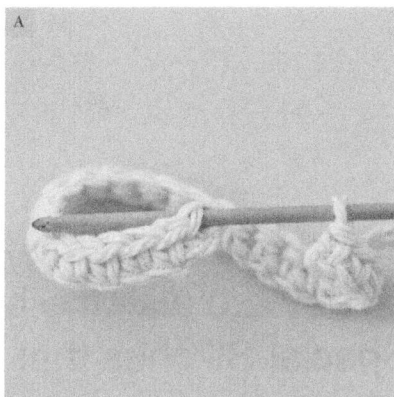

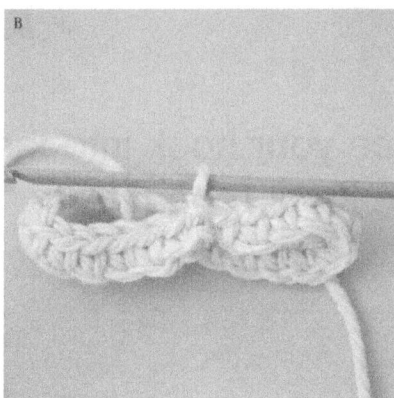

SINGLE CROCHET (SC)

Insert hook into the specified st, yarn over and pull through a loop, two loops on hook; yarn over and pull through both loops on hook A B

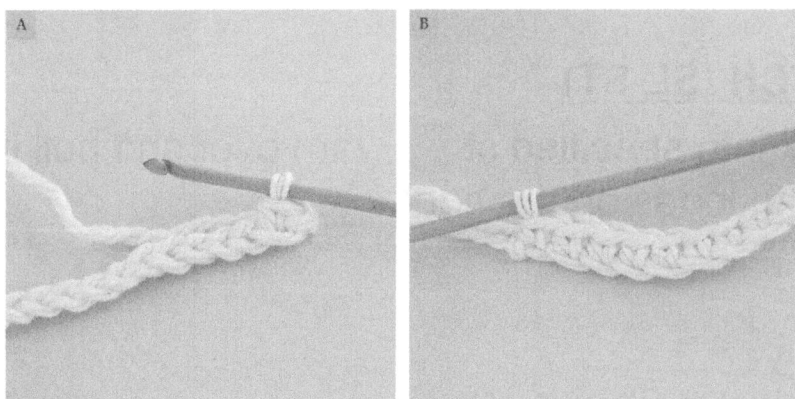

HALF DOUBLE CROCHET (HDC)

Yarn over A , insert hook into the specified st, yarn over and pull through a loop; three loops on hook B ; yarn over and pull through all three loops C D

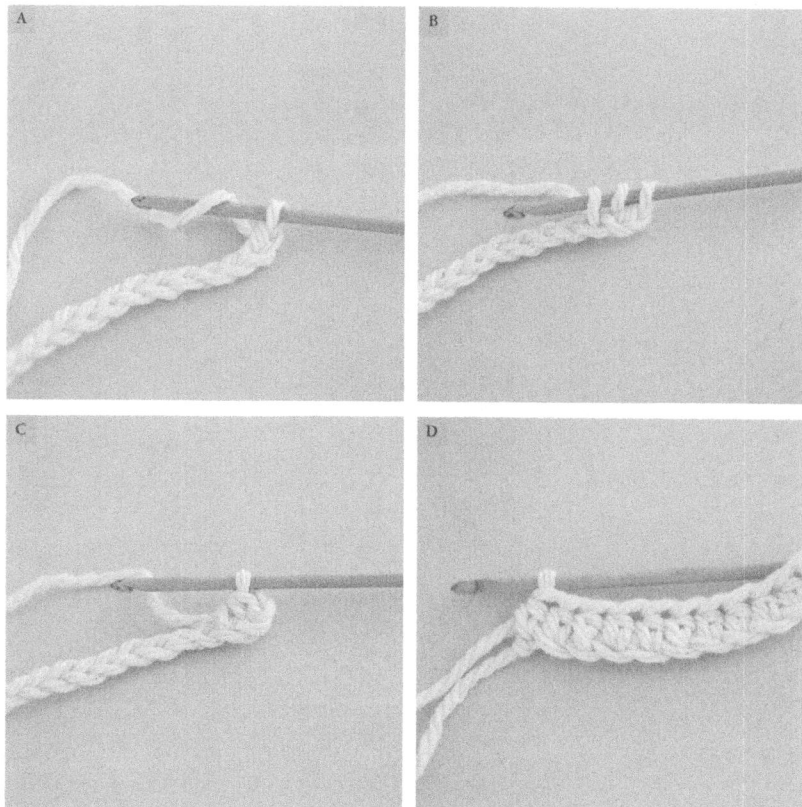

DOUBLE CROCHET (DC)

Yarn over A , insert hook into the specified st, yarn over and pull through a loop; 3 loops on hook B ; *yarn over and pull through 2 loops on the hook* C ; repeat from * once more D E

TREBLE CROCHET (TR)

Yarn over twice A , insert hook into the specified st, yarn over and pull through a loop; 4 loops on hook B ; *yarn over and pull through 2 loops on the hook* C ; repeat from * two more times D E F

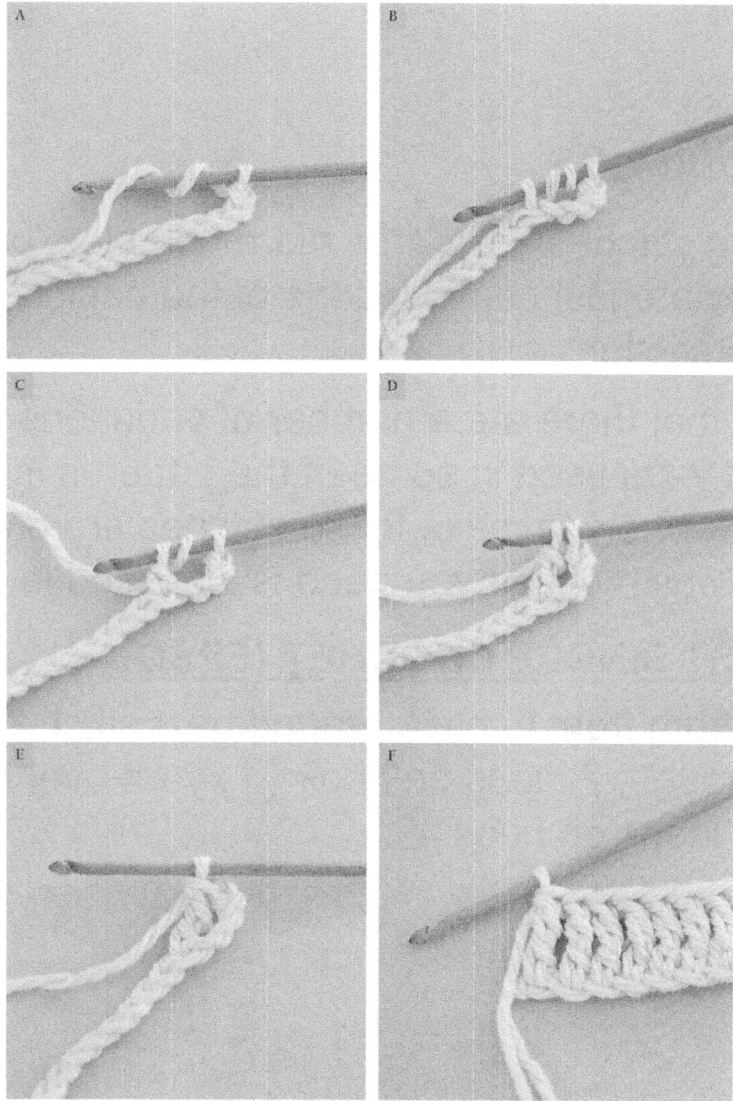

Special Stitches

The following stitches are a little more complex, but in essence they are just combinations of the basic stitches in the previous section.

You will see that there are a number of variations of shells, bobbles and v-sts used in some of the patterns in this book. Instructions for how to make these stitches are given in this section and which option you need is specified in the pattern.

FRONT POST SINGLE CROCHET (FPSC)

Insert hook from front to back around next stitch A , yarn over, pull through; 2 loops on hook B ; yarn over and pull through two loops on hook C

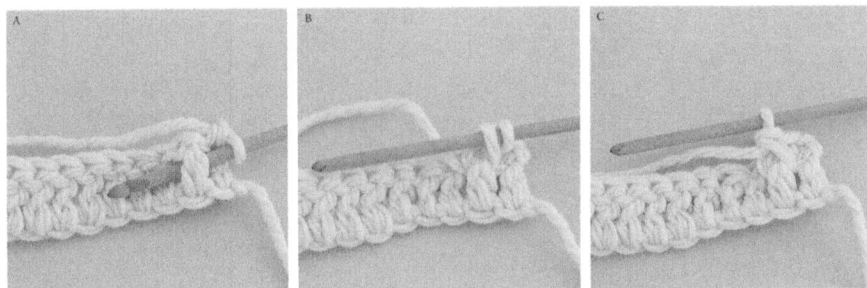

BACK POST SINGLE CROCHET (BPSC)

Insert hook from back to front around next stitch A , yarn over, pull through; 2 loops on hook B; yarn over and pull through two loops on hook C

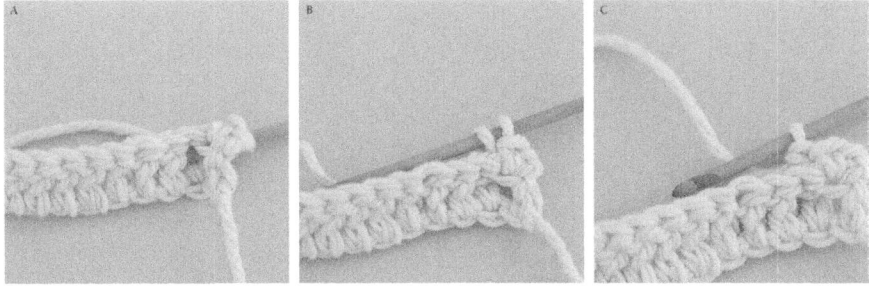

FRONT POST DOUBLE CROCHET (FPDC)

Yarn over, insert hook from front to back around next stitch A , yarn over and pull through; three loops on hook B ; finish front post double crochet as normal dc C D

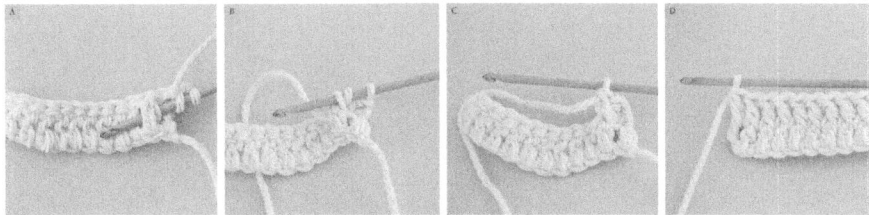

BACK POST DOUBLE CROCHET (BPDC)

Yarn over, insert hook from back to front around next stitch A , yarn over and pull through; three loops on hook B ; finish back post double crochet as normal dc C D

FRONT POST TREBLE CROCHET (FPTR)

Yarn over twice; insert hook from front to back around next st
A ; yarn over and pull through **B** ; *yarn over and pull
through two loops on hook **C** ; repeat from * two more times
D **E** **F**

WORKING IN THIRD LOOP OF HDC

Each hdc stitch has three loops – two main loops in the shape of a V are on the top of the stitch, known as front and back loops; behind the back loop there is a third loop, that's where you have to work when pattern states to work in third loop A B

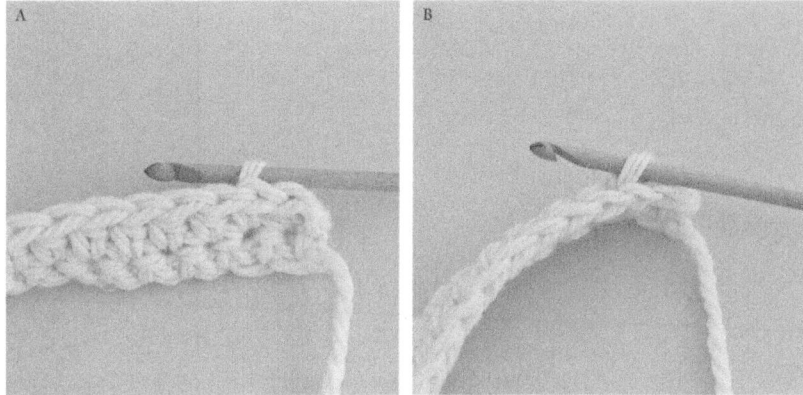

PICOT

Ch3 A , sl st in 3rd ch from hook B C

PICOT SHELL

Work (3dc A , picot B , 3dc) into the specified stitch C

DOUBLE CROCHET 2 TOGETHER (DC2TOG)

Begin to work dc in next st, but don't complete it, leaving 2 loops on hook A , work another incomplete dc in next st, so that you have 3 loops on hook B ; yarn over and pull through all 3 loops on hook C

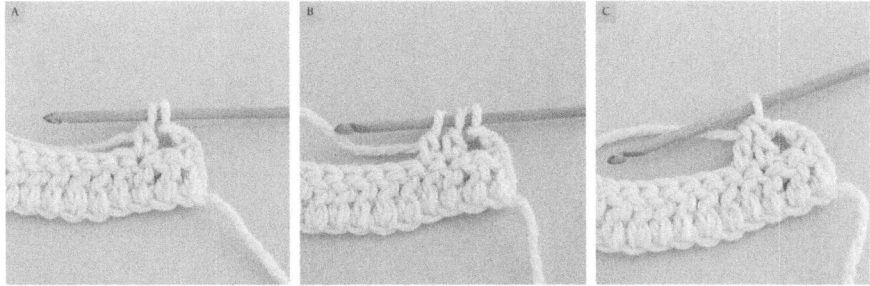

FRONT POST DOUBLE CROCHET 2 TOGETHER (FPDC2TOG)

*Yarn over, insert hook from front to back around the post of the next stitch, yarn over and pull up a loop, yarn over and pull through 2 loops on hook A ; repeat from * once more B , yarn over and pull through all three loops on hook C

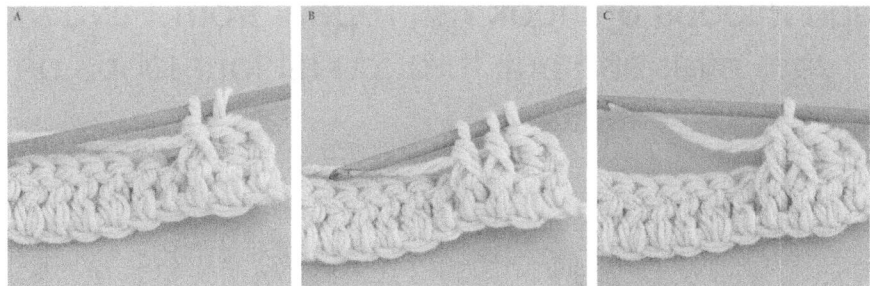

BACK POST DOUBLE CROCHET 2 TOGETHER (BPDC2TOG)

Yarn over, insert hook from back to front around next 2 sts A , yarn over, pull through; 3 loops on hook; finish back post double crochet as normal dc B

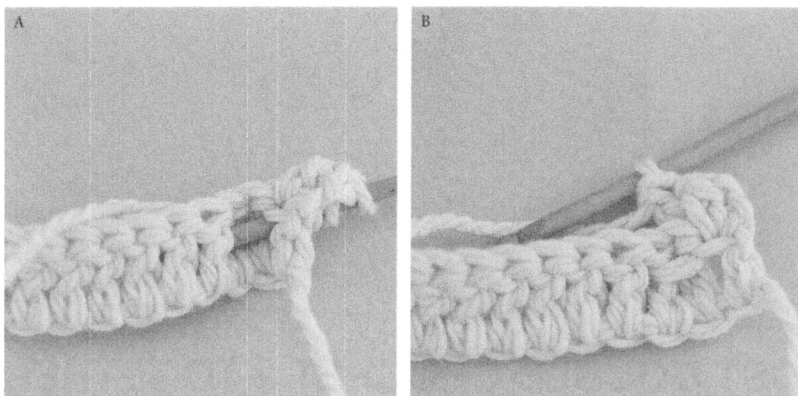

FRONT POST DOUBLE CROCHET 3 TOGETHER (FPDC3TOG)

*Yarn over, insert hook from front to back around the post of the next stitch, yarn over and pull up a loop, yarn over and pull through 2 loops on hook A ; repeat from * two more times B , yarn over and pull through all four loops on hook C

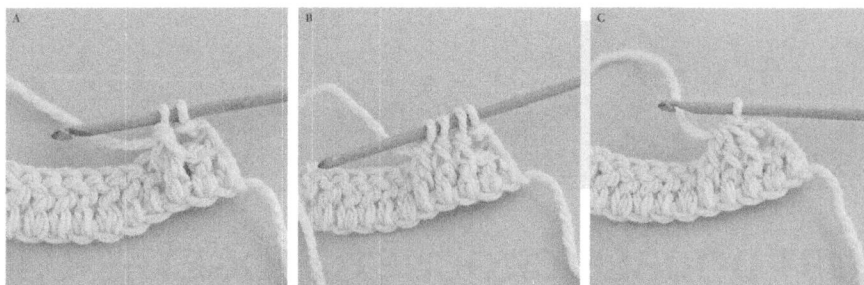

FRONT POST TREBLE 3 TOGETHER (FPTR3TOG)

*FPtr around the post of next specified st, but leave last two loops on hook A ; repeat from * two more times; 4 loops on hook B ; yarn over and pull through all 4 loops C

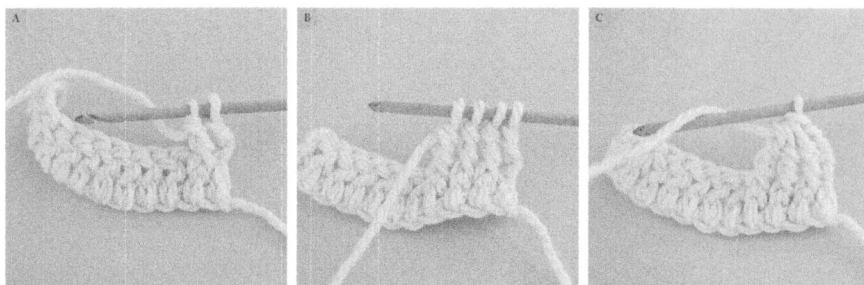

V-STITCH (V-ST)

Work (dc, ch1, dc) into the specified stitch A

TRUFFLE DRESS V-STITCH

Work (dc, ch2, dc) into the specified stitch B

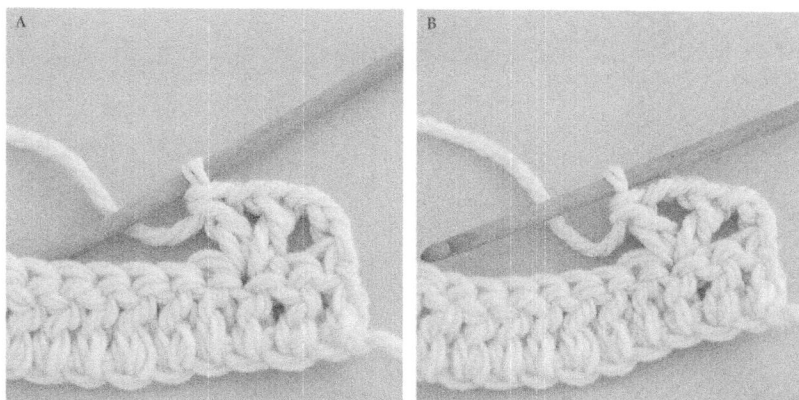

BOBBLE (BO)

There are two variations of bobble stitch used in the patterns in this book. The 3-dc version is used for the Jasmine Sweater, and the 4-dc bobble is used for the Heavenly Sweater, Harvest Cardigan, Angel Romper, Waves Sweater, Classic Bonnet, Cozy Blanket, and Favorite Hoodie. Instructions are given below.

3-DC BOBBLE

*Yarn over, insert hook in specified st and draw up a loop, yarn over and draw through 2 loops; two loops on hook A ; repeat from * two more times working in same stitch B , yarn over and pull through all four loops C

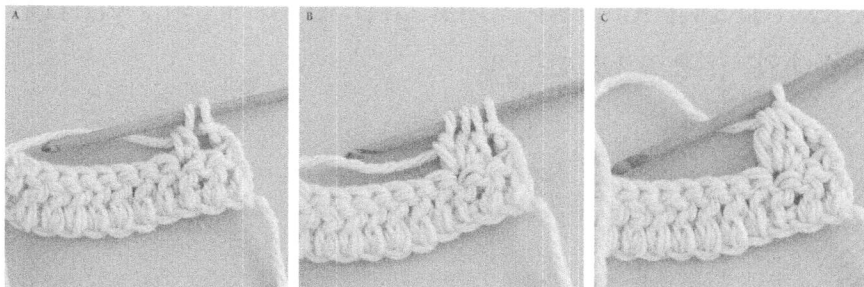

4-DC BOBBLE

*Yarn over, insert hook in specified st and pull up a loop, yarn over and draw through 2 loops; two loops on hook A ; repeat from * three more times working in same stitch B , yarn over and pull through all five loops C

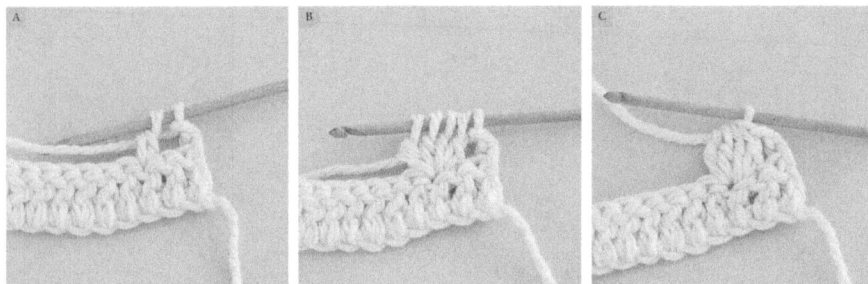

PUFF STITCH

(Yarn over, insert hook in specified st and pull up a loop) A four times; 9 loops on hook B ; yarn over and pull through 8 loops on hook C , yarn over and pull through 2 last loops D

POPCORN

Work 4dc into the specified st A ; remove the hook from working st; insert the hook into the top of first dc of the group of 4; place the working loop back on the hook B and draw it through the top of the first dc of group of 4 C ; yarn over and draw it through the final st D

POPCORN SHELL

Work (popcorn, ch2, popcorn) into the specified stitch A

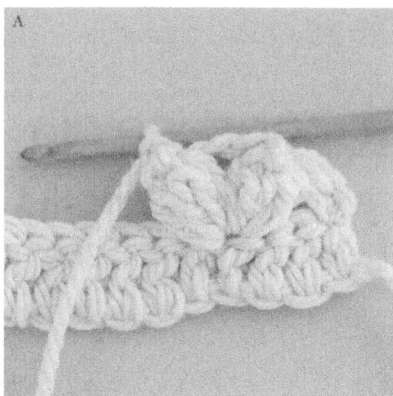

CROSSED DOUBLE CROCHET (CROSSED DC)

Worked over 3sts, skip 2sts, dc in next st A , ch1, dc in first skipped stitch working over dc just made B

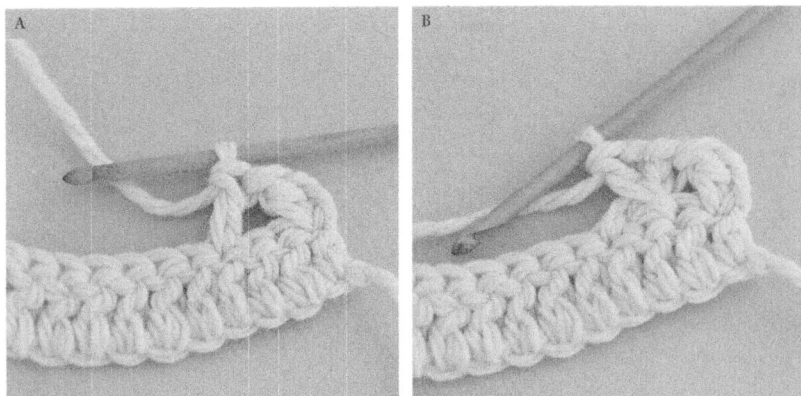

CLUSTER (CL)

*Yarn over, insert hook in specified st and pull up a loop, yarn over and pull through 2 loops; two loops on hook A ; repeat from * once more working in same stitch B , yarn over and pull through all three loops C

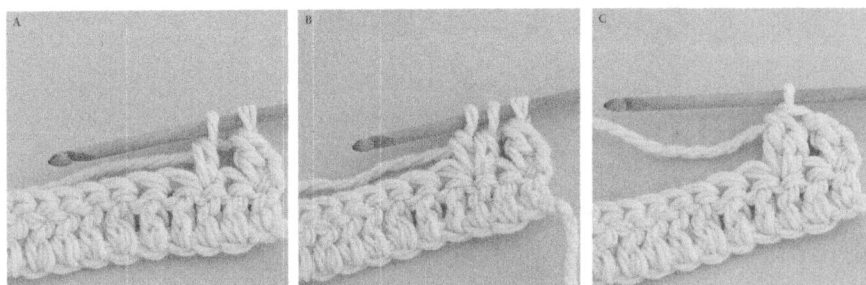

CROSSED CLUSTER (CROSSED CL)

Worked over two sts, skip next st, work CL in next st A , work CL in skipped st working over previous CL B C

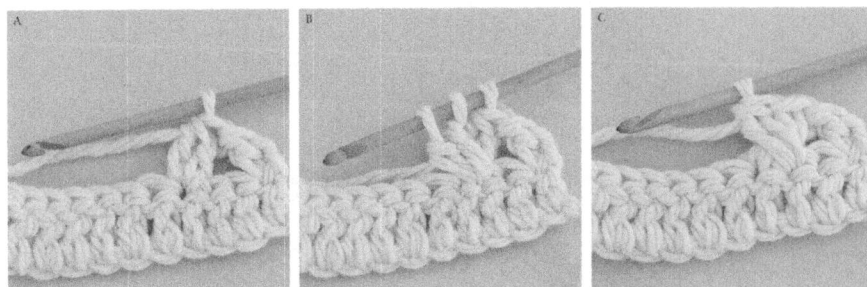

2-DC CLUSTER (2-DC CL)

*Yarn over, insert hook in specified st, yarn over and draw through, yarn over and draw through 2 loops on hook (this is a half-closed dc) **; two loops on hook; skip next sc and skip ch-3, repeat from * to ** once more working another half-closed dc in next st , yarn over and draw through all three loops on hook

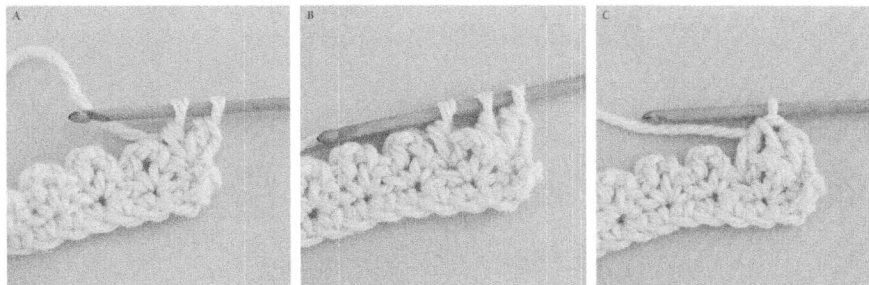

HARVEST CARDIGAN SHELL

Work (dc, ch1, dc, ch1, dc) in specified stitch

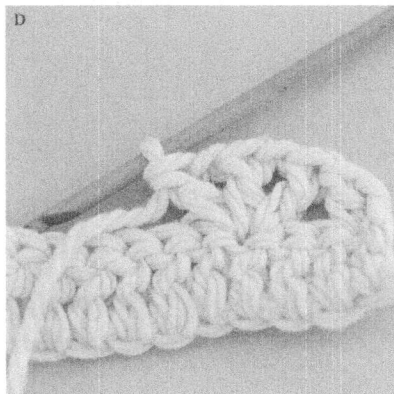

SEMILLA CARDIGAN SHELL

Work (3dc, ch2, 3dc) in specified stitch

SWEET DRESS SHELL

Work (2dc, ch3, 2dc) in specified stitch F

HEAVENLY SWEATER SHELL

Work (2dc, ch2, 2dc) in specified stitch.

Finishing Techniques

Follow the instructions below to complete your crochet and give your garments a well-made, professional-looking finish.

SEWING ON BUTTONS

As I mentioned earlier, buttons can present a choking hazard (see Getting Started: Tools and Materials). For this reason it's possibly better to use buttons with four holes as they can be sewn on very firmly. Make sure you pass the needle through the holes in the button at least twice and secure on the wrong side with a small knot and with small oversewn stitches.

WEAVING IN ENDS

Thread a big tapestry needle with the yarn end and run that needle through a few stitches, changing directions a few times to ensure that the ends won't come out, and matching your weaving to the existing stitches. Always weave on the wrong side of the work. At the end pull the yarn snug, and cut the tail close to the surface of the fabric, but not too close. You should weave in ends before washing and blocking. You can always trim the ends again afterwards.

WASHING

When washing the garment for the first time I recommend doing it by hand. This will allow you to see how the fabric reacts and to control the process. Use warm water and a small amount of a gentle detergent. If you don't have a hand wash specifically for woolens, you can use a regular shampoo. Carefully rinse the garment in warm water, then press out or squeeze to remove as much water as possible. You can also wrap the garment in a towel and squeeze it. The towel will absorb the excess water. Place your garment on a flat surface, for example, on a dry towel, keep it away from sunlight and let it air-dry.

BLOCKING

Not all garments need blocking. Usually letting a garment dry on a flat surface is enough, as long as you lay it out neatly and check on it a couple of times as you will probably need to adjust it while it's drying. Some garments, like the Harvest Cardigan, need light blocking. You can block in the following way. After washing and laying the garment out on a flat surface, use blocking pins to tack down the collar, pin alongside the yoke and sleeves and then let it dry. Additionally you can steam it. In the case of the Harvest Cardigan I would recommend steaming it as well, as it will flatten the leaves a little and make it drape more beautifully. When it's almost dry, cover it with a towel and pass a steamer over it a couple of times, without touching the towel. You can use an iron with a steam setting if you don't have a steamer. Check on the garment to see if any section needs more steam. Do not over do it as this may stretch and damage the fabric. Let it dry completely.

Made in United States
North Haven, CT
11 January 2025